ADVANCE PRAISE FOR *WOMEN, WRITING, AND PRISON: ACTIVISTS, SCHOLARS, AND WRITERS SPEAK OUT*

"This powerful volume is the best possible portal for approaching the vital impact of *the word* in the context of incarceration. The voices of advocates, activists, academics—and, most brilliantly, the voices of incarcerated and formerly incarcerated women—deploy astonishing and effective languages of clarity, truth, and justice. The rational passion on these pages is startling and unforgettable." —**Rickie Solinger**, author of *Reproductive Politics: What Everyone Needs to Know* and co-editor of *Interrupted Life: Experiences of Incarcerated Women in the U.S.*

"This book provides glimpses of prison life that most of us would not otherwise know. As the women write, thoughts guarded so closely come spilling out upon the page. They invite us into their worlds to see them as human beings with human issues they are trying to resolve. I was moved by the beauty of their poetry and the poignancy of their life stories." —**Sister Maureen McCormack**, Ph.D., who pioneered the Ira Progoff Intensive Journal® workshops in prisons and jails across the U.S.

"These writings undermine the very foundation of our nightmarish and shameful prison system. Like crews boring a tunnel from opposite ends, the writers from inside and outside meet in the middle with affirmations of life and humanity that offer a potent antidote to the deathly cruelties of the American gulag. And because the vast majority of women prisoners are incarcerated for non-violent crimes of poverty, this volume exposes the fundamental assumptions of the American criminal justice system as instruments of brutal class control." —**H. Bruce Franklin**, John Cotton Dana Distinguished Professor of English and American Studies at Rutgers University, Newark; author, *Prison Literature in America: The Victim as Criminal and Artist*

"A moving, sometimes unsettling, account of women caught within the prison industrial complex. Weaving together the voices of incarcerated and formerly incarcerated women, community activists, and academics, this innovative anthology reminds us why writing matters." —**Patrick W. Berry**, Syracuse University

Women, Writing, and Prison

Editorial Review Board

It's Easy to W.R.I.T.E. Expressive Writing Series

Robb Jackson, PhD, MFA, CAPF
Regents Professor and Professor of English
Texas A&M University–Corpus Christi

Vanessa Furse Jackson, PhD, MFA
Professor of English
Texas A&M University–Corpus Christi

Peggy Osna Heller, PhD, LCSW, PTR
Clinical Poetry Therapist and Psychotherapist
Potomac, Maryland

Also in the It's Easy to W.R.I.T.E. Expressive Writing Series

The Flourishing Principal: Strategies for Self-Renewal
Kathleen Adams and Rosemary Lohndorf

The Teacher's Journal: A Workbook for Self-Discovery
Kathleen Adams and Marisé Barreiro

Expressive Writing: Foundations of Practice
Kathleen Adams

Women, Writing, and Prison

Activists, Scholars, and Writers Speak Out

TOBI JACOBI and ANN FOLWELL STANFORD, EDITORS

ROWMAN & LITTLEFIELD
Lanham • Boulder • New York • London

Published by Rowman & Littlefield Education
A division of Rowman & Littlefield Publishers, Inc.
A wholly owned subsidary of The Rowman & Littlefield Publishing Group, Inc.
4501 Forbes Boulevard, Suite 200, Lanham, Maryland 20706
www.rowman.com

10 Thornbury Road, Plymouth PL6 7PP, United Kingdom

British Library Cataloguing in Publication Information Available

Library of Congress Cataloging-in-Publication Data
Library of Congress Cataloging-in-Publication Data Available
ISBN 978-1-4758-0822-3 (cloth)
ISBN 978-1-4758-0823-0 (pbk.)
ISBN 978-1-4758-0824-7 (electronic)

We dedicate this collection to the writers, scholars, and activists working tirelessly for social justice, both within and beyond the razor wire

Bless
by Mia

bless the ladies on I-2
bless them for what they're going through
bless all of us in this jail
bless us with low bail
bless us with good things
bless us with the love god brings
bless our family that's in the street
bless us with this mysterious food we eat
bless our sisters and brothers
bless all of us in one way or another
bless us with some spiritual support
bless us when we go to court
bless our sons and daughters
bless this tier and the other living quarters
bless us and bless the men
please, bless us to the end
bless our body and soul
bless us to stay in control
bless us all one more time
but before you bless us, bless our
beautiful minds.

Contents

Section II: Bridging Communities: Writing Programs and Social Practice

Section III: Writing, Resistance, and the Material Realities of U.S. Prisons and Jails

Series Overview: About the *It's Easy to W.R.I.T.E. Expressive Writing Series*

Expressive writing originates from the writer's lived experience—past, present, or imagined future life. Written in the author's own voice, expressive writing creates bridges between thought and feeling, reason and intuition, idea and action. It is equally rooted in language arts and social science, and it takes multiple forms: journals, poetry, life story, personal essay, creative nonfiction, song lyrics, notes, and snippets of thought. Expressive writing is democratic and accessible. No special knowledge is needed, supplies are available and affordable, and research confirms that outcomes can be profound and even life-changing.

The *It's Easy to W.R.I.T.E. Expressive Writing Series* captures the voices of worldwide experts on the power of writing for personal development, academic improvement, and lasting behavioral change. Authors are both theorists and practitioners of the work they document, bringing real-life examples of practical techniques and stories of actual outcomes.

Individually or as a compendium, the volumes in the *It's Easy to W.R.I.T.E. Expressive Writing Series* represent thoughtful, innovative, demonstrated approaches to the myriad ways life-based writing can shape both critical thinking and emotional intelligence. Books in the series are designed to have versatile appeal for classroom teachers and administrators, health and behavioral health professionals, graduate programs that prepare educators and counselors, facilitators of expressive writing, and individuals who themselves write expressively. Workbooks offer well-crafted, self-paced writing programs for individual users, with facilitation guides and curricula for anyone who wishes to organize peer writing circles to explore the material in community.

Each book or chapter author is held to exacting standards set by the series editor, Kathleen Adams, who, prior to her 1985 launch as a pioneer and global expert in the expressive writing field, was trained as a journalist and served as chief editor for a small nonfiction publishing company.

It's Easy to W.R.I.T.E.

*W*hat do you want to write about? Name it. Write it down. (If you don't know, try one of these: *What's going on? How do I feel? What's on my mind? What do I want? What's the most important thing to do? What's the best/worst thing right now?*)

*R*econnect with your center. Close your eyes. Take three deep breaths. Focus. Relax your body and mind. Gather your thoughts, feelings, questions, and ideas.

*I*nvestigate your thoughts and feelings. Start writing and keep writing. Follow the pen/keyboard. If you get stuck, close your eyes and recenter yourself. Reread what you've already written and continue. Try not to edit as you go; that can come later, if at all.

*T*ime yourself. Write for five to twenty minutes or whatever time you choose. Set the timer on your phone, stove, or computer. Plan another three to five minutes at the end of reflection.

*E*xit smart. Reread what you've written and reflect on it in a sentence or two: *As I read this, I notice . . .* or *I'm aware of . . .* or *I feel. . . .* Note any action steps you might take or any prompts you might use for additional writes.

Foreword

To be awake is a precious gift. We can't enlighten ourselves, though, until we find ourselves, or put ourselves, in situations that provide an awakening spark. Then, once awakened deeply inside, we respond. My own waking up had to do with seeing that providing charity wasn't enough, that my calling was to seek justice in the world.

Reading is one way to be awakened, an important way. Reading stories and commentaries like those in this book should bring us fully awake, even rattle us. The kind of rattling that leads to productive action and an understanding that we are all—*all*—connected in this great web of life. What happens to one of us affects all of us. Maybe in minute ways, unrecognizable ways, but over the long haul, those little tugs on the human web create massive ruptures. Or they can wake us up.

And we need to wake up. We need to be enlightened, awakened to the millions of voices, human voices, behind bars.

The fact that our nation is the top incarcerator in the world, disproportionately imprisoning the poorest among us, should shock us. Dry statistics don't always do the job. It's hard to imagine what 2.3 million people look like as a group. It's hard to imagine that every one of those 2.3 million has their own story. Those stories aren't always pretty and sometimes they are pretty ugly, but they are *stories*, and stories remind us what it is to be human—the good, the bad, and the ugly. Stories build bridges that connect our voices and vision in myriad ways.

It's hard to feel connected to those who appear to be radically "Other," and those who are hidden away in prisons and jails are "Other" to most of us. They are surrounded not only by bars and razor wire but also by policies that make it difficult for those of us on the outside to know what happens inside and, most important, who is inside. Despite TV shows like *Oz* and *Orange is the New Black*, the voices of real women and men, parents, sisters, spouses, and children are muffled and, at the political level, we continue to brush all prisoners with the same stroke—predator, criminal, fearsome, dangerous. The stories you'll read in this book give the lie to these images.

A story is a bridge. When we read a story, we place a foot on the bridge and begin to walk across, and where before there was a gulf of ignorance, we cross over into enlightenment, into an awakening. The work of writing in prison and jails is spiritual work, it is work that calls the deepest part of every individual who puts pen to paper and allows them to say, "I am real. I am human. I have a voice and I am worth listening to."

One thing we know is that the majority of people locked in the system are people who have committed nonviolent crimes, mostly crimes related to addictions and the consequences of poverty.

Prison is a terrible place where human dignity is systematically stripped away, even before a conviction in cases of those too poor to make bail payment. In prison and jails, you get a thousand signals a day that you are nothing but human waste. We have 2.3 million people being told that for years. This is a system of daily mental (and sometimes physical) torture and brutalization. And those people are then released into a society that continues to signal their undesirability with laws and shunning that so often leads women and men back to the streets and through the revolving door of the prison system.

Alternatives to incarceration as a first response do exist. Restorative justice allows a person who has committed a crime to make amends and be restored to the community through service, education, job training. Sure, there are people who are so violent that they need to be kept away from society. But most people can and do change, although a system of continual punishment and dehumanization is the worst way to foster that change.

Books like this one need to be read, *must* be read so that we can cross that great divide separating Us from Them. Drs. Jacobi and Stanford have collected stories and poems by incarcerated and formerly incarcerated women that will stun you with their honesty and beauty. They have also included articles by activist-scholars who reflect on what it means to "go in" from the outside with their privilege as free people.

One thing you'll discover as you listen to these stories of the imprisoned is the resilience, intelligence, and strength possessed by the storytellers. In *Women, Writing, and Prison: Activists, Scholars, and Writers Speak Out*, we are treated to stories of resistance, of taking despair and turning it into creative expression, of healing post-incarceration by reaching out to newly-released women, of turning sorrow into gratitude, and of "making a way out of no way."

I hope you will relish the stories and challenges that this important collection holds.

Sister Helen Prejean, C.S.J.
Ministry Against the Death Penalty
Author, *Dead Man Walking* (1994) and *The Death of Innocents* (2004)

Preface

The story might begin with a woman outfitted in orange or white or institutional greens who pauses at the edge of a door. She turns and whispers, "I never wrote a poem before." She grins, clutching her new folder and already fast-forwarding to next week's workshop. Or the story might begin with a silent room, one voice unfolding a narrative of childhood abuse that many in the room share, that many applaud when the end of the page is reached. Or the story might start with a media statistic that leaves a teacher stunned and moved to seek change by going behind bars armed with books, pencils, and samples of suppressed histories. The story of this book begins with each of these scenes playing itself over and over as writing programs and teachers intersect with the world's justice systems.

We envision a wide audience for this collection. We hope the narratives from prison will inspire both incarcerated writers and those who do or are considering work inside; such writings are powerful records of the material and affective conditions that come with being locked away. For teachers and writers, we imagine increased interest in literacy-based activism in sites like prison as well as other social institutions (taking up Foucault's oft quoted claim that our schools, factories, and hospitals resemble prisons). We also hope to reach out to those engaged in the criminal justice community, particularly those interested in imagining change in the U.S. system. Whether working toward increased access to educational programs or toward more radical prison abolition, we believe that people committed to justice work can benefit from dialogue with the voices in this collection and the varied models of writing and writing communities that they emerge from.

Finally, we hope this book spurs responses and conversation among interdisciplinary scholars and practitioners who make writing and literacy the center of their practice. Although neither Ann nor Tobi approach this work from the perspective of formal writing therapy, our years writing with women inside have inevitably resulted in important shifts in our worldviews and self-perceptions. As noted above, we've seen the confidence of individuals and groups rise. We've witnessed women embracing writing with pride for the first time in their remembered lives. We've shared moments when difficult and painful stories about rape, incest, and abuse are spoken and owned across a group of diverse women. These are moments when we've seen the power dynamics of our writing groups shift and reassemble in ways that transform writers—however momentarily—into powerful authors of their lived experiences and designers of their futures.

Like many writing projects, this collection comes together through the work of many. Tobi recognizes and thanks the hundreds of women who turn to and find pleasure, pain, solace, and challenge in the work of writing behind bars. She is humbled to write alongside them each week. Graduate student Lauren Alessi spent countless hours crafting a thorough index. Tobi would also like to acknowledge the support of her family, primarily her partner, Ed Lessor, and aunt, Wendy Adelson, both of whom encourage and support her activist literacy work.

Ann wants to thank Sr. Patricia Schlosser, who got her into this work many years ago and continues to be an inspiration to her and the thousands of women she has touched in Illinois prisons and jails. Also many thanks go to her partner, Marisa Alicea, who is a constant source of joy, support, and laughter. Above all, Ann wants to thank the many women who attended workshops at Cook County Jail and several Illinois prisons. Their resiliency, good humor, and passion for written expression continues to energize and inform Ann's writing and teaching.

Ann and Tobi also recognize the efforts and commitment of series editor Kathleen Adams; her enthusiasm and gracious reminders have been immeasurably responsible for sending this manuscript into the material world. The team at Rowman and Littlefield has provided guidance and support all the way through this process. Thanks particularly to Nancy Evans, acquisitions editor, and Carlie Wall, associate editor, and to Sarah Kendall, who joined the team as the production cycle began. We also thank graphic artist Maria Kaufmann, who translated the core concepts of this book into a cover design.

This collection has struggled through a decade of circulation, expansion, contraction, longing for the stability that can come with print. Through the excitement and dedication of the diverse writers featured in this collection, we are proud to see this body of work on women, writing, and prison become public. We invite your conversation as we work toward collective change for women writing behind bars.

Tobi Jacobi, PhD
Ann Folwell Stanford, PhD

Introduction: Not Much Silence Here

ANN FOLWELL STANFORD

Writing is a matter of survival: if I don't write I forget, and if I forget it is as if I had not lived. That is one of the main reasons for my writing: to prevent the erosion of time, so that memories will not be blown by the wind. I write to record events and name each thing. (x)

—Isabel Allende, *Conversations with Isabel Allende*

To walk past loop after loop of skin-splitting concertina wire, through locked gates that slam behind you, and past the hard stares of frequently distracted and annoyed security officers is much like crossing a geographical border as an unwanted guest. It's all there: the rigid identification procedures, invasive searches, shuffling of required paperwork, and then the crossing over into a new culture, a new language, a new world to navigate. Sometimes mellifluous, mostly cacophonous, the sounds of such a crossing can be radically disorienting. It is so for the women and men who make the journey from the free world into the carceral spaces of prisons and jails daily—the hundreds of thousands, locked up and away from children, parents, husbands, lovers, friends, and the simple pleasures of filling an ice tray or unlocking a door. For some, the space is familiar, if unwelcome; for others, it is a nightmare; for all, it is being consigned to near invisibility to society.

Within all the various noises of incarceration—slamming doors, TVs, shrill voices, rough voices, laughter, cries, loudspeakers—sometimes another noise emerges. As pencils and pens translate thought to poems and stories, it is the sound of women writing.[1] For some, writing is the solitary, passion-driven activity of a mind hungry to tell stories and, in the telling, to make sense of her life. For others, the sound is polyphonous. Writing inside prison may evoke hilarity or the rich hum of silence, the sound of grief or rage, the flowering of gratitude. It is the kind of writing that can make something happen, as communities of thinking, creating women come together in workshops, classes and informal critique sessions. One thing is certain: whether in solitude or in groups, writing happens in jails and prisons across the country—and we on the outside have much to learn from it.

Many of us walk through the big doors and emerge again in a just a few hours, having facilitated a workshop, taught a class, or negotiated clearances for materials with a warden. This book arises from questions we've been asked or that we've asked ourselves: *Why write in prison or jail? What do facilitators from the outside have to say about this cultural work? And what do imprisoned women writers think about the process of writing? What kinds of writing are they doing? What issues do they care about? What about the women who write in solitude? How does the work of incarcerated women writers become visible to those on the outside? Should it? What kinds of circulation practices are ethical?*

Obviously, the answers to these questions are as varied and complex as the human community itself. But they haven't been asked in any collective and public way.[2] Of the collections of incarcerated men and women's writing that do exist, only one focuses on women's work exclusively.[3] Although we believe that such anthologies are urgent, necessary, that is not our purpose here.[4] Instead, we have tried to create a many-faceted discussion by currently and formerly incarcerated women and those who write with them. *Women, Writing, and Prison* is the book we wanted to read, needed to read. It is not a statistical or exhaustive approach to our questions, but it begins a conversation that we believe needs to continue.

Women, Writing, and Prison gathers critical and reflective essays, narratives, and poems written by those from whom we most wanted to hear: community activists, academics, and incarcerated and formerly incarcerated women. The writers in this collection are by turns challenging, practical, celebratory, critical, and even dangerous, for they assert the right of *every* person to use her or his voice and be heard, which is to say, listened to, read carefully, paid attention.

In reading writing by incarcerated men and women, state- and media-imposed stereotypes about the faces behind the bars become a little more transparent for what they are—sensationalized images designed to maintain a culture of fear and punishment in place of compassion and the possibility of rehabilitation, when it is needed. As the writers construct and express the texture and shape of their own multifaceted selves, the frightening faces we see in popular media and the constructs of politicians who stay in office with tough-on-crime stances begin to fall away. As long as prisons and prisoners remain relatively inaccessible, the myth of prisoners' inherently predatory natures can remain in place to justify the brutality of incarceration.

Before going into prisons and jails and actually meeting the women they are writing with, many of our university students repeat the stock line—wishful thinking perhaps—"We all have choices and they have made the choice to use drugs (steal, drink, sell drugs, have babies, be with an abusive man). If you are in prison or jail, you must have done something to *deserve* it." What many will come to realize is that poverty, abuse, and addiction tightly constrict the constellation of available choices. The narratives of those inside create a powerful counter-discourse of human struggle. When the *human* voices from inside what Kathryn Watterson calls the "concrete womb" break through the imposed silence of incarceration, not only do the horrors of our American gulag become visible, but strongly defended assumptions begin to crack open.

We believe that writing from prisons and jails can forge links between those inside and those fortunate enough to read the work from the outside. In constructing this book, we hoped to do three things.

First, we wanted to draw attention to the writing that is emerging from women's prisons, jails, and transitional residencies. Necessarily, the writers in this collection are but a tiny representation of incarcerated women who write and those who write with them.

Second, we wanted to create a volume in which the voices of incarcerated, formerly incarcerated, academic, and community women and men would come together as a kind of jazz piece, where each has her or his solo time, but all the sounds exist and play upon each other to create an energetic performance aimed at challenging public stereotypes.

Third, we gathered this body of work as a means of interrogating romantic notions of the writing teacher or workshop facilitator as transformative agent or savior. Indeed, it is our belief that the workshop facilitator only creates a space within which the women have the opportunity to experience themselves as creating, thinking, and contributing human beings. If workshops run, as we believe they can and ultimately should, the facilitator would be able to leave the room and the writing would continue.

The Context

While state and federal prison populations have seen small declines for the second consecutive year, between 2000 and 2011, the overall population rose by 15 percent from 1,334,174 to 1,598,790.[5] About 70 percent of state correctional declines have a great deal to do with California's Public Safety Realignment program.[6] Almost half of every 100,000 U.S. residents were sentenced to more than one year in prison in 2011.[7] In addition, to the more than 1.5 million people in federal and state prisons, 735,601 people were in local jails, bringing the total incarcerated population to 2.2 million.[8] The United States is the number one incarcerator in the world.

Who is hardest hit? Those who are most vulnerable and visible—poor women and men of color and their children. The Sentencing Project reports that more than 60 percent of the people in prison are now racial and ethnic minorities. "For Black males in their thirties, 1 in every 10 is in prison or jail on a given day. These trends have been intensified by the disproportionate impact of the 'war on drugs,' in which two-thirds of all person in prison for drug offenses are people of color."[9] And yet, while African Americans constitute 9.7 percent of those reporting illicit drug use, whites account for 9.1 percent and Latinos are lower, at 8.1 percent.[10]

Nearly two-thirds of women in prison are mothers, and of them, 77 percent report providing most of the daily childcare before imprisonment.[11] Women bear the burden of what Barbara Owen and other scholars have called "double deviancy, . . . implying [that] female prisoners break both gender roles and the criminal law."[12] In Illinois alone, more than 90,000 children had a parent in prison or on parole as of August 2006. Chicago Legal Advocacy for Incarcerated Mothers reports that 82 percent of women in Illinois prisons are mothers. Bloom, Owen, and Covington (2004) describe the following characteristics of incarcerated or paroled women:

- disproportionately women of color,
- in their early- to mid-thirties,
- most likely to have been convicted of a drug or drug-related offense,
- fragmented family histories, with other family members involved with the criminal justice system,
- survivors of physical or sexual abuse as children and adults,
- significant substance abuse problems,
- multiple physical and mental health problems,
- unmarried mothers of minor children, and
- high school degree/GED, but limited vocational training and sporadic work histories.

It's important that we understand women's incarceration within an unjust system of oppression, one that ignores the anguish caused to mothers and their families for decades to come. In her study of incarcerated mothers and their children, Renny Golden (2005) interviews a woman who had been incarcerated multiple times:

> My incarceration was painful and traumatic for my children. I was in Lincoln Correctional Center, a four-hour drive from my home, which made it nearly impossible for my family . . . to bring my children to see me. It will take them years to heal from this separation. They felt abandoned and hurt, and their reaction was to rebel in school and at home. They have low self-esteem and feel like nothing matters. My daughter is the one who has been affected the most, for we were never able to bond like a mother and daughter should. She was born while I was in jail, and we were separated soon after her birth . . . her teacher has noticed her continuing need for unlimited attention. We need extensive long-term counseling. We can never reclaim that lost time. (Golden 2005, 114)

Those who have spent even a minimal amount of time writing with incarcerated women will attest to the dominance of the thinking and writing about their children and the profound desire to reconnect, be forgiven, and start over.

The Sentencing Project reports that women's numbers in prison since 1980 have increased at nearly double the rate for men. Women in state prisons in 2002 were more likely than men to be incarcerated for a drug offense

(32 percent vs. 21 percent) or nonviolent property offense (29 percent vs. 20 percent), and less likely than men to be incarcerated for a violent offence (33 percent vs. 52 percent).[13]

Why is this so? Among other things, sentencing laws have become harsher and have broadened to cover a wider swath of "crimes." A woman living with a man who sells drugs, for example, can be charged with a felony through "conspiracy to sell" laws. It makes absolutely no difference if the "conspirator" had no knowledge that her friend was involved in drug sales or not. Women are also less likely to have the names of drug contacts that men use to reduce their sentences.

Additionally, 93 out of every 100,000 white women were incarcerated in 2008, while 349 out of every 100,000 black women and 147 out of every 100,000 Latina women were incarcerated.[14] These disparities continue today.

Add to the distressing statistics the fact that women with a history of mental illness represent nearly three-quarters of the population in state prisons. Depending on the study, who is asking, and the kinds of questions being asked, a conservative estimate is that more than half the women in state prisons have been abused, 47 percent battered and 39 percent sexually abused (with many being survivors of both types of abuse).[15] Other estimates, however, go as high as 80 percent for domestic and sexual violence. A full 50 percent of women prisoners have no high school diploma and the 50 percent who were employed prior to being incarcerated never made more than $6.50 an hour (Golden 2005).

When women are incarcerated, their punishment extends to their children. According to Chicago Legal Advocacy for Incarcerated Mothers (CLAIM) (2000):

> Very young children may be severely traumatized by the sudden separation from their mothers, and this trauma may result in developmental delays and later emotional problems. Children's substitute caregivers are stretched beyond their resources. Visits to distant prisons and long-distance, collect calls are the only ongoing contact with the mother available to children who are too young to benefit from letters.

Children who aren't cared for by relatives will face the nightmare of state foster homes, and, as CLAIM states, "often are separated from their brothers and sisters, moved to a series of different homes, and denied visits with their mothers" (CLAIM 2000). Many women face termination of parental rights. With ever widening circles of trauma, huge communities of the poor bear the burden of this nation's insatiable hunger to incarcerate. Women in prisons and jails are vulnerable, not only to the trauma that comes with being watched around the clock, but to abuse from jail and prison staff. Human Rights Watch has focused on the abuse of women in U.S. prisons for several years.[16]

In 1994, when Congress voted to exclude prisoners from Pell Grant funds, education became a luxury to people behind bars. Based on a backlash from those who believed that paying for educations of "criminals" was unfair when they couldn't afford to finance their own children's education, the radical reduction of educational programs for prisoners received wide-spread approval. Given the ever-rising costs of college and university tuitions, voters pressed politicians to get tougher on crime. Cutting education, however, was one of the most shortsighted ways imaginable to reduce crime.[17] Consequently, the programs that do exist—GED, literacy, and college—have waiting lists and, as in Illinois, may exist in only one facility, while there are dozens more separated by hundreds of miles. Only those lucky enough to be sentenced to a prison that houses a college have a hope of taking a course.

As the female prison population has increased exponentially over the past three decades, a few progressive wardens and superintendents have looked for innovative ways to introduce useful programming into their facilities. They understand that education is the number one factor in reducing recidivism, and yet a rare commodity for a prisoner or detainee.[18] They know that reading literary texts and writing poetry, prose, drama, or essays combines imaginative with critical thinking. It allows for the joy of struggling to "get it right."

Are these skills essential to making it in the free world? Many would argue no. The women need job training. Yes. The women need computer skills. Yes. The women need to know how to open a checking and savings account and to balance the books. Absolutely. This does not preclude, however, the expansion of mind and creative problem solving that reading and writing literature encourages. Indeed, critical thinking and problem solving are essential to navigating one's way in a society that insists on continued punishment long after the time has been served (imagine searching for a job or renting an apartment with a felony record).

Clearly, a six-week poetry, drama, or prose workshop cannot hope to provide even a foundation of critical thinking skills or the ability to surmount a past that includes incarceration, but it can open windows and create a hunger for more learning. Although we would argue alongside Angela Davis[19] that the majority of incarcerated men and women should not be in jails or prisons, educational opportunities throughout and after incarceration must be available as long as the prison industrial complex exists.

Dangerous Writing

A focus on writing seems an almost absurd response to the large scale and overwhelming issues facing incarcerated women. And yet, with the act of putting pen to paper, each writer defies and remakes the social constructions that have been made for her. Even those who create work that seems to maintain certain narrowly religious foci on sin and submission defy institutional efforts at silencing prisoners' voices. Words can knit together broken narratives, break through silence and create new worlds, new visions. Within the dehumanizing social practice of the jail, writing becomes an act of resistance, sometimes obvious, sometimes masked. Some of the women write against the official discourse of the jail, some write with it, some do both at the same time.

For prisoners to craft and read or perform their own writing is to rebel against distortions, to reclaim a unique and communal voice, and to declare that they are not dead, not deadened, and most certainly are coming back into society some day.[20] As Gloria Anzaldua (2001) reminds us, "Writing is dangerous because we are afraid of what the writing reveals: the fears, the angers, the strengths of a woman under a triple or quadruple oppression. Yet in that very act lies our survival because a woman who writes has power. And a woman with power is feared" (173).

The writing is also dangerous because it proclaims a making and remaking of selves, despite state attempts to confine, fix, and stabilize identities as *inmates* (compliant/unruly). It is also dangerous because it proclaims a "we" within the confines of prison walls and disrupts the individualistic discourse and practice on which any system of oppression is dependent. It is brave writing, scripted from the front lines of a battle for psychic, spiritual, and even physical survival. It is raw and immediate writing. It is an exercise of power in a place that attempts to deny power. This is work that repays careful attention.[21]

Indeed, the poetry and essays often resemble words penned from the front lines of a war, especially a revolution, where what is at stake is the soul and heart of a nation's people. The words are sometimes urgent and raw and remind us of Martin Espada's (1998) poets of the kitchen:

> Their lives are fogged with sweat, loud with the noise of their labor. To be heard over the crashing of pots, these poets may shout, in a language understood by the other workers in the kitchen, to remind them of their humanity even in the midst of flames. As always with kitchen work, many of the poets are dark-skinned or female; there may be no English, or a new English. The kitchen, for these poets, may literally be a city jail, a welfare office, a housing project. . . . This poetry has the capacity to create solidarity among those in the kitchen and empathy among those outside the kitchen. . . . Perhaps the vocabulary is more urgent than usual, but then again the house is on fire. (Espada 1998, 10–11)

The writings are as varied as human beings. And that is the point, isn't it? Easy to forget, incarcerated women are locked so far out of sight that the only notions most of us have about who lives behind the locked doors we have gleaned from lurid movies, pulp fiction, and daily media—perhaps the most misleading of all. It is with this acknowledgment of our current limited social imagination that we offer the alternative perspectives by women in prison and jail and the advocates who work with them.

Anzaldua could be speaking to incarcerated women writers when she urges women of color to tell their stories, to write. "Write with your tongues of fire. Don't let the pen banish you from yourself. Don't let the ink coagulate in your pens. Don't let the censor snuff out the spark, nor the gags muffle your voice. Put your shit on the paper" (Anzaldua 2001, 312).

The Collection

We recruited essays and creative work from scholars, activists, incarcerated and formerly incarcerated writers. We chose essays that took a critical perspective, addressing political, theoretical, and material challenges of writing in carceral spaces. This book is not a how-to manual. There are such manuals in print, and we wanted our essays to think critically about potentially romanticized notions of "prison writing" and motivate readers to think critically and constructively about ways to leverage writing and creativity for the benefit of both the women inside and the communities outside of prisons and jails.

We have organized *Women, Writing, and Prison* into loose thematic groups, with some obvious overlap. We dedicate this book with "Mia's" poem "Bless," a politically aware and compassionate reflection that challenges us all to bear the responsibility of freedom and social justice.

"Where We Are From," a collective poem, frames the three sections that follow by introducing the multiple identities that women bring to prison. One woman declares she's from "a pack of strong women," and another, "from Hell." The poem concludes with epistemological humility, "I am unsure where exactly I'm from," underscoring the fractured nature that women often feel when they pause to reflect on their lives.

Section One

Section One, "Writing and Reclaiming Self," includes essays, scholarship, and poems that examine the experience of dislocated identities and the process of reclamation. Jessica Hill's essay, "My Words are Brain and Bone Marrow," tells a story of writing being silenced when, as a girl, her locked diary was broken into, and how she reclaimed her writing voice years later. For Hill, words are "heart and heartache," and she writes "because I am not always in the right place at the right time to give of myself. Maybe my words will be there though. . . . On the edge of a bridge where a woman makes a final decision. In the bottom of a bottle that's three too many. In dark alleys and on cruise ships. In prisons and on hospital wards."

In "From Nonna's Table to Book Signings: Under the Influence of the Pen," Nancy Birkla describes her early writing experiences with her cousin, novelist Wally Lamb, and subsequent participation in his book project with women writers at York Correctional Facility as she chronicles her journey as a writer inside and beyond prison. For performer Dionna Griffin, landing in a Detroit jail was far from her notion of where life would take her. In "This Ain't No Holiday Inn, Griffin: Finding Freedom on the Blank Page," she documents her struggles to learn and participate in the discourse of jail, turning to paper and pen to channel emotions of frustration, pain, humor and anger. Griffin's vivid descriptions and engaging dialogue offer readers a visceral window into the liminal space of a women's ward at a county jail, the place where the not-yet-convicted await sentencing and those with short sentences await release.

Shelley Goldman, aka S. Phillips, in "A Symphony of Medicine," asks about the power of nature to elicit a sense of mystery and longing, and declares that when she writes, she is "filling up every infinitesimal part of the abyss that has left me a wounded warrior." Judith Clark, in "The Girl Behind the Smile," writes about using essay and poems to track her journey, through writing, back to herself and her multiple identities. "I am a lesbian, a Jew, a prisoner, but if you put any of those words together with writer, I would add in front of them, 'more than.' Not so with the word, 'woman.' Being woman encompasses all the potentiality I can imagine."

Another form of practice and survival, letter writing, is the subject and content of "Writing to Survive the Madness: Letters from Prison" by Sarah Anonymous and Patricia O'Brien. Compiled by a university professor and a former prisoner, this essay weaves together reflections and excerpts from Sarah's extended correspondence with Georg, a healing practitioner whom Sarah never meets face-to-face. Through the act of writing and receiving letters while inside prison, Sarah is able to cultivate a deep and lasting connection and maintain an essential link to Native cultural and spiritual traditions and practice. Recounting the many identities writing allows her, Crista Decker's "My Voice Through A Deadbolt Door," proclaims that while her body is locked away, her mind is free and that her "poems are [her] spirit being sent out to whoever may hear."

The final piece in this section, Irene C. Baird's essay, "Rolling with the Punches," describes a writing program that grew out of her work with homeless women when she began to offer writing workshops in jail. Baird discusses how women choose to write about domestic violence and to recall the reasons they stay(ed) in abusive relationships. Baird recounts their collective effort to reach out to the incarcerated men at the same jail and create an anonymous exchange of ideas between the two groups, and she argues for the necessity of such interchanges if we are to realize social change in this area.

Section Two

Section Two, "Bridging Communities: Writing Programs and Social Practice," brings together essays, poems and scholarship that examine the te-
leology of writing: Why write in prisons and jails? What use is it? What
constitutes good practice?

In "Good Intentions Aside: The Ethics of Reciprocity in a University-Jail
Women's Writing Workshop Collaboration," Sadie Reynolds describes the
Inside Out Writing Project, a women's jail-based writing program. Reynolds
outlines a critical pedagogy for writing work with imprisoned women. She
includes descriptions of the methods for training and mentoring student interns as well as the strategies employed to put theory into practice, pointing to
some of the ethical dilemmas this work poses for self-reflective activists and
scholars. Indeed, as more and more people become interested in "going in" to
offer workshops or classes, discussions about the ethics of the work become
urgent and, we hope, will lead to collective ethical framing specific to writing
with incarcerated women.

Sandy Sysn's "Jumble of Thoughts" describes her encounter with words
as a young child and meditates on what a good story can do. To her, "words
are the pieces of a puzzle that make up the picture of my psyche, my deepest
desires or my heartfelt hopes, dreams and goals. I write to connect the dots."
Sysn describes the child fascinated with words she does not yet know how to
read and her transformation into the woman fearlessly writing to make sense
of her life.

Tom Kerr turns to the question of audience in his analysis of the rhetoric
of women's letters from prison written to a specific audience. Kerr makes
visible the powerful sense of identity women presented when invited to correspond with his advanced rhetoric university course. He argues that the
"spectre of audience" challenges writers to imagine institutional survival and
resistance.

Wendy Hinshaw and Kathie Klarreich's "Writing Exchanges: Composing
across Prison and University Classrooms," describes the partnership between
Florida Atlantic University and ArtSpring, a Miami-based nonprofit arts
organization serving women in prison and youth in detention. The collaboration between Hinshaw and Klarreich has led to ongoing correspondence
between students at both institutions and their essay describes how they built
the partnership and the ethical and material concerns that inform it.

In "Mothers and Daughters: Meditations on Prison Theater," author and activist Jean Trounstine reflects on the time she lost her mother and how the theater workshops she was conducting in prison took on a new significance, especially as the actors' needs for mothering came to light in their writing and improvisation. This essay weaves personal reflection together with the insights the author gained through developing, practicing, and performing an updated version of Hawthorne's "The Scarlet Letter." Another well-known activist, author, and teacher, Hettie Jones ("Poetry, Audience, and Leaving Prison"), articulates the importance of writing within a prison and of finding a means to take the work beyond prison barriers. Jones writes about the complexities of leading a women's writing workshop in a maximum-security prison and the politics of being asked to leave when a more famous writer/performer expresses interest in teaching such a class in the same facility.

Roshanda Melton's poem, "As Others Stand By and Ask Questions," explains that writing helps her "define" herself "as others stand by and ask questions." She writes "because [she] has a story to tell and only [she] can tell it."

Section Three

Section Three, "Writing, Resistance and the Material Realities of U.S. Prisons and Jails," includes personal narratives, poems, and essays that look at the context of women's writing inside prison or jail and deals with the politics of such writing. Extending the work begun in her landmark collection, *Wall Tappings: Women's Prison Writings, 200 A.D. to the Present*, in "'. . . to speak in one's own voice': The Power of Women's Prison Writing" Judith Scheffler discusses the historical silencing of incarcerated women's writing by the literary and social canon. She points to several contemporary writing opportunities around the country as examples of the emergence of workshops in the 1970s, and argues that the work emerging from workshops provides potentially powerful alternatives to the infantilization women often experience in prison as well as the silent reception of women's historical writing.

Taylor Huey, who is serving a twenty-five-year sentence, writes "because I cannot fly," ("Writing is My Way of Sledge Hammering These Walls") and echoing Scheffler's contention that incarcerated women's writing contains power, claims that "people from the established society could learn so much from women in prison. We have so much to teach, so much to tell. I only wish people would listen." For her, prison "has been a beginning—a chance to stand aside and look" at herself and her value. She writes "about it all—about people I have loved or hated, about the brutalities and ecstasies of my life."

Velmarine O. Szabo's "'You Just Threatened My Life': Struggling to Write in Prison," recounts direct challenges to her writing from prison staff and incarcerated peers. Szabo reflects upon the psychological and physical barriers she faced in trying to compose her memoir of growing up and surviving child sexual abuse. As she traces the complexities of surviving as a solitary writer, Szabo weaves into her essay excerpts of her memoir. Clarinda Harriss, a long-distance mentor for Szabo, introduces "'You Just Threatened My Life'" by underscoring some of the material complexities Szabo faced as she began to write in prison.

The endangered swamp upon which Gretchen Schumacher's facility is built serves as a metaphor in her essay "Out at the Swamp." Schumacher examines the contradictions of prison evaluation and socialization, pointing to the injustices incarcerated women face. Claiming prison activist Angela Davis as a role model, she expresses her desire to make change beyond prison walls, noting that currently, "I am on the inside of nothing." Schumacher has continued to write in the free world and has founded a nonprofit for other women released from prison, described in her essay, "The Dream of Water Under the Bridge."

Using the image of herself as a warrior for justice, Boudicca Burning ("I am Antarctica: I Shriek, I Accuse, I Write") has the official job of law clerk in her prison, writing letters, motions, "pleas for the elderly, clemency for the mentally ill." She "takes on all comers. It is adversarial, it is competitive, it is . . . war." Burning has been in prison for fifteen years and writes about the unspoken abuses she has received at the hands of staff, and lives "in fear of committing the smallest infraction and drawing attention to myself. I never know when the thread will unravel and a sword will fall on my head."

Considering the York writers' experiences, activist, scholar, and novelist Bell Gale Chevigny describes the legal and cultural challenges faced by writers who publish their work ("No Stopping Them: Women Writers at York Correctional"). Chevigny describes the workshop practices and offers writers' observations about the impact of prison writing programs, including those of

Barbara Lane, a participant whose essay drew a great deal of attention from the media and correctional system after she was awarded the 2005 PEN International Prison Writing prize.

Tshehaye Hebert's "Dear Shelly: Reflections on the Politics of Teaching Inside" claims the epistolary mode in which Hebert writes of her experiences teaching literature and writing in a large urban jail. She tries to answer one of the women's questions to her: *Why are you here?* The answers constitute the bulk of the letter as Hebert looks at the broad sociopolitical context of women's incarceration and her own needs and commitments as an artist and teacher. In "With the Stroke of a Pen," Joyce Cohen addresses why she writes, since she doesn't enjoy "the mechanics of writing," but concludes that writing not only frees her but might even "help change a system that is corrupt."

Samsara's "The Prisoner's Lament" poetically reminds us all of the pain being incarcerated engenders. She writes that she has "razor wire in my eyes, number on my chest,/ what my future seems to be, unknown, scary/ as hell." Fear, loneliness, self-doubt, inability to forgive oneself for the pain caused to others, all of this and more is what constitutes this prisoner's "lament." Tobi Jacobi reminds us that we must not only describe and amplify voices and conditions in prisons, but "recognize our collective selves as road builders— and acknowledge the risks that come with such work." Using her own work behind bars as a case study, she asks what abstract notions like "solidarity" and "alliance" mean with women writers in prison.

In the closing poem, "Hope is There," Cree writes against the narrative of victimization and instead calls readers to stop looking "at the ugly" and see "the beauty." She encourages women incarcerated with her to "Believe in your heart/ for a new start./ Hope./ Pass it on./ Hope."

Finally, the appendices contain resources for facilitating prison writing workshops as well as a selected (and ever-expanding) bibliography of work on women in prison and prison writing.

Women, Writing, and Prison provides a wide variety of opportunities for those of us outside and inside to move our writing and advocacy work forward with urgency. As we struggle to create a more just society, we search for what bell hooks calls "an openness of mind and heart that allows us to face reality even as we collectively imagine ways to move beyond boundaries, to transgress" (hooks 1994, 207).

References

Allende, Isabel. 1999. Foreword. In *Conversations with Isabel Allende*. Edited by John Rodden. Austin: University of Texas Press.

Anzaldua, Gloria. 2001. Speaking in tongues: A letter to 3rd world women writers. In *This bridge called my back*. Edited by Cherrie Moraga and Gloria Anzaldua. Berkeley, CA: 3rd Woman Press.

Bloom, Barbara, Barbara Owen, and Stephanie Covington. 2004. *Review of Policy Research* 21, no 1: 32.

Chicago Legal Advocacy for Incarcerated Mothers (CLAIM). 2000. CLAIM fact sheet. Accessed November 29, 2013. http://www.claim-il.org.

Espada, Martin. 1998. *Zapata's disciple*. Cambridge, MA: South End Press.

Golden, Renny. 2005. *War on the family: Mothers in prison and the families they leave behind*. New York: Routledge.

hooks, bell. 1994. *Teaching to transgress: Education as the practice of freedom*. New York: Routledge.

Notes

1. We fully understand that incarcerated men's writing is a powerful force as well, but have chosen to focus this book on women's writing only, given the paucity of work that has done so.

2. Jodie Michelle Lawston and Ashley E. Lucas's *Razor wire women: Prisoners, activists, scholars, and artists* (Albany: State University of New York Press, 2011) gets at some of these questions, but certainly not all.

3. Judith Scheffler's fine volume, *Wall tappings: An international anthology of women's prison writings 200 to the present* (Boston, MA: Northeastern University Press, 1989) is the exception. Maisha T. Winn's *Girl time: Literacy, justice and the school to prison pipeline*, focuses on the writing of incarcerated and formerly incarcerated girls' writing for stage (New York: Teachers College, 2011).

4. See, for example, Gayle Bell Chevigny, 1999, *Doing time: 25 years of prison writing —A PEN American Center Prize anthology* (New York: Arcade); Jeff Evans, 2001, *Undoing time: American prisoners in their own words* (Boston, MA: Northeastern University Press); Wally Lamb and the Women of the York Correctional Facility, 2004, *Couldn't keep it to myself: Testimonies from our imprisoned sisters* (New York: Regan Books); H. Bruce Franklin, 1998, *Prison writings in the United States* (New York: Penguin).

5. E. Ann Carson and William J. Sabol, 2012, Prisoners in 2011, U.S. Department of Justice, Bureau of Justice Statistics, December.

6. Ibid.

7. Ibid.

8. The Sentencing Project, retrieved from www.sentencingproject.org/doc/publications/publications/inc_factsAboutPrisons-Jan2013.pdf.

9. Racial disparity, The Sentencing Project, http://www.sentencingproject.org/template/page.cfm?id=122.

10. Substance Abuse and Mental Health Services Administration, 2011, *Results from the 2010 national survey on drug use and health: Summary of national findings*, NSDUH Series H-41, HHS Publication No. (SMA) 11-4658 (Rockville, MD: Substance Abuse and Mental Health Services Administration), http://www.oas.samhsa.gov/NSDUH/2k10NSDUH/2k10Results.htm#1.1

11. Lauren Glaze and Laura M. Maruschak, 2008, *Parents in prison and their minor children*, Bureau of Justice Statistics Special Report, August: 2.

12. Barbara Owen, 1998, *In the mix: Struggle and survival in a women's prison* (Albany: State University of New York Press), 4.

13. Fact sheet: Women in prison, The Sentencing Project, www.sentencingproject.org.

14. Fact sheet: Women in prison, The Sentencing Project, www.sentencingproject.org 009, 17.

15. 2005, Fact sheet: Women in prison, The Sentencing Project, Federal Bureau of Justice Statistics, May, www.sentencingproject.com.

16. Human Rights Watch, www.humanrightswatch.org/doc/?t=usa.

17. See Michelle Fine et al.'s *Changing minds: The impact of college in a maximum-security prison* (September 2001, http://www.changingminds.ws.) and Stephen Steurer, Linda Smith, and Alice Tracy's 2001, Three state recidivism study, September, http://www.ceanational.org/documents/3StateFinal.pdf; and Wendy Erisman and Jeanne Bayer Contardo, 2005, *Learning to reduce recidivism: A 50-state analysis of postsecondary correctional education policy* (Washington, DC: The Institute for Higher Education Policy).

18. Chevigny, *Doing time.*

19. Angela Davis, 2003, *Are prisons obsolete?* (New York: Seven Stories Press).

20. Indeed, many prisoners are released each year. In 2011, 688,384 people were released from state and federal prisons, and 668,800 were admitted to jails or prisons. E. Ann Carson and William J. Sabol, 2012, Prisoners in 2011, U.S. Department of Justice, Bureau of Justice Statistics, *Bulletin*, December, http://bjs. gov/content/pub/pdf/p11.pdf.

21. For a close reading and analysis of texts by incarcerated women writers, see Ann Folwell Stanford, 2004, More than just words: Women's poetry and resistance at Cook County Jail, *Feminist Studies* 30 no. 2 (Summer): 277–301.

Where We Are From

SPEAKOUT! WOMEN'S WRITING GROUP (FALL 2011)

I am from a pack of strong women
    a place where cultures are hugely diverse
    an energy I refer to as LOVE.

I am from Hell.
    from an image of God, the heaven's above
    mothers' tears
    a broken home.

I am from a wonderful, loving family
    from a Spanish-speaking environment
    the Mile High city
    white snowcapped mountains
    the desert so dry.

I am from fallen grace.
I am from hateful love and chaotic serenity.
I am from a repeating cycle that I'm determined to break!

I am from wherever you think I'd be from.
    beautiful, faraway European Slovakia
    two worlds combined in love
    a better place.

I am from a redneck background
    from four sets of German grandparents
    from two crazy kids who had to grow up
    a strong, loving, beautiful mother
    a shell at the bottom of the sea.

I am from my mother, God help me
    a little boy's hugs
    two beautiful sons
    an Italian family.

I am from a rodeo town
    Hollis, Oklahoma.
    Sacramento, California.
    from where it is too hot for birds to fly.

I am unsure where exactly I'm from.

SECTION I

Writing and Reclaiming Self

1

My Words Are Brain and Bone Marrow

JESSICA HILL

I write because I read things wrong. Faces, body language, conversations. I can't be sure that what I say will come out the way I intend it to, so I write to allow myself the pleasure of erasing spoken errors. Misinterpretations and offenses. Conclusions that I may otherwise jump to because of the immediacy of speaking. I write to temper my passions. Sometimes when I speak with it I am mistaken for being angry. With written words my voice doesn't seem so harsh. So I write to get my point across, to explain myself so that later, when I read what I have written, I understand more of who I am. It's writing to stand strong so that I can stand to be corrected.

As an adolescent I wrote to relieve the pressure building in my spirit, to cast aside the things that threatened my existence. I wrote to dishonor the lies that I was too young to know I lived. The secrets that stole my breath. Secrets I was told. Not to tell. Once, I was given a journal with a precious key hole. I had the only key in this entire world that fit. My diary became the safest place to pen the events that overwhelmed me, and so writing began to be my own Heaven of Release.

One day I returned home from school to find my diary open on the floor of the closet. Her secrets, our secrets, spilled carelessly, running in the crevices of the broken wood floor. Breathless and afraid now, fear quickly seized my desire to write. A long time elapsed before I did so again. Until then I spoke sentences in my head, and I enjoyed them. I would see or feel something and on my mind's own slate I would write a poem. Yet in that very moment, as one word began the previous one would end, and so my work seemed only to exist in mere seconds at a time, a narrated movie that doesn't rewind.

Later, life became too complicated to write, to sit down and construct a simple sentence. My writing then began even more to reflect the life I lived— out of control and almost non-existent. I became a moving target because moving targets were harder to hit. To touch. Destroy. I could not sit still and expect to not be violated. Because I could not express myself, I tried to escape myself. Not writing physically and forgetting to write mentally brought all of my creativity to a standstill.

When I finally felt safe enough to allow my fingers to convey my thoughts I was seventeen years old and facing a lengthy prison sentence. Time. Prison-time kept me still. In the same flow of my life, my words began to move again. Emotionally though, and cold. Withdrawn and lonely. Most times I wrote to fill the spaces that others left gaping. I wrote to make me whole, complete. So that I could feel something when I touched myself, pinched myself and know that I am real. I wrote to exist within myself because I felt that I lived in an illusion. I wrote things as they were, then as I wished they'd been. Is that writing lies? It was easier than my truths. Write with me.

It's 2 a.m. You're cold. You're lonely. With pen and paper in hand you lean against the wall and all the parts of your past leans with you. Weighs you down, heavily until you're sliding to the floor. Cold and uncomfortable you wonder. You wonder if those old secrets of so long ago matter enough to still be secrets, to still accompany you. You ask yourself if you should write. My diary comes to mind, those spilled secrets. Your chest tightens and suddenly writing's not so easy. You stare at your paper and pen poised and though years of thought invade your space, your hand doesn't move. The spatters of tears on blue lined paper jar you into the present. You sigh a little though it hurts a lot. You have to push through it though. So you dry your eyes and put away your writing things. It's all the "writing" you'll do for now. All the secrets you'll tell in tears.

I write to articulate my true self. To believe that my actions twelve years ago were not inherent of who I am today. I write to defy the labels that my peers placed on me in their haste to pass judgment. When literally three seconds of a bad decision decided my life, another's life. I write to right the wrongs I cannot erase, I cannot escape. I write to create a glass-blown vase that will catch my tears when I cry and shatter when I'm done. I write.

Sometimes I don't understand the people around me. The mentality of those that hold me captive; those that judge me, perplex me. So I write. With the emotions and thoughts that their actions evoke in me. Then I sit and ruminate what I have wept to get a better understanding of how I receive my environment, and why I reject it.

I have learned that writing is my most effective route of growth. So I write to mature with the worlds in which I exist. I write my most soulful passions on paper and feel them connect in the depths of other beings—of human beings and in all living things.

I write because my words are brains and bone marrow. Heart and heartache. I write because I am not always in the right place at the right time to give of myself. Maybe my words will be there though. In heaven, on earth, in hell. In hearts, on minds. Where they're needed. For who wants them. On the edge of a bridge where a woman makes a final decision. In the bottom of a bottle that's three too many. In dark alleys and on cruise ships. In prisons and on hospital wards. I write because I can't remember half the things I forgot to say. Without words I wouldn't know in which direction I am going. So I write a path that leads to truth. To walk it means I'm moving, I'm breathing. I'm free.

2

From Nonna's Table to Book Signings

Under the Influence of the Pen

NANCY BIRKLA

"No, I don't wanna play croquet; it's time for my art lesson with Wally." Most often this was my reply, as all our other cousins scrambled toward the door after a holiday dinner at our grandmother's house. As traditional as the pans of pasta and sumptuous meatballs that accompanied every Thanksgiving turkey or Easter ham, were the hours I spent after dinner with my cousin Wally. We'd wait for our Aunt Pal to strip the huge dining room table down to the pads that protected Nonna's fine wooden tabletop; then we'd gather our supplies and ready ourselves for our "work."

Excitedly, I'd bring to the table my own supplies, plunking down odd-sized, multi-colored piles of scrap paper, donated by our Uncle Dom who worked for a local printing company, I'd then go over to Nonna's mahogany storage chest and grab the cache of "house" crayons. The crayons lived in a tin can that had at one time held *Toy Cookies,* which were similar to animal crackers but instead shaped like miniature two-dimensional jacks-in-the-box, dolls, bikes, and teddy bears.

Finally situated at the table, I'd pop the lid off the cookie can and stare down into a pile of broken colored pieces, each tinged with speckles of other colored pieces, some with, but mostly without their paper wrappers. I'd always then take a deep whiff, enjoying momentarily the delightful, sensual, aromatic concoction of crushed crayon bits and long ago snatched up cookies.

Wally's passion, for as far back as I can remember, centered around drawing and storytelling. To a lesser degree mine had too, although as a kid I preferred reading and writing to drawing. Together, though, Wally and I spent many hours toiling away, drawing pictures and exchanging stories around our grandmother's dining room table.

During those evenings at Nonna's, Wally always treated me to special "art lessons." I vividly recall those lessons, during which he'd draw various pictures, step by step, as I mirrored each segment on my own paper, thus creating masterpieces I'd never have managed on my own. One scenic endeavor that became etched in memory for me was of a tiny cabin nestled between snowy hills, with pine trees scattered throughout a rugged terrain. The cabin's roof was covered in white fluffy piles, with the chimney bellowing black smoke that wafted off into a gray sky. Once these particular drawings were complete, Wally told me of an impending "avalanche" and precisely how the family that lived within the tiny cabin could survive the disaster.

That's what Wally did through his pictures and his words; he created disasters and then heroically "rescued" potential victims moments before they should have perished. Back during our youthful visits together, Wally had already attained the ability to adequately express both his brilliance and his sense of humanity. And very early on, he knew what he wanted to do when he grew up—he dreamed of becoming a teacher.

As for me, well, I didn't think much about anything other than surviving one more day without hurting so much, as I held inside secrets the likes of which that no kid should have to deal with. Nobody realized that the extroversion that radiated from my outside was just a cover-up for my truly introverted and introspective nature. And definitely nobody knew about or understood exactly what I was dealing with from a psychological standpoint, after being sexually abused by a neighbor when I was just six to seven years old. These secrets prevented me from dreaming about my future at all. But despite all my troubles, I remember those hours spent with my cousin as being the happiest of my childhood. Wally was then, without a doubt, my mentor, my hero, and also my very favorite teacher.

Over the years my family moved further and further away from Norwich, Connecticut, our hometown. At first my family's visits became fewer and further between. The last visit for me before many years of estrangement from the family was in 1972, when Wally and I were both in college. Our time together during that particular visit was not spent at Nonna's house but rather in a smoky nightclub. And instead of trading drawings and stories, we instead shared pitchers of beer and some very loud rock and roll music.

After that, Wally went on to finish earning degrees and to subsequently become a high school English teacher, while I managed to flunk out of college and stumble forward into eighteen years of alcoholism and active drug addiction. Visits to Norwich and any form of communication with Wally or other family members ceased for the duration of those years. Soon drugs and the music scene became my lifestyle, after which nobody or nothing else mattered much to me for a long, long time.

Once in a while I'd receive word, through my parents, of Wally's achievements. In addition to becoming a successful and popular teacher, he continued writing, winning various contests and prizes, and then eventually his writings began being published. My own writing ceased, with the exception of long dramatic journaling binges, and riddle-ridden, nightmarish, not-so-poetic volumes of prose through which I'd exorcise some of my sadness, angst, and utter misery in life.

During this same period of time, I began "hitting bottom" with my drug addiction. I successfully completed an in-patient, thirty day drug and alcohol treatment and then entered an ongoing 12-step recovery program. But my problems were far from over, as I faced difficult consequences that stemmed from my past, including drug-related charges that resulted in a short prison stint that I served during my first year in recovery.

My only writing during those years was the journal I'd kept while I was in prison—the humble lifeline to sanity that I'd hung on to with all I had, after being yanked from my familiar recovery environment and thrown into one of life's most powerful pressure cookers. Writing afforded me the ability to breathe while I was in prison—literally. The day I got locked up was the day my suppressed memories of childhood sexual abuse began surfacing, provoking debilitating panic attacks. I don't know what I would have done had I not been able to rely on my old friend, pen and paper, to comfort and to calm me during that time in my life. Fortunately for me, the judge ruled in favor of granting me "shock probation," so a couple of months into my seven year prison sentence I was able to gratefully return home and back into my 12-step recovering life.

By this time, Nonna had been dead for years, and the hours I'd spent with my cousin at our grandmother's house seemed like ancient familial history that was buried beneath mountains of more recent trials and troubles. Seeing Wally again at a family reunion sparked something inside me, although at the time I couldn't pinpoint what it was. We caught up with each other, sitting alone at a picnic table out in the park where the reunion was being held. We chatted for awhile as our cousins laughed and reminisced over games of croquet. I experienced a vicarious thrill as Wally relayed to me his recent adventures, from receiving the initial phone call from Oprah, to the sale of his novel for a possible future Hollywood screening. I hadn't been thrilled about anything in years but these shared moments felt exciting and old and comfortable to me, nonetheless.

Wally was by then on his way to becoming a best-selling author, so I also found myself permeated with shame and regret over my own "missing" years and all the things I hadn't done with my life.

After returning home from that visit, I thought and thought about Wally and the life he'd created for himself. I don't come from a family that reveals secrets freely, so I'm still not sure where the courage to make a phone call to him came from, but call him I did. It was during that phone call I disclosed the details of my past. Also during that phone conversation I told Wally that I wasn't sure what I should do about my future. I told him I'd journaled religiously while I was in prison and how that particular writing had felt like my hotline to God; despite all my problems in life, writing was still my one area of interest and passion for me. Writing is the only way I can adequately manage to pull myself inside out and expel whatever it is that is burdening me. Eventually I confided in Wally that I wished to revisit the possibility of becoming a writer, perhaps even writing about my prison experience.

This phone conversation with Wally became a truly inspirational moment for me, a significant impetus for my journey back to a creativity buried deep inside. Wally didn't pull any punches with me, though. He told me before I could even think about writing on a professional level, I'd need to go back to school and learn the process and dynamics of the discipline. He also advised me that unless a person is famous, memoir is not easily embraced by the reading public.

Rather than feeling discouraged by the timeframe he talked about, before I might consider becoming a writer, I signed up for a writing class at a local community college. Then I applied for scholarships, one which ended up affording me a full tuition reimbursement, resulting from the accompanying essay I'd written. In the fall of 1994, I turned in the first assigned essay I'd written in over twenty years; then I marveled over my professor's comments upon its return to me. In addition to citing what he called my "natural ability to write," the professor told me I had talent, and then he wrote the words "thank you" at the end of his critique.

As Wally worked on his second novel, *I Know This Much Is True*, I enrolled in more classes, won more scholarships, and learned more about literature and writing. Before long I was entering and placing first in writing contests of my own. And each time I wrote to Wally, congratulating him on his latest accomplishment, he'd write back complimenting *me* over a story *I'd* written or an award *I'd* won.

On with college and writing I went, and my love of writing made my days as a returning adult student much easier for me. I didn't know of many other students who actually loved writing research papers like I did. Wally surged forward into his second experience as a best-selling novelist, with another book tour and a second visit to Oprah's book club, and then movie deals and screenplay writing, flying here and flying there. Over time, I felt more and more content with my own life, including continuing recovery, a second marriage, a new home, a degree in human services, and a respectable job. Who would want to do all that traveling and be under all that pressure, I wondered. "Surely not me," I told myself!

Imagine my surprise when I received an e-mail from my cousin, in April of 2001. He told me of a project he'd been working on with his writing group at a Connecticut women's prison, and he asked me if I would consider writing a piece, with the possibility of my writing becoming published, if it was "a good fit" with the other writings. I took that summer off from working at a regular job, and I wrote with Wally mentoring me, inspiring me, and teaching me. Not only did he serve as my editor, but he also once again became my confidant and good friend during those months of back and forth as we worked together across the miles that separated us.

Wally began referring to this writing as "our joint project," still bouncing all compliments I sent his way right back at me. He comforted me through the initial resistance and squeamishness of my family. When I had myself convinced that I couldn't go on, due to fear of hurting my parents, Wally assured me that as he'd read my draft, that my folks had come across as "unsung heroes"—that I'd more than adequately expressed my love and gratitude for them.

When I became permeated with fear over signing a contract with a major publisher, Wally told me he'd love me the same, regardless of whether I went through with it or not. Once again I felt overwhelmed by his sense of understanding and his usual kindness, after all the long, difficult, and at times unsettling hours we'd spent working on my essay.

Finally I'd become content with my new life in a little house nestled deep within the hills and woods of southern Indiana, a house and land that ironically resemble the picture Wally and I drew together some forty plus years ago. With my own avalanche in life long since passed, I felt little desire to be anywhere but safely anchored in my comfortable and quiet little world at home. The notion of traveling or gaining any media attention caused me to panic.

Wally left me alone as I thought and prayed over what to do. Before long I realized I needed to trust him the same way I had when he'd counseled me about returning to school and about taking my time and doing things right. I'd done as he'd advised, and my whole life had changed as the result. I knew I might never forgive myself if I gave up out of fear now, so I called Wally back and told him I'd do anything or go anywhere he thought I should. I then signed the contract, and immediately my excitement began prevailing over my fear.

Soon I was reunited with my cousin Wally, as we sat on strange seats at much different tables than the one we had shared back in the days at our grandmother's house when we were kids. Along with other contributing writers, for readings and signings at bookstores and college campuses, we worked together promoting our newly published book, *Couldn't Keep It to Myself: Testimonies from Our Imprisoned Sisters*.

When I met up with Wally in Atlanta, Georgia, for the first of these promotional dates, I couldn't resist bringing along a container of broken crayons and asking him to close his eyes and to take a whiff with me. Then, through the sense of an old and familiar smell, together we managed for a few brief moments to travel backward in time, back to our grandmother's dining room table—back to the days when Wally Lamb first became a mentor, a hero, and a teacher to me.

"This Ain't No Holiday Inn, Griffin"

Finding Freedom on the Blank Page

DIONNA GRIFFIN

Writing in prison saved my life. I spent six months in Wayne County jail penning my anguish, frustration, and anger every free moment I had. There were good days and bad days. Somewhere in between the good and bad, and the countless letters to friends and loved ones, I found my faith, resolve, acceptance, and freedom on the blank page. I served a total of two-and-one-half years during my incarceration and looked at my entire journey as an adventure. It was an incredible ride.

June 17, 1996: I remember when I first heard the verdict:

Guilty on count one.
Guilty on count two.
Guilty on count three.
Four.
Five.

My insides wanted to holler, yell, scream—do something, but I couldn't. I was frozen stiff. Powerless. The courtroom looked exactly the way it wanted you to feel—forty-foot-high ceilings with white European design from the early 1900s, velvet blue curtains that garnished the pristine white walls, and a gigantic American eagle mounted on the edge of Judge Friedman's beautiful wood-stained bench.

The U.S. Federal Courts were intimidating, especially to a young black woman. I grabbed the edge of the mahogany defense table, squeezed my attorney's hand, and fought back the tears that started to rip at the back of my throat. With each echo of *Guilty* from the juror's lips, I sunk deeper into my own personal hell.

Within five minutes after the prosecutor and defense attorney argued whether I should be remanded to custody, U.S. Federal Marshals rushed over and slapped cold, silver handcuffs onto my tiny wrists and ankles. I was escorted out of the courtroom hobbling along in a convict trot. I took one last look at my friends Josh, Larry, and Jeff huddled in a group hug, shaking their heads in disbelief. Tears started to roll down my face as I clenched my stomach muscles tight to keep myself standing. I could feel myself starting to hyperventilate. My chest was rising and my heart was beating fast. The steel against my nylons was starting to burn my ankles. The belly chain around my waist made it difficult to wipe my eyes. My heart was beating faster and faster as I took baby steps into the paddy wagon. I couldn't hold it in any longer. The floodgates swung open. Reality sunk in. I was going to jail.

It all started in Wayne County jail in Detroit, Michigan in 1996. It was the first time I had ever been to jail and that year I was sentenced to fifty-one months on drug conspiracy charges. Detroit was my city of many firsts: I was first in my family to graduate from high school as number three in my class, first one to receive a four-year merit college scholarship, first lover at age twenty-one, first engagement with a half carat ring, first acting contract with The Second City, and the first time I fell in love with a crook and went to jail.

"This ain't no Holiday Inn, Griffin; Pick up your mat and blanket and carry it," scolded a 5'2", brown-skinned, twenty-something-year-old officer wearing tight brown uniform pants.

It hadn't sunk in that I was in jail. I was in a daze. My county-issue XL hunter green pants kept sliding down, the sweat from my palms made the mattress slide from under my arm, and my toes kept sliding out of the mismatched brown sandals that the officer gave me when I traded in my court clothes.

The officer tilted her head to the side as only African American women can only do and waited. I was embarrassed to think I would be valeted to my cell.

This is jail. I am not at a Holiday Inn. I better act like I fit in and get with the program.

"Open cell gate four," said the officer to the deputy sitting behind a bullet proof booth talking on the phone.

The deputy had a perfect French roll, not a hair out of place. Immaculate. Everybody in Detroit gets their hair done.

The gate ground its way open to a slamming halt that echoed in the entire ward. It reminded me of the sound of carnival ride gears screeching to a complete stop at the end. The only difference: I wouldn't be getting off this ride anytime soon.

In an instant, I got a panoramic view of another world. All of the women on the ward were dressed alike, sporting "county greens," just like my hunter green smock, matching pants, and brownish orange sandals. Some of the women fashioned the uniform up a bit, cuffing the sleeves, tapering the pants at the leg, giving them a stylish look. The ward was busy with activity, a naked woman with big breasts and an oversized stomach was taking a shower, four women sitting at the steel tables in the middle of the pod playing a game of spades, one woman getting her hair braided into corn rows, another woman sitting on the floor talking on a pay phone, and a group of three women laughing up and down the corridor as they shuffled from cell to cell.

Scents of body odor, stale ammonia, and mildew filled the air. My eyebrows immediately flinched as my nose adjusted to the foreign smells. I bypassed all of the activity, ignored the eyes and stares. I pretended not to see the woman with the big afro playing cards, whose eyes seemed to follow me all the way to my top bunk.

Act tough.

I dragged my mat into the empty cell with a bit of attitude, as if it was routine. It wasn't. I was faking it. I was scared to death. I threw my mattress on the top metal flat rail, placed the care pack on the shelf below my bunk, rolled the dingy white sheets around my limp pillow making a cushion for my head, and climbed on top. My body was limp and weak, my stomach in a knot, legs ready to give out. I needed to lie down. I faced the cement wall replaying the words over in my head—*Guilty, Guilty, Guilty.* My breath started gasping. I clung to my pillow, blocking out the faint smell of bleach, the bright overhead light, the woman calling her "Boo" on the telephone, the loud click-clacking of the brown sandals smacking the floor, the young girl asking the deputy for a razor, the women slamming black kings and queens in a card game, and the constant swoosh sound from toilets flushing on the ward. I rocked slowly back and forth.

I could feel a stream running full force in my body. My stomach muscles were contracting as I put up internal barricades as I rocked steadily. My eyes shifted, scanning the wall from left to right, inspecting every crevice, corner and crack on the wall. Roaches lived here. Lots of roaches. My abdomen was rising faster as my eyes fixated on the writing staring back at me. Hundreds of words, initials, x's crossing off dates, scripture references, and pleas written in pencil or carved in black ink covered the wall. Many women had spent time here autographing their names, marking their time, in a members-only fashion on the cell wall. The women were gone, but their words remained.

I felt a hundred eyes looking back at me.

My focus was drawn to one message carved in thick block letters that made tears start to well in my eyes: *God, please save me.*

I stared until the words became blurry. This was too surreal—some other woman's pain was now my pain. I pulled the itchy grey wool blanket over my head, shielded the blinding overhead fluorescent light, and shuddered my tears.

I don't belong here.

Outside the Motor City, the streets were moving to a faint hum as dark blue-black clouds filled the sky. The city had an omniscient gloom. My loved ones were mourning: my cast from Second City was recounting the events; Lyn, my producer, was contacting an understudy to fill my role; my college beau Jeff was writing a letter; my grandmother was cursing God; my brother was losing his big sister; and my best friend, my dear mother, was facing the reality that her daughter was not coming home. Not coming home. Not for a long time.

Memories of my mother brushing my hair, my grandmother's sweet pound cake, and the time I raced with my little brother in the backyard, flashed in my head. In an instant, I was snatched from the one thing that my mattered the most—my family.

Thunder, lighting streaks filled the sky, cradling the night into a terrible storm. Dark clouds hovered over Wayne County jail as cell gates closed and lights flicked off at the 10 p.m. count. Officers walked the corridor doing their nightly head count.

My body curled into a fetal position as I continued to rock repeating the woman's handwritten words carved into the wall:

God please save me. God please save me. God please save me.

That night, it rained like it never rained before.

The grinding of the gates opened at 8 a.m., two hours after an "inmate" delivered our breakfast under the cell gate in a brown paper bag. My first meal in jail consisted of two boiled eggs, two stale dry pieces of white bread, a kid size box of cereal, and a carton of milk.

Like clockwork, four women rushed out of three cells on the ward, racing to grab a metal mop bucket, a dirty mop head, and a bottle of Simple Green. They had a system down. One woman mopped her cell; one woman sprayed Simple Green disinfectant onto each sink and toilet on the ward; one woman mopped the shower stall, and the other woman cleaned the lunch tables. The deputy inside the booth slid two maxi pads from the window, and one of the women wiped down the tables and the booth window with the oval shaped pads.

It was morning time and the day was about to begin.

I shook my head in dismay, stepping back in my cell, dropping my breakfast bag on my bunk. My mouth was dry and pasty. I needed to brush my teeth and shower. I opened the care pack issued to me at clothing exchange and was pleasantly surprised to find a soft bristled generic toothbrush, a small tube of toothpaste, a barber size comb, and two medium bars of Ivory soap. It was better than nothing.

I maneuvered the steel toilet and sink fixture and finally got water from the small spout to wet my toothbrush. I looked in the speckled mirror above the sink and sighed. My eyes were puffy from crying all night. Another sigh. Now I had to pee.

"You can tie your sheet on the bars," said the woman squirting a splash of Simple Green in my sink as I urinated. "Ms. B, the deputy, doesn't mind."

I politely thanked her in an awkward fashion as I pulled up my pants and flushed the toilet.

"Can I take a shower?" I asked, talking over the loud, vacuous flush sound the toilet made when I pushed the shiny silver button.

"As soon as Yvette finishes mopping it down, it's all yours. You got in last night?"

I nodded my head.

"Get in early; you beat the line," the woman smiled.

"Thank you," I obliged.

She left to spray the next cell.

"Shower is ready," shouted a woman pushing a metal mop bucket across the floor. I quickly grabbed my face cloth, towel, and soap and rushed to the shower clacking my sandals across the floor.

Nine cells on the ward and one single shower stall. No door. No light. No mat. A waffle-cut wall divided the ward providing a partition between the shower and the common area where everyone ate, played cards, and watched TV.

Water dripped from the shower nozzle and vapors of ammonia made my eyes squint as I took a quick peek inside. Green black and grey streaks of mildew covered the chip painted ceiling. Cement walls that were once a pale yellow looked brown. A deep cleaning was long overdue.

Maybe I didn't need to shower. Yes, I did. My body was sweaty from sleeping under a wool blanket in June. I pulled my shirt over my head, folding it in half, and draped it over the garbage bag.

"Use the garbage bag for a curtain. Take two pieces of soap and stick it in the cracks."

The Simple Green woman was back. She must have read my mind.

"Thanks," I replied, removing my pants, holding my towel up to my chest.

"You've got some pretty hair. Don't get it wet," she said, passing me the garbage bag. She was eager to assist, but I didn't know what I was doing. I had never made a curtain out of a trash bag.

"I'm Sharon. I'm at the corner cell," she smiled, jimmying one end of the trash bag in the wall.

"I think I've got it," I replied, attaching the opposite end.

"Enjoy your shower, girl."

Sharon left, throwing me a wave with her long skinny arms, swinging the Simple Green bottle, singing a verse by Stephanie Mills like it was a bright sunny day.

I removed my bra and panties, placing them under my pile with my pants and shirt. I grabbed my face cloth, new bar of Ivory soap, and carefully stepped in. I didn't want the curtain to fall. I made it.

Oh my God.

Roaches again—one coming out of the drain, one camping out on the shower nozzle, and another one resting in the crack of the wall. This was too much.

None of them was running. Their antennas were moving slowly as their brown little bodies rested comfortably in between the cracks. They were chilling out! These roaches got nerve! Most roaches run. They instinctively know that it's a life or death situation. Not these. They weren't going anywhere.

Ignore it. Get over it. You can do this.

I closed my eyes, pulled the shower nozzle, and took one step back. The water sprayed in full force. Streams of hot steamy water enveloped my body, starting from my neck to the bottom of my feet. I was glad to be wearing sandals.

I inhaled one deep breath and turned a perfect rotation without my shoulders or body touching the wall. White tiny bubbles lathered on my skin as droplets of water played a symphony on my back, chest, and legs. Circles of steam seeped from the stall, making a smoke signal over the homemade shower curtain.

The scent of Ivory soap filled the air as I relaxed. The water did its work—cleansing away the past night, the verdict, the tears, and the emptiness. The water was massaging my soul. I wrapped my arms around my chest and hugged myself. I said a silent prayer. *I'm still alive. Thank You.*

I stood still for ten seconds, taking it all in. I inhaled one deep breath and exhaled the remaining tension and anxiety living in my body.

Small pieces of leftover soap and a clump of black hair partially covered the drain as the water swirled in a small puddle before making its final exit.

One push on the nozzle and the water came to a halt. A faint trickle dripped from the shower head. I grabbed my towel, pulled the curtain back, and placed my soap back into the box. As I exited the shower, I stepped on a roach.

I was clean. It was a new day, and my hair barely got wet.

The routine of jail fell into place quickly. Cell gates open, cell gates close, new women come in, old women leave out, and some women never leave. Highlights of the day: mail call, visit days, laundry exchange, outside recreation, three meals, and commissary. All of us played the waiting game.

"Jail ain't nothing but a spiritual house; either you do the time or the time do you," a woman named Sue reminded me, giving me an extra Bible to read. Sue was the mother on the ward. She was waiting to be shipped out to a women's federal prison camp in Alderson, West Virginia to serve a 15-year sentence. I couldn't imagine what it must have felt like to carry that burden. Sue carried herself well—always smiling, in good spirits, and never looking sad. On Thursday, Sue gave me a fresh set of white clean sheets and a cotton blanket. Goodbye to the wool blanket. It was getting better.

It would be one week until my visitor list and outgoing phone numbers were processed in the system. No contact with my family or loved ones until the information was updated in the database. I busied myself reading the Bible and visiting the weekly church meetings in a classroom located across from our ward. The women shared stories about drug addiction, broken homes, and destructive relationships. The women sang songs of amazing grace and prayed fervently.

My stomach went into overhaul as I adjusted to starchy, high carbs and a high-sugar diet. The presentation of the food was always something unexpected every time lunch and dinner were served. Thick, sturdy brown serving trays with compartmental sections held dry chicken patties, canned stew, mashed potatoes, overcooked vegetables, square chunks of chocolate cake, a carton of milk, and a sweetened fruit punch. I always gave my fruit punch away; it tasted like red sugar syrup. Never enough water. My skin knew the difference. Some of the women on the ward saved their emptied cartons and filled them with water from the steel sink combo in our cells. I mirrored what they did. My adult acne was starting to flare up.

"Commissary is coming! Commissary is coming!"

Sharon went up and down the ward announcing the news of the morning. It was 11:00 on Friday morning, and women were lining up at the opening where the meals were served. Excitement and laughs filled the ward as women gathered their lists, bartered items, and grabbed their brown paper bags.

"Dionna, can you get me a Snickers and two suckers?" asked Sharon, looking at me with excitement as if it were Christmas morning. Sharon didn't have any money on her account and she did favors around the ward—cleaning cells, braiding hair, and being helpful to earn commissary.

"Sure." I smiled.

I hopped down from my top bunk, marked my page in the New Testament, and grabbed my list. The commissary cart rolled around right on schedule as women shuffled to the front and middle of the line. Sounds of a little handheld adding machine and women scurrying to their cells with brown bags of goodies created energy and excitement on the ward. Commissary meant snacks, sweets, toiletries, pieces of normalcy—gifts from the outside world that gave comfort to us on the inside. I waited for the last spot in the line. I didn't want to be rushed.

When the middle-aged brown-skinned woman grabbed her clipboard to take my order, I felt like a little kid getting ice cream the first time.

Life was just about to get better.

"Can you tell me how much I have on my account? My name is Dionna Griffin."

"Eighty-six dollars. What would you like?"

The woman had a pleasant look on her face, which made my shopping experience lovely.

"I'll take Colgate toothpaste, a medium firm toothbrush, Head and Shoulders shampoo and conditioner, one razor, a comb, a hairbrush, nail clippers, emery board, a packet of small underwear—white please, five jerky sticks, five packs of cheese and crackers, a Snickers, two blow pops, two boxes of Little Miss Debbie oatmeal pies. . . ." The adding machine was puttering fast as the receipt tape curled over. The lady kept smiling and so did I.

"And last, but not least—three pencils, 10 stamped envelopes and three yellow legal pads." I finally had something that felt like home—paper and pencil. *Thank you, Lord.*

Journal Entry—Sunday, September 8, 1996: Never thought about or knew how I would spend my 29th birthday until I reached that day. Today, I spent my birthday in jail. No plans to make in jail. I just want it to be peaceful and happy. The girls sang Happy B-Day. Yvette slid me an extra Danish for breakfast under my cell door and Katherine and Graciella sang their wishes in Spanish. Despite my surroundings, I feel good. Of course there are a million other places I'd love to be celebrating, but that time will come. I have much to look forward to. Today, I am thankful that I am alive, healthy, stronger, and wiser. A lot wiser. I've prayed to God to make me the person I was born to be. I feel the growth each day.

Journal Entry—Friday, November 1, 1996: Dear Lord—I thank you each moment I recognize you are speaking to me. Today it was through Richard Bach's *Jonathan Livingston Seagull.* When I sat down at the lunch table to watch the 8:00 movie (which I knew I wasn't going to watch), I saw the book laying there un-owned, waiting for someone to pick it up. It's a very concise paperback with black-and-white photos of beautiful seagulls included. Important notes and quoted from the book: "Each of us is in truth an idea of the Great Gull (God), an unlimited idea of freedom."

Journal Entry—Saturday, November 16, 1996: Eight glasses of water of today—achieve and maintain a clear complexion and good system. 300 crunches, leg squats and exercises to achieve the body I want. Meditation—focus on present circumstance to achieve future goals. Visualize your success. Focus on you, what you want to be. Worked on song, "I'm gonna be free."

> *One of these days, I'm gonna be free. Everything is gonna be alright.*
> *I'm gonna fight, pray, and hold on.*
> *One of these days, everything is gonna turn out just fine.*

As an actress and performer, I had learned to embrace my new environment. There was always something to observe and study. As my grandmother would say, life is a stage and we're all playing our part. Prison is no exception. I made some of my most unusual discoveries by listening and paying attention. Prison is a unique environment filled with sounds, details, and characters moving to a rhythm and beat of its own. The women in prison are the pulse.

Unlike the "free world," each sound and image carries depth and meaning to each individual incarcerated. I took as many mental snapshots as I could to remember this unusual place.

Some of those images included: the colored uniforms worn by the officers and inmates, 4:00 standup counts, jingling keys, the standing lines of women, mothers crocheting handmade crafts, grandmothers leading the prayer circle, wives studying in the law library, and young girls talking to boyfriends and their children at home. And the women's faces. I will never forget the faces—visible facial lines of strain, hurt, neglect, and loss of hope. We wore a mask of aged depression in our cheeks and mouth. It was difficult to smile on the bad days. Those days were few when we celebrated the going home of someone's release. Thunderous shouts, claps, whistles, and tears of joy make a roar in prison when a woman is going home. The sound of freedom is captivating.

Prison is also an environment filled with incredible emotional highs and lows without much in between. It was the "in-between" I filled with my writing, teaching improvisation, and listening to the stories of my fellow incarcerated women. Women from all social and economic backgrounds became my sisters enduring the struggle. Together we shared moments of joy, pain, sorrow, and laughter, marking one of the most profound experiences in my life.

The women were black, white, yellow, and brown—women who transcended race and represented all facets of myself.

As one woman told me early on in Wayne County, "We're all the same, only different."

Pen and paper connected me to myself and the women I met on my journey. The women were my mirror. A world that seemed abnormally foreign and distant became surreal, peaceful, and beautiful, providing solace to my caged soul. Writing was a tool to connect the dots. The dots represented my life. The more I wrote, the more clarity, hope, faith, forgiveness, and understanding I experienced in my life. As I wrote, I gave myself permission to be the woman I was born to be. As I shared my experience and love for the arts to the other women doing time, I remembered I was not alone.

A poignant conversation with a roommate named Maria gave me a rule to cherish. We were in our room on a Saturday afternoon relaxing from a day off from work. I was sitting on my bed writing in my journal. Maria was crocheting a powder blue afghan.

"You think you better than everybody, Dionna. You are no different. You got a number just like everybody else."

I paused with a quizzical look and put my journal down. Maria must have been having a bad day.

"You're right, Maria. I do have a number, 20512-039. The government also gave me a social security number and zip code. I've got plenty of numbers. The difference is that the number doesn't mean a thing to me. It is just a number. It does not define me. Not a jury, an institution, these prison walls, the officers, these blue uniforms, or these work boots—I define who I am every waking day of my life. And that means everything."

Maria rolled her eyes and didn't say a word. She kept crocheting. I picked up my pen and paper and continued to write.

Maria reminded me of one simple universal truth: *Freedom is a choice.*

4

A Symphony of Medicine

SHELLEY GOLDMAN, AKA S. PHILLIPS

Have you ever gone to the Grand Canyon, or any canyon? You stand out on a precipice and gaze in awe at the vast rutted chasm in front of you. Why are we in such utter amazement at the size, depth, and beauty of this natural phenomenon? Why are we awestruck by a large gaping open space that is actually the absence of a scenic landscape? Why does every single person who sees a canyon want to know how it got there? Did a meteor hit there? Was there an earthquake? A roaring river that dried up? Do you want to know how it came to be so beautiful? I know I do.

Why do I write? Well, on the outside I appear to be very well put together. In a pair of jeans and a jersey, "soccer mom" would be an apt description. However, I have a gaping hole inside of me that is screaming to be analyzed, by myself. When I write it is as if I am filling up every infinitesimal part of the abyss that has left me a wounded wanderer. Each word crams closure in a crevice. A paragraph may provide open explanation into a cavern. An entire essay, hell, it could be an all-day hike where I can rappel up and down the sides of the canyon, getting my sure footing on each rock that I use to propel me upward. Once I can use my words connected in a symphony of medicine for my aching heart, I can heal, and become whole.

It is so hard for me to be transparent when I am speaking. I am so very vulnerable and opposed to being exposed. There is so much inside me that I have failed to come to terms with that it creates craters throughout my otherwise solid form. I need to fill up those void spaces that are waiting patiently for me to string together phrases of reflection and introspection that come from a place that flows so freely without fear. I write because I do it for me. I share my writing because every human being is inextricably intertwined with another and we owe it to each other to help bridge that chasm each of us views from our own personal precipice. Many may wonder how my canyon came to be in existence, but only I know. However, when I have the privilege to open up on paper, a whole new beginning exists.

5

The Girl behind the Smile

JUDITH CLARK

It is my journal that keeps me above the surface of the waters. On the days when I feel close to drowning. Drowning in anger that wells up, like a tidal wave, from the pit of the stomach, burning my heart, choking my throat. . . . The walls are closing in, closer and closer. My cell window faces a brick wall, and I wonder if they are sending me a message. . . . But I can't let "them" invade my mind. I don't want to write about "them." I want to write my stories, my poems, my words. My words. (Writing exercise, 10/13/93)

Although I have published numerous poems, essays and articles, I still hesitate to call myself "a writer." How many women writers share that fear of making a fraudulent claim? But I have no problem joining the words, *woman* and *writer*. My journey toward becoming a writer has been a woman's journey, which—like so many women's journeys—began in silence.

> *from* **Panic**
> *Papa, driving the family car*
>   *Debates politics with Saul*
> *Mama, next to him*
>   *Navigates*
> *in the back seat*
>   *Brother pinches*
>   *me*   *scrunched*
>   *between him and Saul*

> *Papa's voice rises*
> *as he turns*
>   *red faced*
> *jabbing his finger at Saul*
> *his bullet words*
>   *flying*
>   *scatter-shot*

My family deified the Word. The books that lined every wall of our home represented the ultimate truth that my parents believed in. Ours was a family of talkers and debaters. Meals, car trips, poker games were all occasions for political discussion and debate. But in this atmosphere saturated with the language of ideas, there were many silences.

I had trouble with my speech as a young child. When I was an infant, my family traveled to the Soviet Union, where we lived for three years. I came to speech in two languages, always knowing which language to use with whom. When we came back to the U.S., I intuited the unspoken message to stop speaking Russian—that it was somehow dangerous. But the echo of that first language left a residue on my tongue. I slurred my r's and l's to the point of being unintelligible.

My parents were told by school authorities to send me to a speech therapist. I can't remember how long I went to him; I only remember that I hated it. His musty, smoke-filled office choked me and my words got stuck in my throat every time he sat, too close, and commanded me to speak into his tape recorder. *"The red bird went round the corner, whirled up onto the blue window ledge."* Somehow, he succeeded in retraining my tongue. Cured of my "speech defect," I emerged with a strong Brooklyn accent unlike anyone else's in my family—and just like that cigar smoking therapist's! His would not be the last disembodied voice I would adopt in order to comply with the expectations of one or another higher authority.

from "there is the girl"
   there is the girl/shouting slogans/there is the girl blindly/ smiling/ there is the girl rocking/ herself to sleep/ there is the girl smiling . . . there is the girl behind the smile/ yearning to be known . . .

No one who knew me in my younger years as a "movement militant"—before the crime, before prison—would have suspected that I was lost in silence, least of all myself. I masked my silence with the strident cacophony of slogans and rhetoric. I disdained words as empty promises. *"Put your money where your mouth is"* was my motto. I was a woman of action. That rejection of a language of communication represented a fundamental disconnect, a nihilism that degenerated into and justified violence.

from "these hands"
. . . these hands clenched
into defiant, upraised fists
pointed accusing fingers
punched, ripped and drew blood
 gripped the careening wheel of delusion
  trembling with fear and fury

and when child, home, lifework
and freedom
  were lost
these hands kept on
 writing, gesturing
desperately drawing
  words in air

until one day
these hands
stopped . . .

In my fifth year of incarceration, I was locked up in solitary confinement for two years. Everything in me wound down to a halt. I lost all energy to write letters and articles full of hopeful revolutionary rhetoric, felt no desire for visits with political comrades seeking to show their solidarity. I lived from week to week for my visits with my father and daughter and from a professor with whom I'd begun to look at myself. I stopped being "a public political prisoner," and went into a seclusion of silence.

My day-to-day company came from reading books, particularly women's writings: Joan Nestle, Audre Lorde, Jo Sinclair, Dorothy Allison, Cherrie Moraga, Barbara Smith, June Jordan, Minnie Bruce Pratt, Maya Aguilar, Grace Paley, and many others. I was drawn to writers who defined themselves and their work in the context of community. Their words triggered memories and images, fomented deep longings, drew me into new ways of posing questions, challenged me to see things from different angles. I had begun to keep a journal and while I was writing to and for myself, it often felt like conversations with these women writers.

The words of these women helped me to feel less isolated—that despite our differences, and how very far out on the limb of humanity I had taken myself, the challenges I faced and the emotions they evoked were not unknown to others. There was a point when I realized that in order to face myself and do some serious psychological work, I had to "shelve" my political assumptions and identity. Reading Alice Walker's poem, "On Stripping Bark from Myself," I was encouraged that there was another person who felt as raw and naked as I did. Months later, after a hard holiday season, I wrote in a poem,

> . . . *Everyone has her nightmares*
> *her prison cell*
> *solitary box*
> *that she alone can enter*
> *hesitantly*
> *fearful*
> *of getting trapped*
> *without the key*

Exploring the varied truths revealed by women writers opened up the possibility in my mind of there being multiple truths. I began writing narratives to explore the many dimensions of my own experiences. Writing about our voyage to the Soviet Union in my mother's harried voice, I felt her intense loneliness and her anger at living in the shadow of my father. And for the first time, the Gordian knot of our conflict was loosened.

Viscerally aware of how these women's words nurtured and challenged me, and how different I felt about my own journal writing, I contemplated the power of words, and my relationship to "the word." I began to appreciate how my attitude, that words were only legitimate if we acted on them, actually eviscerated the power of words to express feelings and desires we would never want to act on. Such literalness robbed me of the potentiality of fantasy and imagination, through which we grow to relate to a world full of conflict, injustice, and possibility.

Words could either illuminate deeply experienced truths or mask and distort reality. Words could either connect or disconnect. I had come to prison cloaked in the mantle of "freedom fighter" and "political prisoner." Words spun from whole cloth, a flimsy fabric that began to fray quickly. In those early years inside, I had written speeches, arguments, and political tracts—a torrent of words that had begun to feel illusory and dishonest. They were words meant to stave off questions and doubt; pat phrases, like *to be a mother is to care about the children of the world,* meant to staunch the hemorrhaging of shame and guilt about my own child.

My search for a new language was central to the choices I wanted to make. I wrote out in bold letters, some lines from Adrienne Rich's "Transcendental Etude":

> *But there come times—perhaps this is one of them—when we have to . . .*
> *pull back from the incantations, rhythms we've moved to thoughtlessly*
> *and disenthrall ourselves, bestow*
> *ourselves to silence, or a deeper listening, cleansed*
> *of oratory, formulas, choruses, laments,*
> *static crowding the wires.*

And I let Adrienne's words light my way through the beautiful darkness.

When I call myself "a woman writer," I am giving homage to all those women writers who kept me alive and hopeful, whose words were like kindling, stoking my own creative embers. I am a writer, able to face the truth and tell my truth because of these women. The "woman" attached to my "writer" is really "women." It is an affirmation of my sense of community, in and outside of the prison.

There are women whose *words* reached me and then there are the women who ventured beyond their own lives, to enter into *this* world and our lives. I learned the craft of poetry writing in a workshop taught by Hettie Jones. For over a decade, until the doors were closed to her, she came weekly to conduct a poetry workshop. Many women passed through Hettie's workshop. But a core of us stayed and wrote and read our work aloud and grew into writers. Ours was an emboldened sisterhood, in love with each other's words. The sacred energy of our circle and our communal silence of concentration generated the beginnings of most of my best poems. Their enthusiastic responses led me to believe that my work had potential.

Hettie taught me the physical pleasure of working on a poem, carving away words, changing and reshaping until the poem emerges. Poetry is about breath. I've had asthma since childhood. I was a fearful child who learned to be ashamed of my fear and to dissociate from it. I thought that fear was the opposite of courage, when in fact, the denial of our fears is a form of cowardice. It desensitized me and limited my capacity to empathize with others. In my poetry, I reclaim my breath and with it, the value of fear and empathy.

> *. . . what I want*
> *is to sink into my heart*
> *   for words that*
>
> *take us to a different plane*
>
> *where lines dividing and defining*
> *melt into rivers,*
> *   oceans that carry us to a*
> *unravaged continent*
> *   of understanding*

In recent years, Eve Ensler has facilitated another workshop, where we write narratives from our lives as a means to explore those parts of ourselves we had disavowed and disassociated ourselves from.

> *. . . It's that place—that miserable, weak, isolated, muzzled part of me—that strangely, I want you to know. . . It is the part of me that makes me a kindred soul to every lost, desperate creature on this Earth. That part of me has known fear and therefore would never want to engender fear in another. . . . She has been alone and voiceless too long. Let me let her speak, to call out her desire for love. Let her be heard. (excerpt from a writing exercise, 1999)*

We've written about our crimes, and we've struggled to own and understand ourselves and to take responsibility. We've pushed each other to find the words to express remorse and seek reconciliation. Our work together helped me to write what may be the most important words I have published—a letter of apology for my crime.

I do not think I could have achieved the shift of consciousness, thinking, feeling and personality necessary to emerge into an honest sense of remorse without my search for a language to express what I was feeling and discovering.

flesh
overflowing waistbands
jiggling under tee shirts

slack chin   heavy breasts
loose, sticky thigh meat

I dreamed of taking a sharp knife,
slicing it away
believing that
*   smaller, I would be*
*   quieter*

*   my tongue tamed*
*   as in a clitorectomy*

*   that other hungry organ*

Writing has been a central means for me to repossess those aspects of myself that I had disavowed, dispossessed, and denied, beginning with my femaleness. When I was young, being female meant being puny and afraid. Later, I grew to hate my flesh and the longings of my flesh. I grew up into a literature dominated by the male voice, from Tolstoy to Bellow. It was not just that they were men, but that the notion of great literature was one that separated the word from the body. Great ideas emerged from great minds and to think great thoughts, one had to liberate oneself from the subjectivity of the body. While I welcomed and enjoyed the explosion of literature and poetry by women in the 1970s, it did not seep into my own soul. It could not change me until I was ready to face all that I was throwing overboard.

> *. . . there is the girl who turns*
> > *into her stillness*
> *creates worlds*
> > > *teeming with sound and surprise*

Today, my words emerge from my body. While I write in varied modes, I feel most at home writing poetry, because it is a language of rhythm, of senses. It flows from the heartbeat, the cadence of my natural rhythms, the sounds that emerge from my vocal chords through my wide-open mouth. All that is okay in poetry. Poetry forgets "shoulds" and leaps beyond literal, dualist meaning. This is not to say that poetry lacks discipline. One has to hold true to the structure of a poem, its shape and rhythm, and to let go of the excess baggage of verbiage. Poetry writing is like labor: hard as hell, also incredibly satisfying.

I am a mother, and more to the point, a mother of a young woman writer. I certainly did not know that she would choose a writer's life. But when she was very young, I knew that I wanted her to have the power of the word, to be able to speak and to write her own truth and to be heard. Watching her grow up, and having to contend with all the negative messages that threatened to deny her a sense of her own potentiality, was at times enraging and disheartening. But she truly has that writer's way of observing and knowing, a capacity to reflect as she experiences life and to use a complicated language encompassing self and other and embracing diversity. Recently, she helped to edit a collection of politically inspired short fiction, and in her bio, gave me a most precious present: thanking me for teaching her "all that words can do."

I am a lesbian, a Jew, a prisoner, but if you put any of those words together with writer, I would add in front of them, "more than." Not so with the word, "woman." Being woman encompasses all the potentiality I can imagine. But also the experience of being Other, of being an observer, of having to reclaim all that potential, and therefore loving it, and valuing it all the more.

Writing to Survive the Madness

Letters from Prison

SARAH ANONYMOUS AND PATRICIA O'BRIEN

Prologue: How We Became Partners in This Writing Venture

Sarah

I no longer recall how Georg[1] and I began writing. Perhaps it was through some spiritual publication, through a mutual teacher, O'Shinnah, or perhaps the time when she offered me a trade of woven medicine type bags.[2] My correspondence with Georg, which began at least three years after I had been in prison already, was a connection for me with the outside world—a world that seemed a bit less crazy than the one I inhabited. Working with Georg on spiritual issues and creating ritual objects for her and others she knew, gave me an opportunity not only to be creative but to contribute to the world at large, to be a part of it. Though I was physically isolated, I had a good deal of time on my hands, even if later in my sentence I had a full-time job outside the prison grounds[3] and though I ran and worked out daily—still there was lots of time to fill. Letter writing to others outside was one way of using that time constructively, but it was not only my writing, but receiving letters from Georg and others that helped me maintain some sort of balance and not get caught up in all the madness occurring around me.

So many of the men and women I lived with in the prison were trapped in struggles created by the circumstances of their own lives. Poverty. Abuse. Drug addictions. The women I lived with had lost (if they had ever had it) any sense of themselves as valuable humans and were not able to see each other as sisters in a struggle. There was much game playing—most were not to be trusted. They too readily got caught up in stealing and screwing each other around.

There were also the watchers—those who worked there who were also caught up in the games. The women had to be careful around the male guards—sexual harassment was rampant—fear hung in the air constantly. Many, I assume, brought all the behavior that contributed to their incarceration into the prison with them, which created for them a perpetual state of being "in trouble." Most had little if any support from outside the prison. They were on their own and hooking up with others who supported them; even if it was not healthy or got them in trouble, it was still a means of survival.

It was easy to get wrapped up in the fear and anger and self-hatred of that place. In addition to living with women who had internalized experiences from their own lives was the weight of never knowing what was going to happen, the constant surveillance that meant you were never alone. I created a bubble of self-protection in my own mind that allowed me to breathe. Having connections with the outside world allowed me to "escape" from the reality of my physical constraint. These connections through the letters became a source of inspiration and encouragement. They helped me maintain hope and got me through incredibly difficult times of grief, loneliness, anger, and frustration. They helped me maintain an identity other than being an "inmate."

Without these connections, resources, and support, I'm not sure how I would have made it out of there as whole as I did. It was not an easy time, nor is it so far removed today, though I try to separate myself from all that happened and all I went through in prison. Still it was more than seven years of my life, more than a seventh of it today. Sometimes it's hard to believe that my incarceration actually lasted that long or that I could have survived it. Don't think I'd be able to today without my anger overwhelming me or sedating myself to maintain some control. The experience no longer gets in my way, but there's still a sinking feeling, a heavy weight in the pit of me whenever I think about those years. If I allow myself to really feel what I experienced during those years, it would absolutely bring me to my knees. The connections with people like Georg helped me believe that I was eventually going to get out of there, and I did.

Patricia

I met Sarah about a year after her exit from prison at the battered women's shelter where she had gotten a job soon after her release. This shelter was the same one with which she had gotten linked in prison when staff members had engaged her and other inmates in a training and education program on the phenomenon of violence in their lives.

I asked Sarah to participate in my dissertation study of women who had successfully "made it" (by their definition) after release from prison and she agreed. Over the last twenty years, the average rate of growth of women in prison in this country has steadily outpaced that of men; by 2010, there were 112,792 women in prison[4] and anther 93,300 in jail.[5] To a greater extent than men, due to their lower level crimes, women are released more quickly and in a larger number. Similar to men, however, about one out of every two who are released from prison "fail," most often due to a technical violation of parole conditions or the commitment of a new offense.

From the interview with Sarah in 1996 I learned some crucial things about how she had both coped with being incarcerated for a long sentence in a state prison facility and how she had managed her reentry from prison. I learned that she had developed a structure of spiritual practice and work that enabled her to "do her time" at all levels of the prison hierarchy (maximum to minimum) without experiencing some of the indignities that others describe. She also took advantage of educational and vocational opportunities, such as they were, within the prison, and she did whatever she could to cultivate external connections with people she never met face-to-face (like Georg) and people who came into the prison to offer services, support, and nonprison food. These external linkages served to "normalize" Sarah's world to a certain extent.

Fast forward to 2005. The dissertation is now a book,[6] and Sarah is a small business owner in a midsize Midwestern city. Her identity as an "ex-offender" is behind her, but I asked her to share the letters that reflect how she managed her daily life in an institution that is established by its daily practices to render her invisible.[7] Note that Sarah is still invisible to a degree, in that she chooses not to use her surname. This is due to the continuing discrimination against people who have committed crimes, even after they have served their sentence, have been discharged from state or federal correctional custody, and otherwise look like (and are) law-abiding, tax-paying citizens. She doesn't know what the consequences might be of having her customers, neighbors, and even most friends knowing that she has been convicted of a crime.

The Letters: Power in the Writing, Spiritual Practices and Communication within Prison

You've likely seen those notices: "prisoners seeking pen-friends," "former teacher seeks letters," "lonely man seeks correspondence, all letters answered." In our e-mail/cell phone, quick-bites culture, letter writing is a bit old-fashioned. Who has time? In prison, the way an inmate does her time is perhaps one of the major determinants of how psychologically healthy she can remain, especially if she has more than the average amount of time to serve on her sentence. In 1993, the average time served for all inmates in the state system where Sarah was incarcerated was twenty-nine months;[8] she served eighty-nine. Sarah will quickly acknowledge some privileges she enjoyed in a state where, though she was a member of a numerically minority category (women in prison), she does not identify as a member of a "minority" race[9] and she came into prison better educated and with more social skills than many women, having spent some time in college and being previously employed as a paraprofessional case manager working at a substance abuse treatment center. These privileges meant that even though she was atypically convicted of a violent crime (most women are convicted of property or drug crimes), she had some choices about how she could spend her time in prison, including opportunities for a "good job" working in the prison education department teaching women reading, writing, and math for their GEDs within the prison initially and then, later in her sentence, outside of the prison in a factory. Working at the factory meant she was paid minimum wage, and though she then had to pay rent and restitution, she was able to save money that was crucial when she was released.

Regardless of those relative privileges, she was separated from all that she had known among family members, friends and coworkers prior to incarceration. She spent the necessary time gradually developing relationships on paper with those with whom she could be absolutely safe simply because they could not control her daily life. One of those people, who saved Sarah's letters and then, years after her release from prison, returned them to her, was Georg, a practitioner of healing arts in Florida.

The letters are not necessarily in chronological order; endnotes provide some explanation for spiritual or cultural references. The power of these letters speak for themselves. We have chosen to present snippets of them so that readers might understand how one woman resisted the pains of imprisonment and the daily deadening of spirit by writing about her current and past worlds, and all the ways they were interwoven. Here, then, are excerpts from Sarah's letters to Georg.

Good day to you, my friend.—And what a fine day—saw two hawk sisters on the way home from work. A good friend, a Potawatomie, once gave me the tail of a hawk: I still have one feather from it, the only one that survived—when I saw the red tail hawk, it took me to those days hanging out on the reservation, visiting the old ones. Hunting deer and pheasant, taking it to those who can no longer hunt. Going to Ike and Suzie's, there was always a pot of coffee and corn soup on the stove and no matter how we protested (we didn't for long) she always made up some fry bread. For winter it was long hours by the fire, she getting out many things that had been in the family for generations—each with story. In the backyard, Ike, getting his tipi up, ready for sweat, gathering spring water and herbs. . . . It was a time of peace and learning.

You asked about dance sticks and it's funny, I've seen many over the years—from many nations, Apache, Navajo, Sioux, Potawatomie, Kickapoo, Yurok, Hupa, Penobscot, and I can't really say what they are except for the two I have made—both represent something I feel connected to—the wolf and the Thunderbeings. Most of the decorations are gifts from folks who have touched my heart, besides being gifts of the creature or plant, and from the Mother. Though I've used neither in a ritual way, I know that the time and place will be that I will. They are both power objects for me.

Last night, at the Indian Culture group meeting,[10] I took the two rattles I've recently made, some bones, and asked another member to bring her rattle and taught the group one of the songs I learned from your tape, The earth is our mother, I believe you said you'd learned it from O'Shinnah. It was great. . . .

The crystals are beautiful—as soon as I looked, I knew which one was for Bahira.[11] Thank you my friend—also there has been another I've been wanting/feeling the need to share a crystal with and have either used on something or given away all that I wanted to part with now. I saw hers too. It will be an honor to bead the hawk feathers for you. She is beautiful—I hope you don't mind, she will live on my altar until she returns. I've always wanted a feather from a red tail hawk—to have this one come to visit—to be able to share my energy with it and then let her go—it is a greater gift.

Greetings to you, hope this may find you well and peaceful.—This past weekend I took my furlough[12] into K. for a few days of relaxation, connection and peace. It was wonderful and a needed touch to this focus/direction of life for me—I've been assured yes there is life after prison—it is difficult to put it into words what that time separate from this place means—it was a true gift giving me more than I would have imagined.

Recently, I got a piece of rawhide. I've never worked with rawhide before but successfully made a rattle—she's beautiful! A couple of years ago I found an old bone, probably cow's—they used to butcher their own meat here and it was lay-ing in a flower bed they were digging up to replant—anyway I picked it up and put it away seeing it as a handle for a fan or a rattle or something someday—it worked perfectly. It's really very plain and simple, sort of round—of the size of this picture—something like stitching a ball with artificial sinew holding the rawhide head to the handle here. Years ago I collected tiny stones that I would use in making a rattle someday—couldn't find them when I made the rattle you have, but came across them recently—just before I got the piece of raw-hide, so they went in—along with a small crystal you sent and other stones and things—she has a wonderful sound—after meditation sometimes, I just sit and listen to her. This is a sparrow hawk wing feather—I rarely get hawk feathers, but wanted to share this one with you.

Did I tell you about getting to take a volunteer training for a J. County[13] women's shelter? J. Co. is where I furlough and will be paroling to. Anyway I believe I'll be able to work it out with my parole officer to spend time there dur-ing furloughs. The program director is a good friend and it may become a job when I am paroled. It is something I want, need, to give myself to.—*Blessings to you my friend. Love and light—Sarah.*

May this reach you with love and blessings.—Though I'm working on something else for you, I wanted to get this feather in the mail—I hope you like it—beaded it 3 times before being OK with it.

Did I tell you about the dream with the fireball? I was in my hometown, living with D.—spent a lot of time walking around town and there was a fog, a dense white cloud resting on the ground. I came across it several times while walking and walked through it twice, while in the midst of it I would breathe deeply, trying to take in some of its energy/power.

I was to meet some friends for dinner in another town south that night—I was running late and tried to call and let them know—decided to drive on country roads and as I left town the sky was awesome, lots of clouds and color and light—heading south there were two long billowy clouds with an incredible light coming from behind—they parted and it was like an aura, in the most wonderful colors of sunset but not normal size—huge, taking up half the southern sky—when the clouds parted, rainbows and streaks of color flashed through the sky—I was awed and somewhat spooked—I turned around and went back into town, wondering if anyone else had noticed—people were on their porches and on Main street folks were dancing. I stopped, asking if anyone wanted to go for a ride 'cause I had to meet these friends but didn't want to be alone. Another woman (Susie) I know from here got in and we headed back south. Again the sky lit up and I headed back into the country—I'd had one opportunity to check this out and had chickened out and even though I still felt somewhat fearful I wanted to not miss the chance.

I parked the car and walked into a field and this incredibly huge sun came down and sat upon the top of a hill and it started rolling across the hills, a squirrel ran through it, then up a tree, glowing with some kind of energy. The sun ball started rolling down a hill and toward me. I felt fearful but knew I must meet this power and ran toward the ball and through it—I felt heat from it but not burning. I turned and it continued on over hill and was gone. Leaving me with a feeling, physical, spiritual and emotional—I cannot describe with words. Susie ran over to me and hugged me—we went back to the car. I reached in my pocket for the keys and pulled out the two-year medallion I'd just received from AA.[14] Got in the car and told Susie I couldn't be in it 'cause it would burn, about that time the trunk burst into flames.

We got out and I headed the opposite way across a field to some bluffs. Sitting on these bluffs were seven horses. I walked to them and began talking with them—one said one of them was a dog. They were just like horses, except at the end of their nose and hooves, straw came out, like they were stuffed. One was talking to me and started talking all about my perfectionism and did a perfect imitation of me getting indignant at work when someone was being slow or not doing things the way I think they should—it was comical and I saw the absurdity of myself being that way. I heard noise from behind the hill and walked back there. There were people and creatures working: they had huge wooden catapults, and they were filling them with large crystals (1 and 2 ft. long) and catapulting them into the air—the crystals would take flight when they were airborne, sailing out of sight. I asked these folks what they were doing—one said they'd been sent here to spend the next 10,000 years seeding the earth with these special crystals.

I awoke then, still feeling the effects of the sun ball and feeling sort of spooky—I went and sat in the TV room not feeling like being alone—afraid to go back to sleep, even afraid to be in my room. This was about a month ago, or a little more and this dream still affects me. The dream or my fears from it, has brought a halt to activity. Since then I've felt very disconnected—so much distance between myself and others, D. also—have a hard time during meditation and ritual, working with beads, creating is difficult and takes so much energy I must sleep even if I've not worked long. My appetite has been at the extreme— often eating much more than I want or need, sometimes not being able to eat at all. I hardly speak to anyone and people don't approach me—sometimes I feel on the verge of something and that I'm just resting, gathering the energy to go through, other times it's as though the energy is draining from me like blood from a deep wound.

Thursday (the next week)—it's been several days—the sphere has lived with me since Sunday—I almost feel like she should have a name, she is so alive—a presence I'm constantly aware of—haven't really done anything with her, just look into her, hold her, put her in a pouch in my pocket—slept with her, she likes my belly, no matter what position I'm in, whenever I wake she is near my belly.

For now I will say good night, the body is weary and the bed is warm and comfortable—*Blessings to you my friend.*

Greetings, my sister—You have been in my thoughts and prayers each day. May your journeys be peaceful and powerful for you. May many gifts and good experiences come to you. Did I let you know I received your packages? The bamboo is beautiful. The leather scraps have been put to good use though none were enough for mocs—please be patient with me on this—I need the measurement to be right where your instep goes down your foot. Also did I tell you I have completed several shields—sort of "practice"—but I felt guided from within. Had the notion/feeling that it may be okay to do one for another but feel some uncertainty with this. You asked me of my intention for making shields. It is all part of a dream/vision and a knowing deep within that I should do this, driven direction is powerful and I feel the need for some outside guidance—a teacher, if you will. And so I seek.

They are putting up a new fence (at the prison)—a very tall one and it will separate this cedar sister from us—so I feel the need to spend as much time sharing her space as I can till the fence is done—they're doing more building—that is their reason for the fence, to cut us off from the construction area—please excuse this sloppy writing—it is very cold and my hand is sort of numb, having a hard time holding on to the pen—need to get some gloves, I guess. . . .

Last weekend our little Indian culture group got to go to a dance in K.—a small dance put on by the Heart of America Indian Center. There was gourd dancing and round dances and a huge supper. It has been over 6 years since I've been able to dance—it did wonderful things to this spirit, to drape a shawl across my shoulders, and dance—to the drum—ah, to stand before the drum, its power filling my heart—it was good. When I was home, I looked for my shawl—it was gone, as are so many of the things I once had. A good reason to make a new one, aye?

Georg, do you know anyone who has access to gourds—to use for rattles? Maybe we could trade—for beadwork, or bags or something. I'm having a hard time finding a source—and commercial sources charge $6.00–$10.00 and I just can't afford that.

—Off to work—I'll get this letter finished some day—greetings to you, dear one—may this day be one of peace for you.—*Light and love—Sarah*

Well, I'm currently surrogate mother to a couple of young sparrows whose home was in a light fixture that no longer exists—they're doing well, eat good and should be ready for the world this weekend. It's hard raising young birds—you cannot handle them as they bond easily and if they bond it is more difficult for them to make it on their own. Sparrows do seem to do better than others. I had a grackle follow me for months landing on me every time she saw me—following me when I ran—sitting on my window sill—even sleeping there at night sometimes.

The crystals you sent are wonderful. I was overwhelmed. I am greatly honored. Thank you for the sage cedar sweet grass and the cornmeal—special gifts. I made a bag for each except the cedar—I have a special place for it. I use a lot of cedar—there is a tree in front of our building. I pray to the tree and the next day the ground is covered with small branches. I have planted a crystal and garnet at her base—she is home for robins each spring. The sage is great—I've needed some for so long—it's been years since I've had any and I've never had cornmeal. I am aware of the significance and ceremony of some Native Nations: What is its significance for you, how do you use it?

No, I am not Cherokee, my people are Northern Arapahoe—now settled in Wyoming. I wish you much blessing on your path with owls. The owls have been deeply connected throughout my life also—I seek to learn more. They have been guardians to me since I can remember—to learn, to heal, and strengthen the bond is the best way to honor. The card you wrote in is beautiful. I have heard of a Mandala[15] often over the years—and saw it in your catalog but I am unfamiliar—please tell me of this Mandala. May this find you well and peaceful and may Solstice be a time of peace and power for you.—*Love and Light, Sarah*

Dear Georg—Good Day to you, dear sister—so very good to hear from you again—your letter touched me so. First let me tell you that I have such strong vision of you and your store—it just feels like where you are or should be. And it would be a great honor to have my creations become a part of it all. Trade still feels better than selling but I'm not really concerned about that now.

Thank you for your sharing on spheres; after I had that dream/vision of the fire ball—somehow being connected to this sphere sister—I put her away and have only had her out a couple times—fear of the power I felt—your words motivated me to bring her back out especially to let her share this space as I work on your sphere bag. Please be patient with me as my leather supply is only scraps right now but surely some will be coming soon it always seems when in need of something, it always comes.

Oh yes, I did get your schedule for your workshops—found it after posting that letter. It was good to have that schedule—put myself into connecting with you all day from this—The connection with energy I felt the 16th at sunrise, and all morning was incredible—the sphere sister joined with me that morning—though I've been a vegetarian for 15 yrs, haven't been strict the past 5 or so, always used the excuse here I needed to consume some dairy product and eggs to get protein etc. which was really crap—anyway, the 16th I eliminated all dairy products and it feels good. Did I tell you I quit smoking and drinking coffee? I did after being a 3 pack a day smoker and a 20 cups of coffee a day drinker and put them both away the 4th of July: that feels excellent!!!

Been working 52 hr. weeks and it's really healing me—don't have to work tomorrow, Sat.—the first day off in a long time—great. I need the time to be peaceful and quiet; I need a long weekend to create.

In August the first weekend, I was in K. on furlough. Where I furlough to is suburbia—an exclusive community—the home of a prominent attorney—she's a good friend and a dear woman—I've always intended to parole there—a prominent attorney and former district judge, former chair person of the Parole Board—an "acceptable" place to parole and definitely to my advantage. This weekend I took a walk around the neighborhood feeling a certain peace from all the neat homes with their neat yards and neat families and I knew that what I needed was to settle down. Till I came to prison, my life had been one of transience—being all over this country and to a couple of others, always trouble, never staying long enough to connect with people—always running.

But walking around that neighborhood, I felt the need to settle down, build a life for myself. This middle-class, middle-American suburbia was not the answer for me and I'd always looked at paroling there as a temporary place—get myself together—gather a few dollars to relocate where I wanted to be—anyway, all this began stirrings deep within—and for a couple of weeks upon returning here, there was a restlessness, and I put myself into praying to be open to my own inner voice and follow her guidance. And then this past Wednesday, as I stood greeting the rising sun and decided it was the day to begin a fast, just felt like the thing to do. And that day at work I began my moon time about 2 weeks early and there were things happening—I don't know words can say the joy I felt—and the notion came to me that there was no reason to parole to K. at all—if, and this is what I'll have to focus all my energy on from now until Nov. 8 when I meet the parole board—if I can find women on land who would be willing to allow me to parole there. That's where I need to be in a community of women and on the land—not in middle class suburbia, piddling away my days dreaming of getting out of there—that's what I've been doing here for 6 yrs.—looking to the day this is over.

I was reading something the other day written by a woman in prison. She said this environment was not conducive to mental health, it was not conducive to physical health it was not conducive to humanity—the struggle is to survive intact. That's been my struggle—and it would be the same struggle with any current parole plan—because to "survive" that environment there would be this—I'd be expected to compromise myself to "pass." I won't do that and then I would have to deal with folks' response. I know what it does to your guts to compromise your own ideals and principles and self and I can't live like that anymore. When I'm out of here there will be much need for healing to get this place out of my guts and K. wouldn't be the place for that. I don't know if any of this makes sense—it's just how I feel. It feels so right to pursue this idea to find a women's community where I can go from here. How I'll find these women, this place, I don't know but it feels so right—it was like a gift of vision put before me and all I had to do was open and see—like it wasn't even my deal and if it's right—then somehow, something will happen.[16] *Peace to you this day, my friend.—Light and Love, Sarah*

Greetings Sister—The rose quartz necklace is beautiful Georg—thank you—you are the third person who has sent me rose quartz in a week! It is that the heart is in need of healing/soothing. I have given her a thorough beating the past year—though balance has returned mostly. Did I tell you this already? In March I let go of a 9-year relationship—one of the hardest choices I've ever made—but a necessary one and a healthy one—after 6 yrs of prison—this woman whom I loved dearly and shared so much with had become my addiction and no longer a lover—I think this was true for her too—I knew if we carried it any further we'd have really ended up doing harm or maybe not. I just had to let it go and it still hurts but there has been healing—it is slow, but it comes.

This little beaded piece—just something I had to do—did it immediately after I opened your package—didn't even finish reading your letter—just had to do this first anyway, thought you might use it on one of your bags or something—the red felt bag—I love it Georg—you have often told me about O'Shinnah's words on wrapping crystals in red natural fibers—little by little I've collected little pieces of red cloth and when I make bags specifically for crystals I see red material inside. In this red felt—I just really like the felt—I remember your speaking of beginning to do this.

The tape is good—I took it outside the day your package arrived (it was in my living space waiting for me when I returned from a field day Sat.—unopened!) Want to get this to you—a heartfelt thanks for your sharing—it is so good to hear from you, dear sister.—*Peace and love, Sarah*

Greetings Dear Friend—Have I told you I am parole eligible this year (or should I ask how many times I have told you this?) in November—it is only February and already I am somehow nervous . . . so many years I have waited for this one. So many changes. So much learning and healing—many gifts, and many give-aways.[17]

Made a cup of my mother's spice tea—tang and instant tea and nutmeg and cinnamon—a lot of sugar but tastes good and reminds me of home—warm, safe spaces—though I was never safe at home, the tea still makes me feel good inside—made with the love only a mother has.

Tuesday is my 3 yr. AA/NA birthday—a time to celebrate—and at full moon—I will sit under the full moon to make Thanksgiving in my heart—for the gift of this life—the gift of sobriety—a miracle after the many years of self-destruction through abusing alcohol and drugs. It is truly a gift to no longer live like that.—*Blessings to you, my friend. Peace and love. Sarah*

Conclusion: How the Letters Nurtured Survival and Healing

What can we conclude from these snippets of time spent in prison, so many years later? Sarah remembers other people at the prison who were also quiet and kept to themselves and perhaps were also involved in spiritual practices. She doesn't recall anyone else who used writing as she did to maintain contact outside and to pursue spiritual support. Though mail call was important, many never received letters. Some of the women maintained correspondence with male inmates across the road[18] or in other states. Prison is a very unsafe place to show yourself; any weakness or even intimate knowledge of oneself is vulnerable to being exploited. The act of writing in one sense was an act of resistance to the prison culture, a way of reflecting emotion and self-knowledge that enabled Sarah to survive her separation from the free world. Writing allowed her "to be [her]self, to be human, to express what [she] dare not express inside that system without fear. [She] trusted Georg explicitly to hold that expression of [her] truest self."

Is Sarah *healed* from her time of incarceration? This is the social worker (Patricia) who asked that question of her. Despite her fears of not being her true self after parole to the suburban area where she worked for many years, she owns a home and a car and many other trappings and privileges of citizenship. She has earned respect among many for who she is and what she does. Prison has left a mark on her that will never be erased. At the same time, it is also an indication of her resilience, her creativity, and her spiritual core that certainly is reflected through these letters written at a time "through the madness" that surrounded her.

Notes

1. Short for Georgette.

2. In a letter Sarah wrote to *Maize,* from prison, she indicates that she creates "medicine bags, from very small for a single crystal, to as large as a woman might want, decorated with beadwork, larger beads, shells, stones, feathers—depends on what I have at hand" for barter for craft supplies.

3. During her time in prison, Sarah, along with other prisoners in the same facility, was transported into town by a prison bus to work in a parts factory as part of a "prison industry" contract the state department of corrections had with the owner.

4. P. Guerino, P. M. Harrison, and W. J. Sabol, 2011, *Prisoners in 2010 (Revised)* (Washington, DC: Bureau of Justice Statistics), NCJ 236096.

5. T. D. Minton, 2012, *Jail inmates at midyear 2011—statistical tables* (Washington, DC: Bureau of Justice Statistics).

6. P. O'Brien, 2001, *Making it in the "free world": Women in transition from prison* (New York: State University of New York Press).

7. M. Foucault, 1977, *Discipline and punish: The birth of the prison* (New York: Vintage).

8. P. M. Ditton and D. J. Wilson, 1999, *Truth in sentencing in state prisons*, BJS Special Report (Washington, DC: Bureau of Justice Statistics), NCJ 170032.

9. While Sarah is partially Arapaho in her lineage, she did not grow up on a reservation. Her upbringing by adoptive parents was very much in line with "white culture" as she grew up in a rural town that was predominantly white.

10. Sarah was selected by the women in the Native American culture group to be the spiritual leader because she was perceived as having a daily practice and because she had power even with the correctional guards: "They let me do things they didn't let others do, because they trusted me and because I didn't cause trouble."

11. Friend of Georg's in Florida.

12. In the last years of her incarceration, Sarah, like other minimum security prisoners in this state and because she had earned good time and was within two years of release, earned furlough weekends away from prison where she could visit with specified family members and friends.

13. The county of the shelter where Sarah was hired to work after her incarceration.

14. AA was another way that Sarah used her connections with others outside of the prison even though she did not consider herself an alcoholic. Volunteers from outside the prison led 12-step groups, including some who explicitly wanted to have contact with inmates for political or cultural reasons.

15. The integrated view of the world represented by the mandala, while long embraced by some Eastern religions, has now begun to emerge in Western religious and secular cultures.

16. Sarah did attempt to find a "women's land" where she could parole to but now says that she was afraid that the parole board would not see that as a viable plan and she already had an offer of work at the shelter and a place to stay indefinitely with one of the shelter staff.

17. This refers to a Native American custom and ceremony to never own more than is needed and to share what you had with those who needed it more than you. The more you gave away to others, the wealthier you were perceived to be.

18. The women's facility at that time was located next to a male facility.

7

My Voice through a Deadbolt Door

CRISTA DECKER

I write because I can be anyone or anything. I can be a bee, a tall tree, or just me. I can be the hero and live happily ever after or I can take a trip across the world and tell you about my greatest adventures through my writing. I can fight the biggest wars with my mighty sword that is just an ordinary pen to some. My poems are my spirit being sent out to whoever may hear me.

Writing allows me to scream, vent, cry and even laugh when I've never had anyone growing up to share myself with. I write because I can be my best friend and play and laugh about my fondest memories or allow my paper to absorb all my tears when a lover has sacrificed me by selfish pretenses. It's been the best way to live, learn and grow into the woman I am today.

I write because I can confide my darkest secrets and not be judged by what I say. Writing has helped me deal and work with things I've tried so hard to stuff and lock away. Things that have haunted me from afar for so many years.

I write because I am the star that you can see no matter where you are. Writing is the mirror that lets me see my true self even when life has put me on a shelf. I write because it's a way to feel free even before I was locked up. Writing has given me a voice while the rest of my physical self has been locked up tight as a deadbolt door.

8

Rolling with the Punches

IRENE C. BAIRD, DED

Imagine yourself in an uninviting multipurpose room, the only one in a county jail that was built originally to house about 500 prisoners, but now contains nearly twice that number of men and about 130 women;

Imagine being in that room with a group of women, many of them victims[1] of horrendous abuse who have volunteered to participate in a process that addresses identity, esteem and empowerment building or, to use author Iyanla Vanzant's words, to find the key to unlock one's personal cell;

Imagine their being asked to reflect on the now infamous February 1, 2004 Super Bowl half-time "entertainment" but to focus only on the act of a man's tearing at a women's clothing or, more specifically, a white man's tearing at a black woman's clothing;

Imagine their also being asked to filter the scene through a child's eyes as to what the child may construe as acceptable behavior or license;

Imagine the reaction, especially from the victims . . . outrage? Anger? Disbelief?

Imagine no evident reaction; instead, glazed-over eyes, the result of embedded, learned behavior within a "culture of femaleness" that prescribes subservience to a male and sexual performance as validation of womanliness . . . a "rolling with the punches"?

During the past ten years, groups of incarcerated women in the cited county jail have volunteered to participate in a program that engages them in exploring, discussing and writing their life stories in order to find the key to the personal cell that imprisons them, emotionally and physically. Since it is their truth that is being addressed in this program, they "own" the process; I serve as facilitator of the program process and as "conduit" for sharing their learning, in their language, with the outside community.

The unexpected reaction to the TV "drama" prompted my rereading and reflecting on copies of their lived experiences where I noted, especially, their adherence to socially constructed gender roles in the context of domestic/intimate partner violence. The following examples stood out:

One prisoner wrote, "I remember seeing the only man I knew as my father beating on my mother, who I love dearly. I started believing that if a man beat me, he loves me." This was not the reaction of all of the women regarding the story of the beating, but most claimed they understood and labeled this as learned behavior within some communities.

Another woman offered that she was teaching her sons to be "real, take-charge" men and her daughters to be submissive because this is the way it is supposed to be. Though the women exhibited strengths in other ways, their discussion revealed an acceptance of their perceived unequal status as women and they often quoted Scripture to make their point.

Someone else decided to add to the conversation by sharing views on how to be a woman who could keep her man. She asked her partner to tell her how other women satisfied his sexual needs so that she could do something different, more exciting, and make herself indispensable to him.

These women recognized the power, control, and entitlement attributes in some men; they also recognized that though some of these attributes might be considered exciting at times, that kind of aggressiveness could lead to violent behavior. They also learned that violence is not just physical, that emotional/psychological violence sometimes can be more damaging because, if repeated often enough, it has long-lasting, damaging effects. Many related hearing from their partners words such as "You're lucky to have me, no one else would want you. You're ugly, too fat—a lousy cook and lousy in bed."

R. Jewkes's 2002 study, "Intimate Partner Violence: Causes and Prevention," confirms this kind of behavior, listing poverty, power, and social norms as contributing to violent behavior. She underscores two factors: "the unequal position of women in a particular relationship (and in society) and the normal use of violence in conflict" and concludes that "experiences of violence in the home in childhood teach children that violence is normal in certain settings. In this way, men learn to use violence and women learn to tolerate it or at least tolerate aggressive behavior" (Jewkes 2002, 1423). This prompts the implication of "rolling with the punches," or of finding a resolution to what becomes part of the personal cell.

A Model for Developing Self-Esteem

A resolution might be reached in a program such as the one in which these exchanges occurred, one that is committed to the issue of un/underserved and marginalized populations. The model was created in 1992 as a pilot project funded by the Pennsylvania Humanities Council and implemented with a group of homeless women at a local YWCA.

The intent of the pilot project was to address women's esteem issues; it was inspired by an adult education study that read women's literature to extract and define themes relating to the development of the will to survive among African American women (Peterson 1991). With assistance from a Humanities Department colleague and two of her graduate students, the project evolved over an eight-week period with the participants, as a group, reading, reflecting on, and discussing the traumas and their resolution of female authors of similar race, class, and experience as the participants. Each woman selected the issue in the literature that was relevant to her own situation and critiqued and analyzed it in writing, in a format of her choice. The nonreaders in the group listened for content and joined in the discussion; nonwriters dictated their responses to the facilitators. These were typed and returned for their use in reinforcing literacy acquisition, along with the humanities learning. The initial, tentative steps produced esteem, identity reflections such as *I must search deep inside to find myself,* or *I am me plain and simple/ That's all I want to be.*

Given the relaxed, nonthreatening atmosphere of the workshop, the homeless women began to feel more secure and invested after the first few sessions; they then began to explore more deeply:

I remember
The pain
The rain
The loneliness
The shame
Finally knowing
From where I came.

Since the objective of the project was to explore all aspects of self-identity and the impact on self-esteem, some dared to reflect on and even name drug addiction as a significant factor in their lives.

I remember when I was first introduced to you
I remember how good you made me feel, the things I would do
. . . .
I remember when it was no longer a good feeling
I remember the denial . . . the terrible wracking pains . . .
Saying, God, let me die!!!

These previously silenced women beamed with pride when each week's output was returned in print form. They took more ownership of the process by competing to read aloud what they had written, to share their thoughts and feelings. They began to create a community, learning also that they were not alone, that there was strength in supporting each other as they rolled with the punches of life.

Reflecting on the evolution of the pilot project, I realized that the majority of the women spoke of being introduced to drugs by their male partners. They did not volunteer to discuss or explain problematic relationships to which they alluded within the drug context, and their privacy was respected.

An Invitation to the Prisoner's World

The success of the pilot project,[2] specifically the writing component, generated a larger grant for community outreach to un/underserved groups of urban women. My target audience became the female prisoners at the county jail whose programming activities were confined to mental health, substance abuse, parenting, and adult basic education. Because of prevailing stereotyping that the women were categorically illiterate,[3] I encountered resistance to a project that centered on creative writing. Its efficacy, however, has been reinforced by the "transformed" Jimmy Santiago Baca, a once illiterate prisoner turned acclaimed poet and memoirist who taught himself to read and write, at age twenty-five, while in a penitentiary. He refers to writing as "chang[ing] both reader and writer; as help[ing] to reflect and understand what happened . . . as (a creative context) for prisoners preparing to reenter society." He adds that since we prefer to keep the prisoners out of our society, through their writing they invite us into their worlds to see them as human beings (Baca 2001a, ix). His words are a significant preface and endorsement of the unnamed program.[4]

Since the fall of 1994, women of different colors and ethnicities and I have met in that uninviting room, with the numbers continuing to increase to the point of necessitating a waiting list. As many as fifty women—African American, Anglo-American, Native American and Latina—may volunteer for one of four ten-week sessions offered annually. Because of the unpredictability of the environment—hearings, transfers, lockdowns, as examples—each ten-week session concludes with about fifteen to twenty women, between the ages of eighteen to fifty, remaining. We start each ten-week session by examining the contents of the personal cell that needs to be unlocked and addressed. This results, initially, in images and feelings similar to those expressed by this writer:

Closed door; lock and key
Cold cell, alone, I feel the pain
Emptiness, the void they call life.

Or, this more detailed perspective:

I look at my life with intense disregard
Can you see my pain? Can you feel my thoughts?
I didn't think so.
It's hard to understand chaos
Even harder to tolerate individuality.
Accept me for me and allow me to mend my broken wing
So I may one day fly again.

The Journey

Thus, the group's journey to find the key to unlock the personal cell begins. Over this period of time, we have met some incredible authors whose insights from their earlier, rocky journeys have provided perspectives, inspiration, and direction toward a different path from the one they once followed and that the inmates were now experiencing. We have parsed Nikki Giovanni's and Maya Angelou's poetry, we have been roused to action by Giovanni's 1970s poetry, along with work by bell hooks and Iyanla Vanzant; we have felt empathy for Patrice Gaines through her autobiography that became our reality show when she was allowed to be our guest. We were into narrative theory before it became a buzzword.[5]

Eventually, through all of the reading, storytelling, and writing, specific themes began to emerge consistently: aspects of identity, addictions, and, most frequently, abusive relationships (family, friends, lovers, spouses). Unlike the pilot project with the homeless women, the prisoners seemed to welcome an environment where they could delve deeply into their relationships, engaging fully in the process to try to understand what was happening in their lives.[6]

Drug addiction has become a noteworthy aspect in the lives of many of these women and has contributed to the dramatic increase in their prison numbers because of the mandated sentences for drug violation. In order to make meaning, therefore, of the prevailing theme—abusive relationships—it is necessary for the reader to "meet" the women, to hear how they see themselves, their relationships, and, from the "users," the impact of drugs on their lives.

Visual identity for the women in the county jail is a baggy beige tunic and pants outfit with the prison's initials imprinted in bold, large letters and an ID tag with their prison number, a seeming throwback to the age of *The Scarlet Letter*. With makeup and jewelry forbidden, hairstyles become the only allowable display of femininity, and what a display of style and color! An appropriate poetic connection has been the reading of Nikki Giovanni's "Make Up" (1996) and its references to the time, place, and the extent of the makeup women use to identify themselves.[7] Some see this as a metaphor for the aliases, the masks they wear to survive.

Using paper plates and crayons, we have engaged in creating a mask of how each one felt that particular day and then reflecting on it. One woman interpreted hers as:

The shame and guilt of what I did
Is why she is so disguised
Hiding not only from people but
The person inside.

Shedding the mask, Maya Angelou's poems, "Phenomenal Woman" and "And Still I Rise" (1978) motivated a different, more positive introspection, one that underscores Peterson's (1991) study on the will of African American women to survive, as this writer demonstrates:

I'm a strong woman standing, still alive
Just like Maya Angelou still I rise.
You may want to keep me locked up in a cage,
. . . .
But you should know this is my heaven not my hell
I'm a strong black woman still alive,
Just like Maya still I rise.

Another Angelou-inspired poem asserts:

I'm not your little toy so don't play with me.
I am not your lost puppy so don't find me a place to be.
I am not inhumane when you talk to me.
Talk to me directly so you get clarity.
Every morning I rise I know I am someone
I am I am I am
Someone who cares about her life.

The following verse indicates that in spite of the serious issues the women were facing there was a lighter side and we could laugh.

I am in all ways a woman; there's none like me the same
. . . .
I have strength, peace and joy
This woman you see is so unique
Praise God I wasn't born a boy!

The naming of themselves as women through their writing is relevant because, as with other stereotypes such as presumed illiteracy, the women defy being essentialized. They have argued among themselves that they are not "in the same boat" but rather "on the same boat." Many also have commented that, inspired by the authors, they were driven to share their experiences to help young women on the outside. As a result, they willingly identified the influences that put them on that boat in order, as Baca (2001a, ix) writes, to invite us into their world to see them as human beings, with human issues they are trying to resolve.

- I grew up believing and thinking that I was less than. Not loving myself.
- I've been looking for love in all the wrong places. I looked for the drug dealer that would and could pay my bills, or the man who would tell me whatever it was that I wanted to hear.
- I've had children to have someone to love me when I was in despair.
- Addiction didn't allow me to be there for my children, and the disease doesn't care about you, me or anybody.

Others struggled to identify the barriers to their valuing themselves. The "aha" moment was often triggered by reading about Maya Angelou's troubled youth (1969) and the autobiographies of Patrice Gaines (1995) and Iyanla Vanzant (1998) who honestly described abusive relationships, the most difficult being when the parent, a family member or friend was the perpetrator. The "aha" moment seemed to occur when the authors commented that, as they grew older, they recognized they were not responsible for the sexual abuse and that it was time to get rid of the guilt. Accepting this as "permission" to expose the situation without guilt, some women shared painful events such as the following:[8]

Mommy, don't hurt me anymore
You slammed me into the bedroom door.
Mommy, don't smack me in the face,
I'm sorry I put my book bag in the wrong place.

And, often, there are "A Child's Cries:"

Daddy touched me down there,
He said he would be glad when I grew some hair.
Daddy said be quiet, it won't hurt,
He said I was "his little girl" not "his slut"
Mommy, why didn't you listen to what I said?

The opportunity to expose situations such as these, to begin to recognize the gender implication and influences, and the need to get over the heavy burden of guilt they assumed became a prologue for their future, a new direction. The women's groups have filled many pages with examples of the damaging outcomes of abusive relationships; each ten-week session provided the contents of a booklet that empowered them personally and served to inform the outside world. They categorized the outcomes as:

Verbal/Emotional Abuse. "(T)he male is telling you that you are ugly, you're a crackhead, no man wants a woman with three kids, and after you hear that every day for five years you actually begin to feel and think these things are true."

Physical/Emotional Abuse. "Feeling the pain of each hit, looking up seeing the bottom of his foot coming down to meet my face; I was nothing; no one would ever love or want me . . . keeping all the dirty secrets of his abuse; lying to cover up the bruises and swollenness of my body . . . he turned my love to hate."

Violent Abuse.
I fought the fight, the score was unanimous:
It was 10 to zero; in the outcome he was the hero.
He was like a mad dog that someone loosed from its cage,
The look on his face, the fire in his eyes
Showed me he was in a heated rage.
I remember waking up in a hospital bed . . .
He was proud that he won the fight.

An outcome of an altercation. Succinctly, "He ended up in the hospital . . . I end up in jail."

Many stories begin with, "In the beginning our relationship was beautiful . . . but then things began to change." When asked why they endured the abuse, the answers offered the following insights:

- It's OK as long as he doesn't leave. I don't want to be alone.
- I was violently abused as a child . . . ; my "sick mind" equated abuse with love.
- I stayed because it never occurred to me that I could do something else.
- Because it's what I saw when I was young. And I thought if you beat me, abuse me mentally and physically, you loved me.

Reflection and discussion precede and follow the creative writing process. For some, the culture of race and class present their own set of issues. Gender, however, is central. The women's observations, perceptions, understanding and "imposed" learning from early childhood about being female are reflected in their dialogue and their writing, in their self-definition, their choices, their expectations of rolling with the punches of life. Even the strong ones, with the determination to survive, have been influenced by society's version of traditional and acceptable gender roles. These issues of gender are reinforced and maintained by a penal system that functions from a patriarchal, militaristic mindset.

When groups of incarcerated women with entrenched traditional gender modeling volunteer to explore these issues and are willing to invite us into their world to share their experiences, something important and profound can happen. As one woman wrote, "I am a woman who is so hurt, wounded and scarred that I don't know where to start to repair my life. But I won't give up. I'll keep on trying. I have a little determination to work with what I have left."

Rattling the Cage

In 1999, due to the program's focus on abusive relationships, the prison administration allowed me to create a similar kind of program for incarcerated males at the jail. The intent was to afford them an opportunity to learn to understand the outcomes of acting out their socially-constructed sense of maleness in a format that did not exist for men at that institution. Shortly after the men's program began, a local theater company staged *Voices Inside*, a play using incarcerated women's written experiences as script. Candidly and effectively portrayed were the painful outcomes on women's identity and esteem from troubled relationships with family and partners. These messages helped in procuring funding from a local foundation deeply committed to the well-being of the community, therefore underscoring the men's program.

For insights into interacting with the men, it was necessary to reflect on the patriarchal context of the penal system. bell hooks (2004) quotes psychotherapist Bradshaw's characterization of patriarchy as male domination and power, and that patriarchy rules still over most of the world's religious, school, and family systems. Considering the characteristics of blind obedience, repression of all emotion except fear, destruction of individual will power, and the repression of thinking when it departs from the authority figure's way of thinking, one could say it is the predominant ruling structure in prisons.

The male volunteers are housed in three cell blocks that are separated from the general population because, according to prison guidelines, these men have qualified for programming. One of the cell blocks houses sex offenders; the other two, men with drug and other offenses. At least thirty to forty men request permission to participate and fifteen to twenty remain at the session's conclusion. They range in age from eighteen to fifty-two and are predominantly African American, as is the entire prison population; the remainder are Anglo-American and Latinos.

Pedagogically, the men's program resembles the women's, following the 1992 humanities-oriented model: reading, reflection, and discussion and subsequent writing on gendered issues relevant to each learner. They, too, are introduced to Vanzant's (1998) admonition that we are all doing some kind of time, and that it is the responsibility of each one to find the key to unlock the personal cell. Initially, they read mostly the women's abuse writing and Gaines's (1995) and Vanzant's (1998) autobiographies. Gaines, in addition to graphically describing abusive relationships, candidly shares her earlier, boyfriend-initiated drug addiction, which led to her incarceration because the drug paraphernalia was stored in her purse.

In an effort to try to understand male/female interaction, an exchange of anonymously written questions and answers was initiated between the men's and women's groups; though their programs run simultaneously, prison rules forbid face-to-face meetings. My role has continued to focus on bringing in reading resources with occasional visitors such as Patrice Gaines. As each of the four ten-week sessions draws to a close, the men select from the writings that have been typed for them, draw a cover, and choose a title for their booklet comprised of the writing based on their lived experiences.

Defining Maleness

Coincidentally, *Up from Here, a* Vanzant book written for men, appeared in 2002. It uses seven case studies to illustrate its process for change methodology comparable to what we have been doing—that is, defining the issue, acknowledging and accepting it, and then striving to resolve it. In our program, as a prompt, we adopted her book's observation and premise that:

> (M)en [were] taught what men do . . . and if you don't do enough . . . the right way you feel worthless . . . unvalued . . . you get angry and afraid . . . [you] break into all sorts of harmful actions. (Vanzant 2002, 4)

Vanzant's quote helped the prisoners to focus more clearly, to zoom in on the root causes of acting out their learned behaviors. As an example, one inmate defined his manhood this way: "It always meant to be in control over everything, and never show your feelings or what we would call your weak side because if we did we would think it's a chump move or something so I always wanted to be in control and never let anyone control me and never showed my feelings." Another inmate shared that, "If I'm with my homies and my demanding chick approaches I'm expected to slap her around, to maintain my status, power, and control, to show I'm not a wimp."

The men acknowledge anger and fear as being two basic emotions that haunted them and drove them in their behavior. Alternatively, in response to Dyson's 1999 article, "Behind the Mask" that encouraged looking behind the mask worn as a shield dropping such "posturing and fronting," there were flippant young comments such as:

- I am pretty cool as a man.
- I am a winner, first and foremost, headed toward success and nothing else.
- I'm funny and easy to get along with.

And this candid boast:

- I am a Leo, got six kids, a down-to-earth personality. I want what I want when I want it. Sometimes I can be hardheaded.

As the men struggled with Vanzant's concept of doing and being, they were introduced to Travis Hunter's *The Hearts of Men* (2000) and embraced it. It is the story of a handsome, popular young man on the brink of disaster at his job because of irresponsible work ethic and behavior with female employees. An older respected male mentors him through his erratic behavior to stability at work and in marriage, and in a commitment to a boys' club. The book, written in a style the men related to, presented messages so effectively that the men reflectively paused in the reading and started to relate the story to their own lives. Unlike the mentoring in the Hunter novel, they talked about their early lives and what they were taught to do. "My father introduced me to things that a father should stray his son from . . . I am 22 years old . . . I am not a thug or an angel but I live the life of thuggery as a result." Another wrote of needing another role model when his father died. A relative filled in by introducing him to alcohol and teaching him street survival skills. "He roughed me up to make me a man . . . to make a cub into a lion or bear . . . at age 13."

In discussing and writing about their perception of maleness, the men admitted to feeling superior to women. Society, TV, rap gave them permission; they were entitled. There was pride in their sexuality, in fathering many children as soon as possible. "What took you so long?" one father asked an early teen son. Another young teen shared that "she looked like a red apple to be picked . . . she could have had her first baby to me . . . but her mom got her an abortion . . . she would have been the first to have my baby." They spoke of fathering being essential to their identity. Macho, manly—this was an essential aspect of their socially constructed gender and they acted it out at a very young age because they were taught it was expected.

Sister Souljah (1996) expands on and confirms inmates' pervasive patriarchal attitudes about maleness relating to women when she writes of her father—his wanting to be a man's man, of ruling the household. He believed that women must work hard at being beautiful; that she must make her husband as comfortable as a king in his own castle; that she perfect her skills in housecleaning and cooking and have a lot of babies. After all, he figured, she had all day to correct any flaws in her appearance. Most of all, she must be fully dependent upon him, the source of her money, love, sex, strength, and center of her existence. A postscript to failing to comply— rolling with punches?

The men also assert that their "superior" status allows them to refer to women in any fashion they choose, favorites being *my chick, my bitch, my old lady.* Underneath the uproar, some revealed a fear of change, and they rage at how society perceives and treats them. Some rage at having been sexually abused as children. Until now, what has been obscured is the male sexual abuse story and its implications in their sense of their maleness, their behavior/acting out. Reflect on the following poignant male experience:

> As a child . . . oral sex and doing things to me that a woman in sex movies won't do. I was too ashamed to tell anyone. And besides, I am a man and that doesn't happen to us. They not only raped me, physically and mentally as well, causing me to search for love and acceptance wherever I could find it. Rape is devastating . . . for her because her innermost self is violated. For a man his manhood is ripped from his soul. . . . I freeze and snap at female partners . . . fearing they may see me as weak or undercover gay. It took years to prove to myself I am a man. To tell makes me feel better. I will not let them take away my future.

He Said, She Said

The anonymous written exchanges contained revelations. Paradoxically, when asked the kind of woman the men would consider for a potentially long-term partner, they refer to a traditional model: "A decent girl I could introduce to my mother, . . . not the kinds that are in this jail." At the same time, the men anxiously participated in the anonymously written question and answer exchange with the women's groups in an attempt to understand the others' thinking and behavior.

There are repeated questions about trust and commitment. And how do the men define love? "It is pain, it hurts, it is a word that is used quite often which is confused with trust and once you have received the fruit of the vine you often discard the root. Love is powerful."

And what makes men angry about a woman? "She always wants her own way, is controlling, is always criticizing everything I do." Alternatively, in being asked when they felt powerless, the women answer, "Not having a voice, not being taken into consideration, being dominated, being talked down to." The men want to figure out what is on her mind, even those who have negative opinions of incarcerated women; the women want the kinds of answers that will teach them how to be appealing and accepted without being victimized.

Conclusion

Theories abound about why incarcerated men commit acts of violence. Researchers compile data, but one of the missing links may be to turn to Jonathan Katz's book, *The Macho Paradox: Why Some Men Hurt Woman and How All Men Can Help* (2006). The embedded patriarchal learning in the men's stories tells why they hurt women. For twenty-plus years Katz has been addressing these kinds of stories at, for example, schools, the Marines, and the NFL. He advocates finding some good men to take leadership roles, to discourage sexist remarks and pornography. Another lesson could be taken from Jimmy Santiago Baca's learning experiences with the *doing* and *being* concept (Baca, 2001b). His transforming moment came at age twenty when, serving time at a penitentiary he straddled another prisoner, poised to kill him. The "aha" resulted from his reflecting on his being, on recognizing that he couldn't be a poet like Pablo Neruda if he didn't respect humanity and act responsibly. That may well be the missing link: In order to act responsibly, we must rattle and dismantle the inhumane patriarchal cage that victimizes humans.

References

Angelou, M. 1969. I *know why the caged bird sings*. New York: Bantam Books.

——. 1978. *And still I rise*. New York: Random House.

Baca, J. S. 2001a. Foreword. In *Undoing time*. Edited by J. Evans. Boston: Northeastern University Press, ix–xii.

——. 2001b. *A place to stand*. New York: Grove Press.

Baird, 1997. *Unlocking the cell: A humanities model for marginalized women*. Washington, DC: AAACE Publishers.

——. 1994. The humanities for homeless women: A paradox in learning. *Adult Learning* 5 no. 3: 13–15.

Dyson, M. E. 1999. Behind the mask: Helping African-American men feel secure. *Essence* 30 no. 11: 21–22.

Freire, P. 1996. *Pedagogy of the oppressed. New revised 20th anniversary edition*. New York: Continuum Publishing Company.

Gaines, P. 1995. *Laughing in the dark: From colored girl to woman of color—A journey from prison to power*. New York: Anchor Books.

Giovanni, N. 1996. *Selected poems of Nikki Giovanni*. New York: William Morrow and Company.

Hill Collins, P. 1990. Defining black feminist thought. In *The second wave: A reader in feminist theory*. Edited by L. Nicholson. New York: Routledge, 241–59.

hooks, b. 2004. *The will to change: Men, masculinity and love*. New York: Washington Square Press.

Hunter, T. 2000. *The hearts of men*. New York: Strivers Row.

Jewkes, R. 2002. Intimate partner violence: Causes and prevention. *The Lancet* 359 no. 9325: 1423–29.

Katz, J. 2006. *The macho paradox: Why some men hurt women and how all men can help*. Naperville, CA: Sourcebooks.

Newman, A., W. Lewis, and C. Beverstock. 1993. *Prison literacy: Implications for program and assessment*. Bloomington: Indiana University. Technical Report. TR 93-01. Copublished with ERIC Clearinghouse and Communication Skills.

Peterson, E. 1991. *A phenomenological investigation of self-will and the relationship to achievement in African-American women.* Norman, OK: Adult Education Research Conference.

Rappaport, J. 1995. Empowerment meets narrative: Listening to stories and creating settings. *American Journal of Community Psychology* 23 no. 5: 795–807.

Sister Souljah. 1996. *No disrespect.* New York: Vintage Books.

Vanzant, I. 1998. *Yesterday I cried.* New York: Fireside.

———. 2002. *Up from here.* San Francisco: HarperCollins.

Additional Resources

Baird, I. C. 2004. Rattling the cage: Incarcerated men, gender and the construction of maleness. In *Proceedings of the Joint Conference of the Adult Education Research Conference and the Canadian Association for the Study of Adult Education.* Edited by D. E. Clover. Victoria, BC: University of Victoria, 43–47.

———. 2002. Violence against women: Looking behind the mask of incarcerated batterers. In *Proceedings of the 41st Annual Adult Education Research Conference.* Edited by T. Sork, V. L. Chapman, and R. St. Clair. Vancouver: The University of British Columbia.

Notes

1. The incarcerated women offer their definition/distinction between being a survivor and a victim. To them, survivors are those who were victimized, who finally understood the gendered power/control factors that prompted the abuse and are striving to avoid being abused again. The victims, alternatively, cannot see or understand the pattern, what is happening and why. They believe, instead, that they did not do enough the right way to please their partner. In blaming themselves, they allow themselves to be victimized and blamed; they also assume a heavy burden of guilt that is further victimization.

2. In 1994, *Adult learning,* an American Association of Adult and Continuing Education publication (AAACE) featured the pilot project and its humanities orientation as a paradox in learning (Baird 1994). In 1997, AAACE published *Unlocking the Cell,* a monograph that describes in detail the program—its inception, development and suggestions for implementation (Baird 1997).

3. A Newman, Lewis, and Beverstock study (1993) is among the criminal justice publications that refer to the high illiteracy rates among the incarcerated— implying they are categorically illiterate. The media often cites high levels of illiteracy among inmates and the community and even faculty peers have shared this same kind of stereotyping.

4. Although I have referred to the program by titles such as "Unlocking the Cell," the "Inward Journey" and "Writing Myself," in prison reports it is referred to as the "Reading and Creative Writing Program." Often even that is abbreviated to "Creative Writing." I feel that the program needs/deserves to own its own identity just as the women do.

5. The program content and theoretical support has been influenced by Freire's (1996) work in which oppressed people resist by identifying themselves as subjects, by shaping their identity, naming themselves, their history and telling their story. This same philosophy is found in the work of Patricia Hill Collins (1990) and bell hooks (in Hill Collins 1990) who maintain that black women must assume responsibility for defining their own reality because they live that reality and have those experiences. Finally, according to Rappaport (1995), narrative theory is about the stories that tell us not only who we are but where we have been and where we can be. These perspectives seem to be more evident now, in our confessional age (Oprah, Montel, and Dr. Phil, as examples) than when I first became involved in a process under the humanities umbrella.

6. I note the omission in homeless women's writing and discussion regarding their problematic relationships. Were the inmates more open because there was a greater level of trust established by my tenure at the jail? By knowing I tend not to be judgmental? Or by the fact that they were always being "grilled" about their lives? I don't know the answer. I do know that any story line that resonates with their experiences stimulates lengthy comparison in discussion and writing. Then again, it could be something as simple as currently having more effective books for their program process.

7. Unlike a one-on-one counseling session where questions are asked directly to address traumas, reading and reflecting on the problems of another, especially a

successful and recognized author, seems like a less threatening way to identify issues and, using that author as a mentor, to see hope in resolving life crises.

8. During discussion about influences and barriers, the women tended to move closer to each other; they sometimes placed an arm around the one who had been painfully abused, an "I feel you" moment. During those times, I listen respectfully and empathetically but refrain from interjecting myself into the interaction.

SECTION II

Bridging Communities: Writing Programs and Social Practice

Good Intentions Aside

The Ethics of Reciprocity in a University-Jail Women's Writing Workshop Collaboration

SADIE REYNOLDS

Why Write?

Summer of 1976

She came roaring into my sister's and my room. She was screaming and complaining at the same time. It was terrifying. It was sooooo hurtful. She called us names. Told us how worthless we were, home-wrecker she said to me. I did not understand, I was only eleven years old. She swept everything on our dresser off the top with her right arm throwing a lamp at me with her left. You wrecked my happiness she said to me, my dream of having a home. She grabbed my arm and hit me all over with her open hand. She said, because of me she has to sacrifice everything. She left the room. My sister and I both cried and looked at each other in fear. She shouted clean up that mess and stop crying or I will give you something to cry about. I wrote my first poem that day—out of fear and frustration toward my mother:

> *Why was I born*
> *My soul is tattered and torn*
> *She hates me to the bone*
> *I feel utterly alone.*

I wrote poems like puzzles with double-edged meanings. I was so afraid to tell anyone about her. I was so afraid she would see it. Writing became my secret. My voice. My ventilation system. A cry on the wishful wind. I ripped up everything I wrote the first year. After that I hid in the words so even she could not be sure.

—Sophie (Inside Out Writing Project participant)

When You Look at Me
You may think that it's sad,
because I'm addicted to drugs.
You may think that I'm bad,
because I'm attracted to thugs.
You may not think that I'll
ever change my way.
But you may change your mind,
if you listen, to what I've got to say.
Despite the things you see,
the tracks and scars I bare,
what you can't see is my beautiful heart,
no matter how hard you stare.
Looking at my low budget casual street fashion,
you can't see my desire or
the depths of my passion.
But I really can't say what you think,
when you take that look at me.
Just remember that there's more to this woman,
than just what you see.

—Luz (Inside Out Writing Project participant)

If you have come here to help me, you are wasting our time.
But if you have come because your liberation is bound up with mine,
then let us work together.

—Lilla Watson, Australian Aboriginal Activist, Artist, and Academic

The Inside Out Writing Project

The idea did not come suddenly. It was more of a slow arrival at a deep certainty that I wanted to focus my dissertation research on women prisoners and writing, and that I wanted to bring writing workshops to women inside as part of the research. I was fiercely passionate about this topic, given that my first exposure to adult education was while serving time in a county jail twelve years previously, and that higher education in sociology and feminist studies—and finding a voice through writing—had been so empowering to me.

Going back inside to share the gift of writing and critical knowledge with others who might benefit from it felt personally necessary. And I wanted to learn more and create new knowledge about an under-studied and misrepresented population with whom I felt a deep affinity. Gaining access to prisoners for the purposes of research is notoriously difficult in closed institutions such as prisons and jails. But that didn't deter me. I had a vision, and I planned to promote it at correctional facilities as far and wide geographically as necessary to give it life.

Sometimes events line up in my life as though there were a grand design. Such was the case with this project. Shortly after submitting my dissertation proposal I was given an opportunity to start offering writing workshops in a local jail, within blocks of my home. In 2002 I founded the Inside Out Writing Project (IOWP) and began offering weekly writing workshops in the women's minimum and maximum security facilities in Santa Cruz, California.

In groups ranging in size from three to sixteen, we explored technical and substantive aspects of autobiographical writing, poetry, essays, and fiction, with an emphasis on learning through practicing reading and writing. The program's founding goals were:

- to assist participants in improving their written and oral communication skills,
- to nourish their critical thinking and analytical abilities,
- to expose them to diverse genres of writing, emphasizing writings by people who had been marginalized in dominant culture and society,
- to support personal healing and growth through creative expression and reflection,
- to create a venue for developing confidence and voice.

Another important goal was to affirm the humanity and inherent dignity of participants, who were undergoing an experience that most found dehumanizing in the extreme. Finally, I envisioned the project as a bridge from the university to the jail and back—creating connections across a divide too infrequently traveled.

During the first year I conducted research for my dissertation in sociology and feminist studies with a small subset of the women who came through the workshops. I established the project as an organization from the beginning because I intended to devote my energies to sustaining its work long after the research was completed, as a way to counteract the exploitive nature of much social research. Too often researchers from privileged socioeconomic backgrounds study disadvantaged groups of people and leave little or nothing behind. They take time and information from members of the communities in which they work, and leave to produce knowledge that enhances their careers but that doesn't always benefit or ring authentic to the people studied. I wanted to avoid this, so in various ways I worked imperfectly toward reciprocity with the women who participated in my dissertation research. By building and sustaining IOWP in its early years, I tried to leave something valuable to the population of women who shared their lives so generously with me for my research.

In years two and three of the project I began spending less time in the jail classroom and investing my energies in training and supervising university students and volunteers from the community as interns, and expanding and strengthening the project so that eventually it could operate in my absence. During those years I trained and supervised more than fifteen interns. I obtained office space, a paid undergraduate internship, and 501(3)c status under the University of California, Santa Cruz Women's Center.

Our group established a reentry project to provide resources for women upon release from jail. We expanded our curriculum to include art. We secured funding for writing and art supplies from the community and university. We organized events on campus designed to promote critical awareness of the issue of women's imprisonment. One year we created a Women in Prison Awareness Week, including a public education campaign and performances by interns on campus; another year we organized a Prison-Industrial Complex Week featuring public education, film screenings, and a keynote speech by Angela Davis; and one year we invited the San Francisco–based

Medea Project, a theater project of and for incarcerated women, to perform for the campus community.

Through the support of the UCSC Women's Center and the energy of a continued influx of interns, the project was positioned for longevity.[1] In 2005 I transitioned out of leadership in the organization. Having nurtured the project for more than three years, I placed it in the capable hands of a small group of women who were committed to sustaining its important work.

Since then, IOWP has been run by revolving sets of volunteer interns from UCSC, the community of Santa Cruz, and Cabrillo College—the local community college where I currently teach. It has expanded into the men's units in the maximum security jail, and a handful of men have served as volunteers. Interns have a created a project blog online and a zine that showcases writings and drawings from workshop participants, and they engage in the community by participating at local events and connecting with statewide activism to change correctional policy. I served in a consultant role for several years. At the time of this writing my role in the organization is minimal. I am the workshop scheduler, I facilitate workshops during summer and breaks, and I host occasional intern meetings to lend support to the organization.

In this chapter, I offer some thoughts on the ethics and politics of facilitating women's writing workshops in a county jail, discuss how these ideas have informed my work with IOWP, and lay out some of the ways that project interns and I have worked toward developing relationships of reciprocity with workshop participants.

It bears noting that my thinking about this work derives directly from a confluence of my unique life experiences and academic training. As a girl and young woman I lost my way. In the aftermath of trauma resulting from violence and in keeping with the behavior I saw in my immediate family, I used illegal drugs heavily. I became entangled in the criminal justice system at an early age—appearing in protective services court; serving short stints in juvenile hall, foster homes, and a group home; and leaving home by the age of fifteen. I turned eighteen years old just as the "war on drugs" was escalating, and spent the next few years in and out of adult facilities—both county jail and prison. I was on the precipice of life. But during my most recent incarceration, I earned a GED and took my first college courses. Upon my release, I enrolled part-time in community college and became an avid student. Higher education became a much-needed anchor and my life's work.

By the time I launched the project, I had been in graduate school studying sociology for several years, working consistently throughout that time as
a teaching assistant in sociology, community studies, and women's studies.
Thus, I came to the workshops with first-hand experience of the pains of
criminalization and imprisonment; broad exposure to feminist theory, critical criminology, and critical race theory; and years of teaching experience in
the social sciences and humanities. I also came with considerable privilege—
as a well-educated, white woman from a mixed-class background in a heterosexual marriage. All of these aspects of social location shape my approach
to the work of facilitating writing workshops with women in county jail and
their reception of me.

Building a Program Based on Solidarity

The Problem with Rehabilitation: A Deficiency Model

Educational programs in institutions of detention are commonly designed
and implemented with rehabilitation in mind. But it is important to note
that the notion of rehabilitation is based on the assumption that prisoners
are "ill or deviant in some manner" and in need of moral or psychic transformation—the goal being "to restore well being through various therapeutic
models and education" (Ross 1998, 127). While the United States is in a hy-
perpunitive moment in its penal history, rehabilitative discourses continue to
thrive, if muted by calls for incapacitation and retribution. And rehabilitation
is widely considered a politically progressive, philosophical and practical approach to imprisonment. Its critics tend to be those advocating more punitive
approaches to imprisonment. However, as Luana Ross (1998) points out, in
practice, rehabilitation programs for women prisoners are often more about
maintaining tight control than healing or genuinely supporting prisoners.

A major flaw in the notion of rehabilitation as commonly conceived is that
it implies deficiency; educational programs based on this model are grounded
in a perception of prisoners as inherently defective. It became clear to me
early in my work inside that the women who come to my writing workshops

are, overwhelmingly, anything but deficient. Many have experienced severe poverty, violence, and racism—with all their insidious effects. Most have been arrested on minor charges—drug possession, under the influence, shoplifting, or violating the conditions of probation or parole by failing to appear at meetings with probation and parole officers or producing "dirty" urine. Within the context of lives shaped by harm and lack of opportunity, their conduct actually makes sense, and this is true also for the relatively few women whose charges are more serious. These are people who have demonstrated remarkable survival skills, fierce adaptability, and creative forms of resistance to injustice. As human beings, the women with whom I have worked demonstrate a vivid range of personalities, worldviews, and personal strengths and foibles. But as a group, they are personable, resourceful, and intelligent—roundly defying popular stereotypes of incarcerated women. Their powerful writing provides a glimpse at their dynamism and the depths of their humanity. The poems and writing that open this chapter exemplify this reality.[2]

Critiquing the rehabilitative model shouldn't minimize women prisoners' need for access to social resources. Indeed, systemic lack of access to resources is probably the most pressing issue facing many of the women with whom IOWP works. Nonetheless, the project's work starts from the premise that workshop participants are not deficient but people who have dealt remarkably competently with destructive social-structural forces of state violence and inequalities based on race, class, gender, and sexuality—people who have responded to often brutal life circumstances with remarkable strength and courage. A radical departure from a correctionalist discourse, this starting point is more conducive to building trusting and affirming relationships in the jail classroom.

The Problem with Charity: Good Intentions Are Not Enough

Much contemporary charity and service work is tinged with discourses of colonialism and does nothing to change underlying power relations (Wagner 2000). However well-intentioned, privileged individuals who help less fortunate people often do so without critically examining their motives. The blinders of privilege show up as an unacknowledged sense of superiority and condescending ways of communicating and relating with the people they are trying to help—sometimes subtly, sometimes blatantly. Many believe they know the character traits needed for the unfortunates to extricate themselves from their troubles—for example, a better work ethic or more self-discipline. Or they think that they can "save" "these poor people." This kind of thinking slips into the minds of even critically trained service providers and educators who congratulate themselves for being progressive allies—so engrained is it in popular discourses of helping. One must be vigilantly self-reflective if one is to hope to repel it.

In working with prisoners, refraining from succumbing to a mindset of superiority, pity, or saving is of paramount importance. Such thinking is poison to a politically and ethically sound practice that is guided by a desire to create mutually affirming relationships with incarcerated workshop participants. Maintaining a keen awareness of this is difficult; in a culture that elevates charity as the highest form of altruism, it is all too easy to forget.

The minimal scope and impact of most charitable work are noteworthy. Soup kitchens are the quintessential example—seen by so many Americans as the pinnacle of good works. But serving soup does nothing to eradicate the root causes of hunger and poverty. At best it serves as a Band-Aid—a stopgap measure that has only short-run utility. At worst, it justifies the status quo, provides the giver with a sense of moral superiority, fosters dependency, and forestalls more fundamental change—for example, a more equitable distribution of social resources such as food.

The Importance of Solidarity

IOWP seeks to build solidarity with women prisoners rather than rehabilitate or provide charity for them. While the project provides services to women prisoners, interns strive to see that their efforts move beyond a typical service approach. By bringing in writing workshops that explore diverse writers' work and encourage critical thinking and the development of voice, the project strives to build social awareness and to nurture critical reflection and social action. By striving to create with participants free spaces in which all present are affirmed as thinkers, writers, and human beings, it poses fundamental challenges to predominant correctionalist discourses and practices that would strip people of their agency and humanity. By sharing critical knowledge with participants it is extending a potentially revolutionary tool to a group that, overwhelmingly, has been systematically denied access to education.

There is also the dynamic exchange that happens between women from the university, college, community, and jail. These groups of people are not mutually exclusive. But to a considerable extent, women from these different groups remain in separate spheres.[3] This inside/out outside/in exchange is potentially valuable and educative for all involved, particularly women from the outside. It can help them see the interconnectedness of their lives and communities with people inside, giving them a insider glimpse of the prison industrial complex and showing them how profoundly this pernicious institution affects us all. Finally, IOWP couples its work inside with work outside that seeks to disrupt the logic and practices of mass incarnation. In this way it resists becoming a cog in that machine, fundamentally challenging the work of the prison industrial complex through public education and advocacy work in the community.

The Politics and Ethics of Access and Social Change

Access

The most challenging aspect of working with IOWP for me has been negotiating my role as a program provider in an institution of repression. This has been an ongoing source of personal distress, as I have been compelled to stifle my political affiliations in the interest of preserving access to the jail. Interns generally find this to be a particularly difficult feature of working inside. Among the primary aims of jails and prisons is enforcement of discipline and creating a punitive environment. Repression is the *leitmotif* of carceral spaces, and as program providers granted access by gatekeepers of the institution, IOWP interns are expected to follow along.

The written training materials distributed at jail volunteer orientations rely on and reinscribe negative stereotypes of prisoners and provide a sense of the punitive ideological context within which we work as writing workshop facilitators. At my first orientation I was given a document that refers to prisoners as "seasoned manipulators," "drug dealers, . . . rapists, child molesters." An orientation document developed later includes several pages outlining a theory of criminality. The "extreme criminal," according to the theory, "divert[s] attention from self by introducing irrelevant material and by invoking racial issues." Racism is deeply structured into the U.S. criminal justice system, and U.S. society and its institutions more generally. The notion that "the extreme criminal" exists is highly suspect in the first place. And the argument that she or he invokes racial issues to avert blame might easily be seen as a trope to divert attention from the structural racism embedded in the jail itself as an institution, and to preempt or repress complaints about it.

Interns have been instructed not to touch prisoners, convey any messages from one prisoner to another, make phone calls for prisoners, criticize the justice system or staff in the presence of prisoners, or write letters to prisoners' judges reporting upon their participation in IOWP. We watch women led to the strip search room from our workshops, knowing that many of them find the experience highly traumatic. In fact, for survivors of sexual violence—and more than 80 percent of the women from workshops who I interviewed for my dissertation research reported histories of sexual violence (Reynolds 2008)—the strip search is often experienced as a retraumatization.

I decided early on that I could not in good conscience follow all the repressive rules laid down by jail staff in every single instance. But continued access depends upon generally following rules and giving the appearance that I am in accord with them. It also requires that I conduct myself as though I object to neither jail staff's characterizations of prisoners nor their treatment of them, when the truth is that I often find both objectionable. This is a source of ongoing internal dissonance, as I am obliged to deny what I believe are reasonable requests from participants, to shun any physical contact with them, and to rein in my critiques of the criminal justice system and its agents. I occasionally break a rule or protocol, for example by critiquing the criminal justice system and practices by guards in the company of participants, quickly hugging a woman I haven't seen in a long time when she gestures to do so, or putting a hand on her shoulder if she is crying in the classroom and my intuition tells me it should be done. But restraint is necessary. Following rules and keeping my protests to a minimum are strategic compromises made in the interest of preserving the continuity of IOWP.

Social Justice: Working toward Revolutionary Reform

The anguish brought about by the compromises made to do this work has led me to question its value and wonder if working outside the system to fundamentally challenge it would be more consistent with my ideals. Providing services to incarcerated populations is an exercise in reformist politics. It seeks to improve conditions for imprisoned people, working within the existing institution. While advocates of reform suggest that working within existing institutions is desirable because it is realistic, many of those advocating more fundamental change argue that reform tends merely to buttress the status quo.

Antonio Gramsci, an Italian socialist thinker writing in the early twentieth century, argued that reform serves as a concession that solidifies the consent of the people and thereby entrenches the hegemony of the powerful (Gramsci 1971). With respect to reform in the criminal justice system, a radical approach points to the deeply and historically entrenched racism and class biases that are built into the institution, suggesting that these can never be fully rooted out, and advocating decarceration and the establishment of viable nonpunitive alternatives to incarceration for all but the most violent among us.[4] Such an approach argues that reforms only strengthen the criminal justice system by improving it—bolstering its coercive power and control over human lives. But does this negate the value of all service work with incarcerated women?

Karlene Faith argues that reform is necessary in the short run because real women occupy real prison cells and are subject to grave human rights violations inside. But she makes a practical distinction between what she calls "revolutionary reform" and "reformist reform." According to Faith, revolutionary reform has "liberatory potential to challenge the status quo," whereas reformist reform "may ease the problem temporarily or superficially, but reinforces the status quo by validating the system through the process of improving it" (Faith 2000, 164). Women prisoners benefit from revolutionary efforts, while correctional discourse and practice is bolstered by those that are reformist.

This distinction has been useful, helping many volunteers reach a measure of resolve on this ethical and political dilemma. We examine our practices on an ongoing basis to determine if our work reinforces or subverts the criminal justice system. While we are sanctioned by the jail to facilitate writing workshops inside and are largely beholden to its rules, there are many ways in which our practice is subversive.

Our approach poses fundamental challenges to correctional perceptions of women prisoners as morally degenerate "criminals." We treat the women who attend our workshops with respect and kindness. We view them and encourage them as critical thinkers, as writers and artists, as historical agents. We expose them to written materials selected to support them in building analytical skills, communication skills, and self-determination. We create a space with them for healing and connection in the confines of that dreadful place. We try to stay mindful of the larger goal—contributing to the creation a more just and equitable society—letting it frame the bulk of our work inside which focuses on more modest and immediate goals. And we complement the work inside with work outside that is geared toward public awareness and resistance to mass incarceration.

Putting it into Practice: Working toward Reciprocity in the Jail Workshop

There are a number of ways in which we try to conduct ourselves that are consistent with and remain mindful of these larger ethical and political concerns. The most basic feature of IOWP's approach is that its primary goal is to work toward reciprocity with project participants.

Language

Language is important. In the project's early years, I always suggested that interns think about referring to participants as prisoners rather than the more commonly used but ideologically encumbered referents "inmates" and "offenders." The term inmate is sanitizing, euphemistic, and depoliticizing. By contrast, a *prisoner* is clearly someone who is *imprisoned.* Inmate is the preferred term of jail staff, one that is eschewed by many critical antiprison activists. *Offender* is also very commonly used by criminal justice officials and so-called "experts." It is a normative designation with a derogatory ring, much the same as the clearly deprecating *criminal.* Both terms contradict a notion of crime and criminality as socially constructed, and culturally and historically specific, a premise of the work of IOWP.

This may seem like a mere matter of semantics. But the ways people talk about prisoners has significant bearing upon how they think about and conduct themselves with them. Also, importantly, many women in jail are awaiting sentencing or trial and have not yet been duly convicted; their status as "offenders" is as yet undetermined. At the same time that these designations have political significance, it is crucial to remember that they can also be overdetermining and totalizing labels. The women we work with tend to define themselves more in terms of family, work, and friends on the outside than their status as prisoners. Thinking of IOWP participants primarily as prisoners rather than mothers, sisters, partners, friends, workers, and so forth—as human beings—is reductionist and does a kind of epistemic violence to them. In recent years I have come to refer to the women inside as *workshop participants*. This kind of awareness and sensitivity to issues of language are important in IOWP.

IOWP interns are titled *facilitators* rather than *teachers*. What we offer are *workshops* not *classes*. The concept of facilitating workshops has very different connotations than that of teaching classes. It moves away from hierarchy and toward horizontality—suggesting that the workshops belong to participants and facilitators together, and that facilitators are there to support and encourage prisoners as all present create engaging and enriching writing workshops. It challenges the unequal power in typical classrooms and places interns on a more equal basis with participants.[5] In addition to facilitating, interns also participate fully in workshops—writing and sharing their work alongside participants.

Self-Disclosure

Self-disclosure can be a powerful tool in breaking down hierarchy in the workshop. Many educators receive personal disclosure from students but refrain from sharing personal details of their own lives in return. Mutual self-disclosure between facilitators and participants in jail-based writing workshops helps create the trust and connection that can make them healing and transformative spaces. Self-disclosure, a basic tenet of feminist pedagogies (see hooks 1994), has been a guiding principle in my work facilitating writing workshops inside as well as my teaching at the university and community college. To create a workshop promoting personal and intellectual growth, participants must feel validated as human beings with unique viewpoints and experiences. They must be comfortable with some level of vulnerability. When facilitators practice vulnerability by revealing their hopes and dreams and fears and suffering, it sets a tone that invites participants to do the same.

I often call upon my experiences as a girl and young woman—of gender violence, substance abuse, criminalization and prison, or freedom through education—in workshops. I try to place these experiences within historical context, construing them as part of much larger systems of violence against women, economic injustice, and a burgeoning criminal justice system that continues to consume larger and larger numbers of people. Workshop participants tend to think of their experiences in individual terms—even experiences that are systemic in nature like sexual violence, poverty, and racism. I talk about our experiences in social terms, conveying a language of the social that I hope is destigmatizing and affirming. I am trying to disabuse participants of the shame they have learned from the culture to attach to their life trajectories. Unfortunately, some of the women I meet inside are very self-critical, blaming themselves for making poor choices, when in fact their choices were quite limited from the start. I know because I did this for many years, until I began to develop an understanding of the social determinants of individual outcomes.

I have developed four "rules of disclosure" to guide my decisions to open up in the workshop on a case-by-case basis.[6] First, I ask myself, "Am I healed?"—or at least, "well on my way in the healing process?" I self-disclose in the workshop if I can answer this question with a reasonably confident "yes." Feeling and expressing strong emotions in workshop is not necessarily inadvisable. To the contrary, it often forms the basis for trust and connection and creating a safe space inside the jail. Losing my composure entirely while facilitating a workshop, however, would do a disservice to participants. I would lose my ability to facilitate. Participants might feel compelled to take care of me. And it could set an inauspicious tone for focused discussion and writing.

Second, I ask myself, "Is it relevant?" There should be a purpose in self-disclosure in the workshop—such as connecting with participants, conveying inspiration or hope, or illustrating a point related to workshop content. I often use myself as an example of how to analyze how written workshop materials apply to our lives, or discuss my experience confronting obstacles and the important life lessons learned in the process.

Third, I ask myself, "Is it safe?" This is an intuitive matter, and there will be some days with a particular group of students or workshop participants in which it just doesn't feel right. I always respect my "gut" on this question and go only as deep as feels appropriate.

Finally, I tell myself, "Keep it brief." I refrain from lengthy excursions into my personal past or present in an effort to avoid dominating the workshops or making them overly focused on me. Time is precious inside and there is writing to be done. I developed these guidelines while working in the university classroom, and I find that they work in the jail and community college as well.

Reciprocal Learning

Breaking down the hierarchy typical in student-teacher relationships is essential to creating a democratic space inside the confines of the jail, in which women as thinkers, writers, speakers, and human beings, are validated and affirmed. Dialogue has been one of my prime strategies for working toward equalized relationships in the classroom and for learning reciprocally and across difference. I am as much participant as facilitator in workshop; as participants share their perspectives, experiences, and analyses, I learn about their lives and worldviews, their ideas and perspectives on specific topics. And I learn about facilitating— what works well in the jail workshop and what doesn't.

In spaces of reciprocity, each member must fully participate, and must feel a responsibility to take part in the creation of a classroom community (see hooks 1994). Each must be acknowledged, her or his voice heard and emphatically affirmed. This has been an essential strategy for my practice. In every workshop, participants are asked to introduce themselves and check in with the group, to participate in the day's discussion, and at least once during the workshop to read their written work aloud. This helps create an inclusive setting in which all present feel invited to contribute as full participants. I never *require* that anyone participate in these activities; women in jail have enough structure imposed upon them.

Listening skills are essential for this work. It is imperative that facilitators do not dominate discussions, a mode that is easy to slip into when one is leading a group, but one that is antithetical to reciprocity in the classroom. Skills facilitating discussion are also vital, to help move toward equal participation among participants and focus and depth in the quality of dialogue created.

Reciprocal learning requires flexibility on the part of facilitators, helping them to be responsive to participants' ideas and interests as they develop in the course of a workshop. Participants often take discussions and writing exercises in unexpected directions, and it is the responsibility of facilitators to follow as well as lead. This requires spontaneity, fast thinking, and a readiness to go in new directions on any given day, in any given moment. We often set aside our plans for the day to follow participants' leads, redirecting discussion and devising new writing assignments accordingly. Avoiding rigid formulas for instilling writing skills, we advocate practicing reading and writing in a supportive, engaging context as the most effective route to building literacy.

Creating opportunities for participants to determine curricular content is another important feature of reciprocity (Freire 1997). Interns regularly take requests for topics and authors around which to devise workshops, and we respond to them. We have given participants the opportunity to devise their own workshops. The workshops designed and led by participants thus far have been very well conceived and delivered—for example, one on color and personality that I attended—if small in number. I have frequently invited participants to critically assess my work facilitating in written evaluations that note strengths and point to areas for improvement, and I take feedback seriously, incorporating it into future work.

Critical Reflection and Cultural Competencies

Perhaps the most important way in which IOWP interns work toward reciprocity with project participants is through continuous, critical reflection, and the application of that reflection to our work. The story of the project's name illustrates the importance of this. At its inception I titled the project the Literacy Instruction for Empowerment (LIFE) Project. This title worked for a couple of reasons: It fit with the way I packaged myself to the jail in the proposal I wrote to gain access, and it was catchy so I thought it would help participants and donors to remember the organization—thereby aiding in however small a way its potential for strength and longevity. After a number of months working in the jail and reflecting on the purpose of that work, I decided that the initial title had a problematic ring, suggesting that somehow I would empower participants by instructing them in literacy. But people empower themselves. Efforts to empower others—however well intentioned—are based on a deficiency model that makes them potentially damaging for all involved.

The new name better represents Inside Out Writing Project's founding goals; to the extent possible, we are trying to break down hierarchy, create connections across the barrier between inside and outside the jail, and create relationships of reciprocity with project participants. We see ourselves as learning and benefiting from this interaction at least as much as participants in the process. That I had chosen such politically problematic language in the first place, even with my training and experience, demonstrates the insidiousness of colonialist discourses. That I recognized and addressed the problem early on demonstrates the value of critical reflection on practice.

Much reflection takes place with respect to identity and difference. For example, while I regularly call upon my experiences of interpersonal and state violence in the jail classroom as a teaching tool, I am keenly aware of the privileges I bring there. Because we are women, participants in my writing workshops and I, have all experienced sexism. And participants generally have a clear lived understanding of gender-based inequality. But experiences of sexism are shaped profoundly by race, class, sexuality, age, culture, nationality, and ability. It has been essential to my practice to reflect continuously on my social location, both internally and sometimes verbally the classroom. I am white. I am in a heterosexual relationship and married. I am a documented citizen of the United States. While my class background is mixed (my mother's family is middle-class, my father's working-class), and while I have experienced extended periods of lack of access to resources, my more recent educational efforts place me squarely in the middle class. My race, class, and sexuality have eased my trajectory from jail and prison to the academy, smoothing my movement through dominant institutions.

These combined privileges make my experiences in the world very different from most of the women who participate in my workshops. The majority grew up in families that struggled economically. A large minority are women of color.[7] Many identify as lesbian or bisexual. To my knowledge none have reached the educational level that I have.

Remaining mindful of the privileges I bring to the classroom keeps me sensitive to difference and its radical impacts on individual experience. Ideally, it prevents erroneous and harmful assumptions of similarity and paternalistic modes of workshop facilitation. Speaking about my social location in the classroom allows me to demonstrate tangibly to students the power of gender, whiteness, class privilege, and heterosexuality in shaping life experiences in a society that is structured by racism, nationalism, capitalism, heterosexism, and male dominance. It counters discourses of meritocracy and colorblindness so pervasive in U.S. culture, to which participants in my workshops are not immune. It helps participants develop critical and holistic analytical frameworks within which to examine workshop materials and their own lives.

When I was training interns, the importance of continuous, critical reflection on identity and difference was the most dominant theme. The potential for harm in this work is considerable, particularly if interns are uncritical of their privileges, assumptions, and practices in the classroom. Many of the women and men who have worked with the project over the years have been white, middle class, and heterosexual. But a large minority have been women of color, and a large minority have identified as lesbian/gay or queer. About a third had grown up poor. More than a handful of us have had family members or partners entangled in the justice system, and several of us have been arrested and done time. Importantly, most have enjoyed the privilege of attending a four-year university, an opportunity the vast majority of our participants have been denied.

Whenever privileged people work with those with fewer privileges, the potential to reinscribe patterns of unequal power—racism, sexism, heterosexism, for example—runs high. A proactive commitment to militate against this tendency is essential. When I was building the project, all new interns underwent a rigorous orientation and ongoing training and support for their work as writing workshop facilitators, with a view toward minimizing the potential for causing harm in the classroom. They were provided with a reading packet of scholarship examining women's imprisonment and mass incarceration, and introducing antiracist and critical feminist pedagogical and organizing approaches—all with a view toward encouraging critical reflection on the dynamics of power and privilege in writing work with women inside.[8] The current leadership employs a similar training process.

That most of the facilitators who worked with IOWP in the early years did so for university credits that counted toward degrees poses an ethical dilemma, even though many decided to continue volunteering long after they had ceased to be enrolled for credits. It was essential that interns reflect critically on the nature of this relationship. I tried to impress upon them that they are in college, in one sense, *because* prisoners are imprisoned. In any system, the various parts work together to constitute the whole. Mass incarceration relies upon a certain subset of the population being locked away. One cannot fully understand the whole without a grasp of the relational nature of how the various parts fit together. In the United States, there are well over two million adult prisoners today. Why are they imprisoned, and not in college? The most important factors are social-structural. The lack of opportunity most prisoners have faced is the opposite side of the same coin of opportunity that provides interns with access to higher education.

To address these realities, I asked interns to be honest about their motivations with project participants, making it clear in each workshop that they were earning credits for the work. I urged them to continuously reflect on power and privilege in the classroom and in their relationship to project participants and the prison industrial complex. I encouraged them to move past guilt to apply the insights gleaned through this process to work toward reciprocity in the classroom and to challenge the larger structural injustices that create a situation in which privileged people tend to go to college and poor people tend to be imprisoned. One way to address this dilemma and create reciprocity in terms of university credits would have been to offer university credit for workshop participants. Unfortunately, there are too many logistical impediments to make this a reality, but IOWP continues to explore alternative means of creating positive and meaningful experiences for participants inside and out.[9] In recent years IOWP has moved away from for-credit internships and the standard is for interns to work on an entirely volunteer basis.

My career has been bolstered by my work for the project. I conducted my dissertation research through the writing project in its early days, and in fact started the project in an attempt to approach reciprocity with women prisoners who shared their lives with me for that research. While I have been never been paid for this work, I earned a PhD with completion of my dissertation, my curriculum vitae is fuller than it was before I started IOWP, and this chapter itself will add yet another line. I see challenging injustices—in the criminal justice system and throughout society—as my life's work. Through my written work, teaching, and community engagements, I hope to devote my life to contributing, in admittedly small ways, to creating a more just society. In this way I hope to use the power and privilege gained through my academic work constructively. Continuous, critical reflection is the most important single ingredient in a solid foundation for this life's work.

Ongoing, critical reflection has taught IOWP interns that we cannot achieve complete reciprocity with the women who participate in our workshops. While we seek in various ways to work toward it, we remain aware of the important fact that hierarchy and different access to power are always present in the jail workshop. We don't mean to pretend that they don't exist or that they are easy to overcome. To the contrary, we let this awareness temper our efforts with transparency and respect.

In Closing

IOWP is in a continual process of growth and development, persistently seeking to sharpen its approach through engaged practice in the jail workshop and ongoing, critical reflection on our work. The knowledge that we will always be learning is a basic premise of our work. This openness helps us remain receptive to new insights gained in the process of facilitating writing workshops, in dialoguing with participants in the writing project, in exposing ourselves to the ideas of critical scholars and activists, and in critically reflecting on all aspects of the work.

As the U.S. criminal justice system continues to grow, consuming ever larger numbers of women and men, swallowing up whole communities even, critical work from a variety of angles is urgent. Writing projects for women prisoners have considerable potential as interventions in the dehumanizing experience of incarceration, and as positive interventions in lives marked by violence, social neglect, and educational disadvantage. But they run considerable risks of causing harm through enacting paternalistic and colonialist discourses and unequal power relations. A critical view of rehabilitation and charity, a commitment to working for solidarity, an awareness of the ethics of access and the politics of social change, and a practical commitment to working toward reciprocity with women attending writing workshops under lockdown can help minimize the risks of harm associated with this work. They have guided my efforts to create democratic spaces in the jail and build mutually affirming and emotionally connected relationships with workshop participants. And they have been useful in training interns as workshop facilitators and building IOWP to practice a politics of reciprocity in our work.

Working with women prisoners in writing workshops has been one of the most personally rewarding and transformative experiences I have ever had. The courageous, extraordinary women I met inside have taught me, inspired me, and transformed me. Project interns reflecting on their work inside have frequently expressed similar assessments of the experience—as educative, meaningful, and life-changing.

References

Faith, Karlene. 2000. Reflections on inside/out organizing. *Social Justice* 27 no. 13 (Fall): 138.

Freire, Paulo. [1977] 1997. *Pedagogy of the oppressed.* New revised 20th-anniversary edition. New York: Continuum.

Gramsci, Antonio. [1926] 1971. *Selections from the prison notebooks.* New York: International Publishers.

hooks, bell. 1994. *Teaching to transgress: Education as the practice of freedom.* London: Routledge.

Reynolds, Sadie. 2008. "Writing against time: The life histories and writings of women in Santa Cruz County Jail." Dissertation. University of California, Santa Cruz.

Ross, Luana. 1998. *Inventing the savage: The social construction of Native American criminality.* Austin: University of Texas Press.

Wagner, David. 2000. *What's love got to do with it?: A critical look at American charity.* New York: New Press.

Notes

1. I am extremely grateful to Roberta Valdez, the UCSC Women's Center's Director throughout the early years of the project, and Stephanie Milton, Director in more recent years. Both have been the project's great benefactors through staffing, housing, and helping fund the project.

2. See my dissertation for a collection of writings produced in association with the workshop in its early days (Reynolds 2008).

3. There are some eerie connections that deserve mention, for example, the fact that many state prisons are contracted by state boards of education to supply furniture, as in the case of California's state university and state prison systems, or the fact that funding for public education and other social services is being gutted to pay for corrections.

4. Restorative justice programs, hundreds of which have been launched across the nation in recent years with much success, are one such viable alternative to mass incarceration. Primarily in use with juveniles at this time, they show great promise for curtailing the United States' overreliance on imprisonment—of adults and children alike—that characterizes the contemporary moment.

5. I am not suggesting that equality can be achieved between workshop facilitators and participants. As I will argue later, I believe that there are enormous power differences there, and that these need to be fully acknowledged by facilitators and carefully considered in planning and implementing workshops. Indeed, a predominant theme in IOWP meetings is power in the workshop and in interns' relationships with participants—how it plays itself out, and how interns can remain critical and avoid misusing it.

6. My thanks to Bettina Aptheker, whose ideas I borrowed in formulating these guidelines.

7. In terms of race, Santa Cruz County Jail is unusual relative to other U.S. jails. A majority of prisoners are white, a reflection of the demographics of the county. Still, mirroring national trends, African American and Latino/a prisoners are overrepresented inside. As of 2000, African Americans comprised 1 percent of the county population but 4 percent of the jail population; Latino/as comprised 27 percent of the county population but 36 percent of the jail population. By contrast, whites are underrepresented in county jail. In 2000, they comprised 66 percent of the county population but only 58 percent of adult prisoners in the county. See Santa Cruz County Assessment Project, 2002, Public safety issues, http://www.appliedsurveyresearch.org/products/CAP8_Public1.pdf, and U.S. Census Bureau, 2000, American factfinder. Quick tables: Santa Cruz County, California, http://factfinder.census.gov/servlet/BasicFactsTable?_lang=en&_vt_name=DEC_2000_SF1_U_DP1&_geo_id=05000US06087.

8. Writings include the following:
- Amnesty International. 1999. *United States of America Rights for all: "Not part of my sentence": Violations of the human rights of women in custody.*

- Anti-racism for global justice: Building movement for collective liberation. A reading packet prepared by Challenging White Supremacy Workshops. Unpublished.
- Banks, Gabrielle. 2003. Learning under lockdown. In *ColorLines: Race Culture Action*. Spring: 12.
- Critical Resistance. 2002. What is abolition? http://www.criticalresistance.org/index.php?name=what_is_abolition.
- Davis, Angela. 2003. *Are prisons obsolete?* New York: Seven Stories Press; Davis, Angela. 1998. Racialized punishment and prison abolition. In *The Angela Y. Davis reader*. Edited by Joy James. Oxford: Blackwell; Davis, Angela. 1997. Race and criminalization: Black Americans and the punishment industry. In *The house the race built*. Edited by Wahneema Lubiano. New York: Vintage Books; Davis, Angela. 1999 [1974]. Selections from *Angela Davis: An autobiography*. In *The Angela Davis reader*. Edited by Joy James. Oxford: Blackwell.
- Faith, Karlene. 2000. Reflections on inside/out organizing. *Social Justice*. Fall 27 no. 13 (Fall): 138.
- Freire, Paulo. 1997 [1977]. *Pedagogy of the oppressed*. New revised 20th-anniversary edition. New York: Continuum.
- Girshick, Lori. 1999. Women in prison. In *No safe haven: Stories of women in prison*. Boston: Northeastern University Press.
- hooks, bell. 1994. Selections from *Teaching to transgress: Education as the practice of freedom*. London: Routledge.
- Mohanty, Chandra Talpade. 1993. On race and voice: Challenges for liberal education in the 1990s. In *Beyond a dream deferred: Multicultural education and the politics of excellence*. Edited by Becky W. Thompson and Sangeeta Tyagi. Minneapolis: University of Minnesota Press.
- Rodriguez, Dylan. 2000. Locked UP, Beat down. In *Color Lines: Race Culture Action* (Winter).
- Ross, Luana. 1998. *Inventing the savage: The social construction of Native American criminality*. Austin: University of Texas Press.
- Wagner, David. 2000. *What's love got to do with it?: A critical look at American charity*. New York: New Press.

9. For one, many of our participants haven't earned high school diplomas or GEDs. Students could not earn university credits without this documentation. Second, the population is highly transient, with a large proportion of participants serving shorter sentences than earning credits would allow. Third, importantly, we would have to find considerable resources to cover each participant's tuition.

10

Jumble of Thoughts

SANDY SYSYN

The room around me feels so large and vacant. My feet don't touch the floor and that's okay because I know the tile is ice cold. The tiny radiator on the wall spits and sputters as steam fills its coils. I shiver a bit as I look down at my dangling little feet, thankful for the socks I wear. As I do this I notice the newspaper lying on the floor and I am mesmerized by the words upon the pages. I want so badly to know what they say and I lean forward to get a better look.

I am puzzled by the knowledge that I know the words to say something but I don't know what and I can't make sense of it all. I am only a little girl sitting in the bathroom. The words are alluring and secretive like a hidden code and I want to know how to decipher them. The different size letters catch my eye and I am sure the bigger ones must be more important somehow. I feel a sense of frustration in not knowing what the words say, but I am so amazed that they do say something and I am suddenly driven by the desire to know how to read. I decide the words can mean what I want them to mean and I imagine what they say. Like, "Daddy saves Lefty the hamster from near demise," or "Aunt Alice is coming to stay with us," or better yet, "Little girls no longer have to take naps during episodes of Peyton Place." Then I can't help but wonder: How long is it going to take them to paint that place anyway?

In my mind I am already a writer, but I don't even know how to spell anything but my name. When my brother comes home from school, I'll ask him to teach me. He knows how to read.

As you can see, the jumble of thoughts that fill my head are formulated by old emotions and ideas. To me, words are the pieces of a puzzle that make up the picture of my psyche, my deepest desires or my heartfelt hopes, dreams and goals. I write to connect the dots, fill in the spaces, find explanations for my emotions or attempt to put things in chronological order. To me, words are the medium with which an artist blends and mixes to create fabulous illusions in the mind. Words strung into literature and stories excite me, change my mind and help me escape from the present nagging thoughts and troublesome fears and pains. A good story can be timeless and tireless, allowing the reader to fall in love or revisit it over and over again. I write because I want to remember the past and change the future.

Incorporeal Transformations

Audience and Women Writing in Prison

TOM KERR

At my desk late one evening, surrounded by pets and familiar objects, my wife and daughter reading together quietly in the next room, I was overwhelmed by the first of several letters my college writing class had received from incarcerated women being held in various prisons around the country. The letters had begun to trickle in during the week and I had saved them for a quiet moment. My course focused on the writing and rhetoric of social movements in general and of the Critical Resistance movement in particular, and my students and I had expressed our desire, via a widely distributed query letter, to learn about America's prison industrial complex from an insider's point of view.

I knew enough about conditions behind bars to know that respondents would certainly have painful tales to tell. But I could not have prepared myself for the cumulative effect of the powerful voices of a half-dozen women who were sharing their personal histories and traumatic experiences, describing the oppressive, often violent condition of prison life, and critiquing the underlying ideology of the system that had condemned them. It was hard to reconcile the depth of thought and feeling, not to mention the courage, demonstrated by these women in their letters with the cold, frequently brutal fact of their confinement.

My reaction, however, sprang more from the improbable connection the letters represented, one that promised so much in the way of recognition, understanding, empathy, and even political action, and yet one that seemed so tenuous, so frail—even as it formed: hardly a match for the law and order ideology and state penal apparatus separating "us" from "them." This is our predicament, a separation in a world, a society, deeply marred by social injustice. What could such marginal correspondence ultimately amount to, ultimately mean, in such a world?

Separating "Us" from "Them": Prison Correspondence and Audience

"Greetings!" opens Kirby Warner's letter.[1] "I'd like to thank you for choosing me as one of the prisoners to correspond with. Many of us do have voices that need to be heard. Society tends to forget that as human beings, we feel pain, anger, and cry tears. They forget that we are human; they forget that we have personalities and have placed labels against us, when most of us are genuinely good people, who have chosen the wrong roads in life's journey."

Linda Caldwell begins her letter to the class in a similar vein, noting that she is "honored that you all are interested in the people 'behind the wire' and 'on the other side.'" "Actually," she continues, "most prisoners here refer to society as 'in the world.' That alone has a strong emphasis when you think of 'people' not being in the world.'"

Thus, suddenly, my class and I were invited into the intimate circle of several incarcerated women's most pressing concerns—their deprivations, achievements, daily struggles, their hopes and fears. By the magic of rhetorical exigency, by positioning ourselves as readers for whom those concerns would matter, we were, in a sense, "re-membering" those who wrote to us, situating us through our correspondence together "in the world." By giving some shape, however vague, some human definition to ourselves, we had called forth writing that was (and is) both prolific and profound.

Over the next weeks and months, many more letters arrived and we responded, as best we could. The imprisoned women became *our* reason to write, *our* motive for reaching out beyond the confines of our own circumstances—that is, a capstone senior seminar in the Department of Writing at a predominately white, upper-middle class private college in New York State.

The experience was in many ways profound for my students, and me, and I'll touch here on the effects on my class of the correspondence,[2] but I'd like to focus in this essay on the letter writing of women in prison, and especially on the critical role audience plays in that writing.

The distinction, made in composition studies variously by Linda Flowers[3] and Peter Elbow, and by now many others, between "writer-based" writing and "reader-based" writing goes a long way toward explaining the nearly magical transformation that can occur when a writer shifts her conceptual orientation successfully from Self to Other. While the reader, or audience, can indeed be, as Elbow (1987) points out in "Closing My Eyes as I Speak: An Argument for Ignoring Audience," an inhibiting, even silencing agent—no more so, perhaps, than for incarcerated people—it can also be a liberating force, as the letters my class received attest.

The benefits that Elbow enumerates of ignoring audience at strategic points in the composing process, or in life, are indisputable. In writer-based prose, writers can free themselves from the often coercive demands of audience, from the pressures of "society." They can nurture and nourish and give solace to themselves without regard to what others may think, and they may therefore *think* in ways that others' presence can stifle. They may also be perfectly honest with themselves, and perfectly self-pitying or perfectly heroic, as occasion warrants. They talk to themselves and no one else—save for the voices that have always and already been introjected—the proverbial demons/angels inhabiting our psyches. In writer-based writing, writers are alone with their thoughts, however comforting or disturbing they may be.

In reader-based writing, on the other hand, writers are "in the world," very much interested in effectively conveying information, persuading, or entertaining, and the bulk of one's rhetorical decisions are thus made with a reader or many readers—with an external audience—in mind. Of course, it is perhaps most useful to understand these distinctions as tendencies rather than categorical types: One's focus may tend toward oneself or tend toward one's readers. A novelist, for instance, may fictionalize scenes from her own life with the intention of entertaining her readers while simultaneously writing for herself—making sense of an experience via her fiction.

Likewise, an incarcerated journal writer may keep a journal with the explicit intention of expressing private thoughts and feelings *privately*, nonetheless mindful that her words may well be read by prison officials, mindful that no text generated by a prisoner of the state who has been stripped of her right to privacy can be strictly "private," or writer-based, unless the writer destroys the text as she creates it. A prisoner's writing may tend, in a given text or at a given juncture, to be writer-based, but some decisions about what to write and how to write it are likely to be "reader-based"—made to protect oneself from the prying eyes of the state and its agents.

Antagonistic Audiences: Students and Inmates Compared

When it comes to the specter of audience in relation to self-expressive writing, student and incarcerated writers face different challenges. When asked explicitly in a writing assignment to produce reader-based prose in the form of an academic essay, for instance, free student writers can, if they choose, disregard rhetorical constraints and write mainly for themselves (or to the universe) as a form of direct or indirect resistance (that they may be more or less in control of, despite their decision to set audience demands aside) to institutional authority.

On the one hand, in order to give freer rein to self-expression, it is not uncommon for student writers to forgo the impersonal demands made by "members of the academic community" as defined in the assignment; the authority represented by such an audience may be perceived more as an obstacle to self-expression than as a threat to the self. Incarcerated writers, on the other hand, may write for and/or to themselves not in defiance of convention but rather as a rhetorical strategy of survival—self-reflective, writer-based writing serving both as a way to make sense of their predicament and to render themselves present/visible—at least to themselves. Too, it can be the case that few people in the lives of incarcerated writers have paid either sufficient or appropriate attention to their thoughts and feelings, making their expression of these in some form a healing imperative.

Both groups have a natural tendency and good reasons to write mainly for themselves, but if they hope to connect to readers effectively—to live in the world successfully and responsibly—all writers, free and not-free, must learn to gauge and address "audience." But for incarcerated writers, the personal stakes are much higher. For both groups, a shift between writer-based prose and the reader-based prose generated by public correspondence can, to the extent that it situates writers in a supportive if remote community, mitigate psychological and social isolation and so create unique opportunities for emotional growth and political action. But for writers in prison these benefits can make the difference between life and death—emotional, political, or physical.

For many prisoners, especially women, audience in the form of "society" has often been covertly or overtly hostile, either passively unreceptive or actively antagonistic. In addition to our "backlash society" and its many patriarchal subcultures, in which the reactionary suppression of women's strong and independent voices takes many forms (e.g., criticism, shaming, abandonment, violence), a preincarceration audience also frequently includes neglectful caregivers, indifferent teachers and/or employers, abusive relatives or acquaintances, social service bureaucracies, police, courts, and so forth. Once imprisoned, "audience" looms as an oppressive punitive system that includes correctional officers paid to vet mail for "contraband,"[4] inscrutable parole boards, court-appointed defense attorneys, and other prisoners—some of whom may be allies, some enemies. For incarcerated women writers, then, the act of moving between writer- and reader-based prose is momentous and risky.

The force of radically different realities and related rhetorical situations faced by students, on the one hand, and inmates, on the other, cannot be underestimated. Any kind of connection, much less transformation in relations, is hard won. As Linda Caldwell indicates in the introduction to her letter, fundamental misconceptions exist from the beginning:

> And in all honesty, I was a bit insulted and a lot of prisoners would be by questions that question my humanness. However, I know no offense was meant. Prison life makes one defensive when they are asked if they can live amongst the citizens of society being a productive human being. Maybe you can tell me why we get offended?

The questions Linda refers to here, posed by a couple of students (e.g., Do you think you are ready to leave prison and become a productive member of society?) signal class and race-based ideologies that correspondents on either side must contend with since what constitutes "productive" and "society" depends very much on where one is positioned. Yet were my college students and inmates to meet on neutral ground, unawares (at a mall, say), class background and ethnic/cultural differences would likely make communication complicated, at the very least. Were they to come face to face in the "free world," our racist, stratified society might very well keep them from speaking to each other at all. Lived experiences and age also make the prospect of meaningful communication between both groups, even in a neutral space, exceedingly slim.

For these reasons, it would be naïve to suppose that correspondence between students and prisoners is likely to lead to long-lasting, sustainable connections, although this cannot be ruled out as a possibility. Neither should one suppose that letter writing could transform the physical living conditions of inmates, though this is possible, or for that matter, induce immediate ideological shifts in students. The potential, however, for "incorporeal transformations" in both groups of writers is great, and such transformations may have profound consequences, especially for those behind bars.

Forging Relationships through Correspondence: Writer- and Reader-Based Writing

The notion of an incorporeal transformation, as described by Deleuze and Guattari, is useful in understanding relationships forged through correspondence. As their prime example of an incorporeal transformation, Deleuze and Guattari, citing the linguist Ducrot, point to the moment an accused person is transformed into a convict by the judge's sentence:

> In effect, what takes place beforehand (the crime of which someone is accused), and what takes place after (the carrying out of the penalty) are actions-passions affecting bodies (the body of the property, the body of the victim, the body of the convict, the body of the prison); but the transformation of the accused

into a convict is a pure instantaneous act or incorporeal attribute that is the expressed of the judge's sentence. Peace and war are states or interminglings of very different kinds of bodies, but the declaration of a general mobilization expresses an instantaneous and incorporeal transformation of bodies. Bodies have an age, they mature and grow old; but majority, retirement, any given age category, are incorporeal transformations that are immediately attributed to bodies in particular societies. (Deleuze and Guattari 1987, 80–81)

Incorporeal transformation, then, describes that dizzying moment in which one is the same yet different, the moment perhaps captured best in animated cartoons when the character has run over the cliff but does not immediately realize that all has changed irrevocably. Such a transformation requires all the elements of the rhetorical situation: a speaker, a message, a context, and an audience. One cannot affect an incorporeal transformation on one's own; an Other is necessary. Just as I cannot convict myself of a crime in such a way that I will be recognized as a convict, neither can I single-handedly affirm my positive social value outside of a social context. In both cases, for either conviction or liberation, one must speak, and be heard and spoken to in a meaningful context.

As incarcerated writers invariably attest, writing of all kinds is important to them, and journal writing for and to oneself provides a sanctuary for self-reflection and critical analysis. The journal is both intimate friend and political/spiritual ally. In an invitation to collaborate with me on a conference paper about our correspondence, I asked the women who had written what they would like to say about their experience to a room of college writing instructors.[5] One incarcerated women writer who wishes to remain anonymous, puts it this way,

> Since my unpredicted incarceration, writing became my only friend. There was someone I could tell my deepest secrets to—without being criticized for being human.
>
> Unfortunately, the environment that I find myself in daily is dead of any real warmth. Therefore spirituality plays a key role in my life. However, there were times I have felt that God himself has even turned his back on me. During one of those times is when writing became a form of salvation.
>
> Once I was able to reflect on paper what "today" is like for me, I was able to learn and maybe change it. If nothing else I was able to move on.

For some reason "tribulations" seemed smaller on paper. They were easier to overcome. This is how I cope. I write, reflect and deal with whatever comes my way.

I am certain that writing saves lives. Especially among the incarcerated. Without writing the suicide rate would be much higher. We are able to express on paper how we really feel. There is no sugar coating or masks, only reality.

For me, to write is more than communication. It's a liberator. One of the few constant things in my world. Without it is to truly be in hell.

While this writer does not indicate whether she is referring to journal writing exclusively (one supposes not), her second sentence makes clear the value she puts on writing to and for herself. In her cell, alone, confined, she is able to *feel* free, for a moment, from criticism. The private journal has of course served this purpose for everyone who has ever kept one, but its value is clearly elevated when it constitutes the *only* private and/or free space available to a human being. For inmates without the ability or will or interest in journaling, there are few alternatives, and psychic implosion becomes a very real possibility.

Victoria Nevarez explains that "First and foremost, [writing] has become my outlet for pain, fear, insecurity, loneliness, and love. I write to express myself in a positive way. So [that] my emotions don't cause me grief or hurt anyone else." For Victoria, writing allows the positive expression of emotion; more than just venting for relief, writing becomes a means for structuring emotion, for making choices about how she will and will not experience/ express it. Self-control is one of the only forms of power a prisoner has, and writer-based writing is a personal technology of self-control.

Whether they begin keeping a journal prior to incarceration or during their incarceration, writing to and for oneself in hostile, often chaotic living conditions, is a means of self-nurturing and structuring one's experience in positive ways. But a journal, as mirror, has limits: It cannot acknowledge, recognize, celebrate, commiserate, empathize, analyze, or reciprocate. Although it may lead to social interaction, a journal is, finally, no substitute for constructive dialogue with others. In certain respects, a journal can even accentuate one's isolation, insofar as its contents are so glaringly *not* shared. Thus there is a need for incarcerated writers to move beyond writer-based journaling. In the following passage, Cheryl addresses the value of both journaling and letter writing, both writer-based and reader-based writing:

I have become very reliant on letter writing and journaling. The journaling process has awakened an inner sense of strength that I didn't know I had. I write about 5 or 10 letters a week to various people in prison and out of prison.

I have a Christian mentor/pen pal and she has been writing to prisoners for close to 20 years. She's very inspiring.

In my personal opinion, if every woman in prison had an "outside" person who wrote faithfully, believed in them and challenged them to believe in themselves, the recidivism rate would be drastically reduced. I have spent the last 19 months of my life writing everyday and I feel that writing has opened new doors that I really didn't expect. I acquired many positive attributes to grow on while being in prison.

Both writer-based and reader-based writing are clearly important to this writer; her journaling sets the stage for connection through correspondence that creates conditions necessary for incorporeal transformation—for a meeting of minds that can change social relations for writers and readers. Many incarcerated writers stress the value of such connection, such dialogue, and none more eloquently than Dee Garcia:

Corresponding with your class was another great experience for me. I was allowed to feel connected to a group of very talented young people. One of your students and I became "curious friends"—seeking to understand life through each other's eyes. Thank you—thank her—for the humbling sensation to have met such a talented, wonderful young woman—free to be honest—seeking her life's direction. Writing connects and opens wide the soul to seek-question-understand and continue on and on.

Writing my experience now is the only way I have to share my life. As I put these words on this paper—they come from my heart and through my mind. My emotions and deep passion for the very lives of these women and myself drives me to honestly and openly speak the truth.

A person cannot quit writing—it is our only means of expression, of crying out. Our voices are but a whisper—you are the lion's roar for us. Allow us to give the facts to you—throw us a lifeline—save us from drowning and disappearing into this system. Help the weak become strong, the illiterate become intelligent, the raped and abused feel worthy, the aged and disabled be able to live in appropriate housing.

We struggle each day behind these walls—don't turn your back on us—don't ignore us—don't leave this room and forget us—for you now know of our existence, our cry—and you have the responsibility to add your voice to our cry. Let us roar the truth until justice prevails.

Dee celebrates the social and political values of writing. Corresponding with people beyond the walls lifts her out of her isolation and creates a sense of hope and possibility. The "curious friend" she mentions becomes, in this one instance of her writing life, an audience who can recognize and affirm Dee's experience and humanity. A twenty-one or twenty–two-year-old college student likewise finds an audience who values her honesty and can affirm her voice, as well as the relative value of her own anxieties and prospects. I do not know how long the friendship Dee describes lasted—whether for one or two letter exchanges during the semester or for longer—but duration is irrelevant when it comes to incorporeal transformation. The incorporeal contact and the words exchanged are sufficient to "transform" each writer.

The Three Dimensions: Political, Psychological, Social

For both free and confined writers, the transformation can be broken down into three dimensions: psychological, social, and political. If we consider first the benefits for students, the psychological may include what I might call the effects of the de-infantilization of schoolwork, since in such correspondence the gravity of the situation/relation calls for mature, responsible interaction. After all, prisoners are experiencing what, as Zygmunt Bauman explains, the rest of us desperately fear: "abandonment, exclusion, being rejected, blackballed, disowned, dropped, stripped of what we are, not allowed to be what we wish to be . . . being denied company, loving hearts, helping hands" (Bauman 2004, 92–93), and college students are asked to recognize and mitigate such fear. Media-driven stereotypes held by students about who occupies jails and prisons are also likely to be shattered in the course of correspondence. Such stereotypes, of course, obliterate the possibility of constructive social relations, thereby reinforcing class and race divisions and stratifications. Finally, a student corresponding with a prisoner can very well be "rehabilitated" from law and order ideology and/or the unexamined belief that, in general, people basically end up where they belong: students at school, criminals in jail. The political consequences of free people learning to empathize with incarcerated people are incalculable, since empathy opens the door to support for reforms based on the principles of restorative versus punitive justice.

Incarcerated Writers: Shifting from Writer to Reader-Based Writing

The social and political benefits of finding and cultivating receptive audiences are even more profound for imprisoned writers. For Victoria, writing has become a means to interrogate oppressive social and political conditions that funnel many women into prison, and dialogue—audience—is essential to such work. As she explains,

> I have found numerous letter/journal and publications concerned with women's issues in prison. A main topic I read and write about is the injustice women in our penal system are suffering across the U.S. If only more women listened to their hearts and told their stories, maybe we would be heard. As prisoners, women are doubly punished by society for their crimes. There's a shortage of educational opportunities, mental health treatment, therapy, parenting programs, abuse groups and drug addiction programs. Without these, we will continue the vicious cycle in our prisons. Then there's the continued crimes against our bodies, minds, and souls by the guards who are paid to protect the public and us. It's commonplace to hear about or know a female prisoner involved with or raped by a guard. They help continue the cycle of abuse, drug addiction, and prostitution.
>
> I [have] participated in two writing workshops since I have been in prison, each with volunteers from our community. I have met many women who have a tremendous ability to write and express themselves. We need more volunteers willing to go in and open the minds of these women. Many have never thought about writing as a tool for recovery. It's a rewarding experience to help someone else write about their lives and dreams.
>
> My experience with Professor Tom Kerr was rewarding also. I was unaware of college courses concerned with women in prison or the social injustice throughout the U.S. I hope more people will take the time to reach out to women in prison. We need positive role models and tools to use in here and in our communities that will lead us to productive lives. Writing has changed my outlook on life and given me a new, brighter perspective on who I am and will become when I leave these walls.

Victoria describes a complex causal chain of relations here, one that begins with writer-based and ends with reader-based writing and her appeal for "more people [to take the time] to reach out to women in prison." She experiences the power of writer-based expression in workshops taught by volunteers, meets other incarcerated women writers in the process, and becomes, along the way, aware of a wider circle of writers and activists focused on her experience as an imprisoned woman and on fighting for social justice both within and outside of prison. Finally, she underscores the need for and value of dialogue with the wider community, as represented in this case by the students in my class and me. It is clearly important for Victoria—or any other person fighting the good fight—to know that she is not struggling in complete isolation, that there are people in the world who will give a hand when she reaches out as well as people who will reach in, such as the volunteers who ran the workshops she mentioned.

Rhonda Leland, Margaret Majos, and Barilee Bannister echo Victoria's experience. Each writer in her way remarks on the shift from writer-based to reader-based and audience-specific writing.

Rhonda:

I received a letter from Professor Kerr in 2003. I couldn't believe a Professor would be interested in what I had to say. Although, I had previous reasons to believe in myself, my self-esteem was still damaged. I realized a new voice within myself and another door that was opened to me. I found that I could give something back in my writing by helping students that will become our future. To understand perspectives they may have never realized otherwise.

When I was turned down for a College Scholarship, I took action. I wrote a Professor at Roosevelt University and I have participated in her class for quite some time. I don't receive credits for this work, however I do send my homework in and I have learned so much. I am excited to see the page marked up. I know, I will have to work hard and prove myself and that is ok. I have had several of my pieces of work published. I never imagined this possible six years ago.

We, the incarcerated, live in a self-abandoned state in life. I am one of the determined ones. I will reach my goals and struggle to overcome all of my obstacles. However, I may have not accomplished this had I, along with some very special people, not recognized that I had something special to offer. I see women every day in this community that want to find a way. Unfortunately, they have nowhere to turn. Remember us and we will never forget you!

Margaret:

Many express themselves in words speaking, but neglect the importance of writing, that is what connects the whole entire world together. We may be thousands of miles away from one another, and written words bring our minds and hearts to its place, the spoken words can't reach all at the same time, but written words can. Through my incarceration in the last 13 ½ years I have learned the importance of conversing through mail and expressing the details of everyday life in a place of despair and pain. Yet, one can and should strive to achieve the goal of meeting the deepest potential. Every human being possesses the ability to be what they desire to be but everything requires work, energy and ambitious determination. . . .

I am proud to say that last year when I was asked by professor Tom Kerr to write an article about the prison system, and the value of writing (corresponding) with the outside world. I have learned a lot about the students and their values. I've met many interesting people in that way, and they have changed my life.

In the struggle for social justice, writing plays a major role. In spite of the language barrier (I'm Polish) I didn't give up. I reached from inside out, writing articles, fighting legally (in court), helping others to stand and not sink in the madness of prison's sicknesses or mistreatment.

I express not only my own feelings, but also the truth (the facts) through the pen and paper. Can't see another way. The truth is, I write every day. It's a huge part of my daily living. Some think, the food is more important, other—exercise, or writing. I need it all to function properly, body, mind and the spirit is the make-up of a human being and we can't neglect them. I want to keep my mind alive and not stagnated.

The most valuable thought I wanted to share is "How important it is to write or know how to write while in prison." Not just for legal reasons, but to simply keep your relationships growing and alive. My children live to hear from me. My only plea to a free society is to help women prisoners to pursue their education, and not diminish it, as the system tries. We (I) must fight, free or not. Too many talents are already wasted away. How sad.

Barilee:

Writing is a way to pass time, to escape the confines of prison, and the debilitating ailments of life within a man-made hell. If I can write about what happens in my world, and about what I am surrounded by on a daily basis, I can in some way put on my boxing gloves and enter the ring; and in many ways, fight and win. Writing helps to lift the reluctance to attack the corruption, deception, disorder, intimidation, oppression, and violence that not only plagues the prison

*system, but also many aspects of this world. It is a way to free myself, and share
with others my thoughts, opinions, ideals, likes and dislikes. Writing, for me,
especially while incarcerated is great first amendment right that I exercise on a
daily basis. I strongly believe that everyone has a story to tell, something to share
and is in need of someone who will listen and offer some kind of support and/or
understanding. It is important to me that women in and out of prison find the
power of their voice either verbally or by writing.*

For Rhonda, Margaret, and Barilee, the enormous political value of writing—"a great first amendment right"—very much depends on audience, on
people who "will listen and offer some kind of support and/or understanding." Writer-based prose, such as journaling for oneself, can be enormously
useful for people who are psychologically, socially, or physically isolated, but
only reader-based prose, in which one represents oneself and one's experience for an Other, for Others, provides the energy required for incorporeal
transformation. If it were not so, writers of all stripes would not be driven to
publish, would not care whether they were read or not, and readers might not
exist. The connection a writer makes with an audience creates energy no less
real than energy produced by nutrients in the body, and such energy fuels
change, the nature of which depends on the kind of social relation, either
positive or negative, formed by the act of written communication.

I could not have guessed, prior to undertaking this rare trans-institutional
correspondence, how much each audience, each set of readers, might mean to
the other, or even how much writers in both places had to say to one another.
Rhonda, Margaret, and Barilee's profound observations about the experience,
particularly as regards the power of embodied audience, of "audience addressed," to inspire and motivate confirm the singular value of reader-based
writing in struggles for social justice wherein mutual recognition and empathy are paramount.

Critical Resistance through Writing: Bringing Together "Us" and "Them"

While students may exist in a different experiential realm than prisoners
and so cannot, perhaps, be expected to do more than correspond within the

context of a class, the correspondence itself is sufficient cause for incorporeal transformations on personal, social, and political levels. Anyone who has undertaken work with people locked away in America's prisons knows the difficulties presented by the bureaucracy and the risks of exposure, both for inmates and students, the ideological and logistical, as well as personal and so-cial, barriers are great. However, in my experience, and in the view of the many college students and women who participated in the correspondence I have described, positive personal, political, and pedagogical outcomes far outweigh the problems and risks, not to mention all the finer questions concerning pro-priety of representation and address associated with reaching into prison and/or conducting inter-institutional conversations with the people held there.

Were every college writing class in the United States to reach out with letters to our incarcerated counterparts, the audience for institutional and cultural transformation of the criminal injustice system would, as it must, expand exponentially. To expand this audience is to resist America's gulag. Each letter exchanged among teachers, students, and imprisoned people becomes an integral part of the Critical Resistance Movement that, as we know, aims to transform both the oppressive political and material—that is, the *corporeal*—conditions of our criminal (in)justice system and its massive prison industrial complex.

As with all social movements, the movement against retributive justice and for restorative justice ultimately requires the forging of alliances between people suffering the injustice directly and people who likely "benefit" from it, between the "them" and the "us." College-prison writing projects like the one described here clearly fosters such alliances.

References

Bauman, Zygmunt. 2004. *Identity*. Cambridge, MA: Polity Press.

Deleuze, Giles, and Felix Guattari. 1987. *A thousand plateaus*. Brian Massumi, Ed. Minneapolis: University of Minnesota Press.

Elbow, Peter. 1987. Closing my eyes as I speak: An argument for ignoring audience. *College English* 49 no. 1: 50–69.

Jacobi, Tobi. 2003. "Contraband literacies: Incarcerated women and writing-
   as-activism." PhD dissertation. Syracuse University. New York: ProQuest
   Dissertations & theses (PQDT).

Notes

1. Some of our correspondents wanted their names attached to their words, others
did not. For the latter, I've used initials.

2. I have written about this class at some length in 2004; Between ivy and razor
wire: A case of correctional correspondence, *Reflections: A Journal of Public
Rhetoric, Civic Writing, and Service Learning* 4 no. 1 (Winter): 62–75.

3. See Linda Flower, 1979, Writer-based prose: A cognitive basis for problem in
writing, *College English* 41: 19–37.

4. Tobi Jacobi (2003) has suggested in her dissertation "Contraband Literacies:
Incarcerated Women and Writing-as-Activism" that critical writing in prison
constitutes what she calls contraband literacy.

5. I presented the paper, a collage of the women's responses, which I photocopied,
passed out, and read, at the 2004 Conference on College Communication and
Composition in San Antonio, Texas.

12

Writing Exchanges

Composing across Prison and University Classrooms

WENDY W. HINSHAW AND KATHIE KLARREICH

In 2012, Professor Wendy Hinshaw initiated a partnership between Florida Atlantic University and ArtSpring, a Miami-based nonprofit arts organization serving women in prison and youth in detention. The pilot program instituted a correspondence project between university students and ArtSpring students incarcerated at a Florida women's prison. The collaboration, directed by Hinshaw and freelance journalist and ArtSpring facilitator Kathie Klarreich, has turned into an ongoing correspondence between students at both institutions. Below, Hinshaw and Klarreich describe how they built their partnership, the ethical and material concerns that informed it, and the tremendous impact it had on the participants.

Separated by some eighty miles, the only thing that two classrooms with the same curriculum seem to share is a syllabus. One room is dank with subarctic temperatures that, when the metal chairs and tables are removed, is used for the facility's dog training program; the other is furnished with mesh-backed chairs on rollers and state-of-the-art audiovisual equipment. In the former, seven women incarcerated at Homestead Correctional Institution have enlisted in a new Advanced Creative Writing class offered by ArtSpring, an organization providing arts in corrections programming in Florida since 1994. All of these women are ArtSpring alumnae and have participated in writing, dance, drama, music, and visual art classes. But this class will be unlike any they have taken before: they are preparing to read alongside, and correspond with, fourteen graduate students whom they have never met.

In the second classroom, the graduate students are enrolled in a new Florida Atlantic University (FAU) course, "Rhetorics of Incarceration," designed to create a dialogue about prison writing and to examine how social, institutional, and personal contexts shape writing. It is intended to create a platform where issues of incarceration and social justice can be addressed in a sustained way that includes the voices of locally incarcerated writers.

The partnership was built around a shared examination of writing by and about prisoners to create change through dialogue and collaboration. It also intended to provide participants an opportunity to form new understandings of themselves, each other, and society. Mindful that this was a new partnership between the prison, the Department of Corrections, ArtSpring, and FAU, we took great care to proceed cautiously and establish practices that would accommodate everyone's needs. We took inspiration from best practice models, informed, in part, by the Inside-Out Prison Exchange Program. This Temple University and Philadelphia prison partnership was created in 1997 by Lori Pompa and has been adopted internationally as a model for providing dialogue and education across prison walls: inside and outside, students equally share materials, space, and ideas.

Our new partnership aimed to employ the ethics of these and other community-based learning programs, where outside students are not, as Pompa describes, "'helping' the participants who are incarcerated; it is not charity or service of any kind"; rather, "everyone involved is seen as having something vital to offer the learning process" (Pompa 2013, 129). However, given that the distance between the two institutions made a traditional face-to-face partnership difficult, we sought ways to build connections through correspondence.

In addition to Pompa's program, we borrowed from scholar Tom Kerr, who argues for the "power of direct correspondence to establish connections, however tentative and transient, between middle-class, American college students and incarcerated people" (Kerr 2004, 62). Adapting programs like Inside-Out, Buzz Alexander's Prison Creative Arts Project, and other prison-university partnerships that prioritize direct, in-person contact between inside and outside participants, our program aimed to incorporate written correspondence exchanges as a means to build understanding and connection, thus blending models for direct and distance partnerships.

Establishing the students' identities as writers was a crucial component to the success of this program, but so, too, was our direct and consistent involvement as facilitators. We traveled regularly to each other's classroom and communicated outside the boundaries of the written exchanges. Wendy first visited an ArtSpring class several months before the start of the partnership to get to know some of the students and explain the proposed course. This visit provided her with a clearer picture of the institution, the ArtSpring philosophy, and the women themselves. In turn, Kathie, along with ArtSpring's founder and Artistic Director Leslie Neal, attended the first day of Wendy's class, enabling Kathie to understand the FAU students' investments in and expectations of the writing exchange. These visits continued on a monthly basis, bridging the gap and building trust between the two classrooms. Kathie was able to carry student writings in and out of the institution and send the material to Wendy electronically, thus bypassing the delays and complications of prison and the postal systems. This greatly reduced the turnaround time, making it possible for students to send and receive feedback on their writing within a three-week period. It also allowed the instructors to oversee the writing for any sensitive or otherwise potentially compromising material.

While these visits created a sense of proximity, the space and anonymity of written correspondence provided privacy for the students and control over their own identities, which translated into safe and thoughtful explorations of each other's identities and ideas. The first exchange began with personal "Why I Write" essays and continued with responses to shared readings including *Exit, Civilian* by Idra Novey (2012), Wally Lamb's edited collection *Couldn't Keep It To Ourselves* (2003), and selections from *Razor Wire Women*, a collection of art and writing by and about incarcerated women edited by Jodie Michelle Lawston and Ashley Lucas (2011). The readings introduced the students to a range of first-person accounts and interpretations of the prison by contemporary incarcerated women writers, as well as a range of critical texts examining various aspects of the modern prison system. For each assignment, students composed their own essays and then exchanged with, and provided feedback for, writers in the other class.

Withholding certain information was both mandated and discretionary. Outside students used only their first names. All of the inside students were required to use pseudonyms and were forbidden from revealing information about their crimes but had editorial discretion for whatever else they wanted to disclose regarding their lives before or inside prison. Writing for faceless graduate students provided the inside students an opportunity to testify and forge connections, but what was not said was, at times, as significant as the material shared. The silences and disclosures negotiated by inside and outside students in their exchanges throughout the course revealed the power of silence that Cheryl Glenn theorizes in *Unspoken: A Rhetoric of Silence*, as they reshaped and were also shaped by the politics of "who can speak, who must remain silent, who listens, and what those listeners can do" (Glenn 2004, 9). As an outside student, Student A, commented in an e-mail to Wendy during the course:

> One of the reasons I believe I am comfortable with our arrangement with ArtSpring is because it gives our incarcerated pen pals an opportunity to engage us from an identity that they are comfortable with instead of from what they know will be a preconceived notion of who they are. "Prisoner" and "convict" are very fixed identities; those identities are at least stereotypes, but I think that in our culture they may even be archetypal identities. That is a terrible place from which to begin a relationship, intellectual or otherwise. Allowing the ArtSpring prisoners the opportunity to construct their own identities for this project allows us to engage them on a more equal, if not more intimate level. We have the luxury of constructing multiple identities and manipulating those identities as we wish; allowing them to construct identities is about as egalitarian as we can be under the circumstances.

Written correspondence provided the students a critical distance from which to examine cultural and institutional formations of identity, and also solidified their identity as writers. It was the first essay, however, designed to introduce students to each other as writers and reinforce the role that writing would serve to facilitate their connections to each other, which sparked the first seismic shift in both group's thinking.

Why I Write

The "Why I Write" essay, inspired by the PEN Prison Writing Program's publications of prisoner writing and accompanying author interviews, gave both sets of students the opportunity to reflect on the role that writing plays in their lives. Bell Gale Chevigny, editor of the PEN Prison Writing collection *Doing Time*, suggests seven motivations that drive prisoner writing:

- to bear witness,
- resist institutionalization,
- know oneself or come clean,
- sustain relationships and recover feeling,
- resist racism and cross cultural barriers,
- use as an alternative to violence, and
- to live in the face of death (Chevigny 1999, xxiv–xxxii).

We saw many of these impulses in the ArtSpring writings: they described writing as a way to access things they couldn't say and to better understand themselves and the world around them. For some it was a survival mechanism; for others a way to stay connected to a world otherwise unavailable. For example, Student B wrote:

> I write to articulate my true self. To believe that my actions 12 years ago were not inherent of who I am today. I write to defy the labels that my peers placed on me in their haste to pass judgment. When literally three seconds of a bad decision decided my and other's life. I write to right the wrongs I cannot erase, I cannot escape. I write to create a glass-blown vase that will catch my tears when I cry and shatter when I'm done. I write.

For those who lost their sense of self when incarcerated behind steel doors, that very first exchange opened a new door. The majority of the ArtSpring essays were personal, as the writers were accustomed to writing for and about the self, though not necessarily with the intent to share. While details of their personal history, crimes, even tattoos became a matter of public record when they were sentenced, they still retained control of their inner thoughts. When given the opportunity, however, they trusted the written exchange process enough to reach through the razor wire and carefully reveal parts of themselves. The women saw the chance to share their writing not as an academic assignment, but a rare opportunity to be heard in an otherwise voiceless environment, a chance to be recognized for something other than their crime and validated in a setting deliberately designed to diminish their dignity.

Unlike the ArtSpring students, for whom writing was primarily personal, the university students were accustomed to the conventions of academic writing, including assignments specifically directed toward teachers and tied to an evaluation or a grade. Twelve of the outside students were English graduate students, enrolled in an MFA or MA program, one was in visual arts, and one was a nondegree student. The creative writers were also accustomed to broader audiences for their writing, honed to the "the promise of readership" (Student C). Like the ArtSpring students, they described the ways in which they used writing to think and process or for work. A few shared details about the role that writing had played in their lives, particularly creative or personal writing, but students also struggled to imagine the audiences they were writing for and to put themselves into their writing enough to help that audience get to know them.

The exchange of essays and responses that followed gave shape to the absences and gaps in each other's knowledge about themselves and each other. Outside students who imagined nascent literacies were met with elegant prose, vivid images, and a sophistication they couldn't have envisioned. One outside student (Student D) reflected:

> I was frankly blown away by the relative sophistication of the "Why I Write" essay we ([Student C] and I) read. I guess I was expecting something far more disjointed, less literate. Assumptions. Dangerous. This writer had some rich and [un]expected images—for example, "A thought that is as frail as a spider web that is tatted into lace," and "Give me words that I might knit a wardrobe of my own choosing." Thematically, she talked about "beginnings" to be "retooled," that are "never finished," and concerns to be "revisited."

Another (Student E) wrote:

> What surprised me most is how poetical (Student F)'s writing is. Some of her turns of phrase, such as "convoluted nest of neurons" were gorgeous. I think, deep down inside, I expected these women to be like my developmental [writing] students. That they are not speaks volumes about my stereotypes and biases.

The writings and subsequent class discussion also brought to the surface veiled prejudices, exposed preconceived notions about race, gender, incarceration and social class, and challenged long-held beliefs and philosophies.

The outside students' bias about the literacy rate among the inside students were, for some, a revelation. One university student praised his writing partner for technical aspects "as good as, and in many cases better than, the students in my Freshman Composition class" (Student A). He had no way of knowing that she was not only highly educated but in her job as prison law clerk routinely filed legal briefs. Outside students struggled to recognize their own privileges and assumptions, and to account for their own authority as writers once they recognized those privileges. One outside student (Student G) reflected in a journal entry that in the beginning she "found it challenging to respond at all. I didn't feel like any of my thoughts did this situation justice, and as a person living a privileged lifestyle, how can I appropriately speak to this person's writing?"

Students in both classes struggled to respond to the writer as well as the writing, and to form a sense of identity—of themselves and each other—on the page. One student (Student E) described in her journal her difficulty:

. . . removing my professorial cap and responding as a peer. I struggled with tone. I didn't want to sound effusive or insincere or pedantic. I also struggled with reconciling my preconceived notions with what my partner revealed about herself. I hesitated to read too much between the lines. For example, I didn't want to assume she may have esteem issues, though she wrote about feeling inadequate as a verbal communicator. I wrote, "Your essay fills me with hope because writing also appears to have buoyed your sense of self and helped you not only find merit in your thoughts and ideas but in your ability to express them," but originally had a stronger sentiment—something about finding the value in herself. However, I didn't want to belittle her or intimate she had not found value in herself. My pedagogical tendencies did slip through a bit, and I offered some advice.

The outside students began their writing exchanges expecting to be teachers; as graduate students most of them were already teaching in some capacity, and they saw themselves as emerging professional writers. Wendy worked hard to debunk traditional notions of service-learning: rather than focusing on learning through serving, her class centered on building a mutual exchange through dialogue. But as the outside students began to question what they thought they knew about prisoners, particularly incarcerated women, they also began to question their own reading and writing practices: Was it safe to "read too much between the lines," knowing that such readings are framed by the (limited) experiences and cultural knowledge we bring with us? How was praise from a reader, moved by a particular image or passage, shaped also by assumptions of authority and expertise over writing?

Other students struggled to find an appropriate response in this unfamiliar territory. When one inside student wrote about how writing served as a lifeline for her during her thirteen years of incarceration, her outside exchange partner struggled for a way to respond, commenting: "I knew intellectually that many prisoners have been (or will be) incarcerated a long time, but to see such an example in black and white was still shocking" (Student H). His own unease with the length of her term stymied him and, unable to get past her sentence, he could not find an appropriate response to her essay.

When Kathie visited the graduate classroom following the first exchange, she shared that the inside students had felt distanced by the graduate students' academic approach to their "Why I Write" essays, and encouraged them to put themselves into their writing more in the way that many of her students had done. That feedback gave the university students permission and confidence to be more emotionally honest in their writing, examining their own writing practices and the extent to which they had been shaped by their disciplinary and institutional experiences. One outside student (Student I) reflected:

> In terms of what I learned about writing and the writers, I was reminded of the healing nature of writing. In workshop, we are told that writing is NOT therapy, especially nonfiction writing, and we should not use writing as a way to "get our feelings out." In order to be a professional writer, we must move beyond that and focus on what is "good" literary work. Our emotions can blind us to producing as well as seeing "good" work. The ArtSpring writers, however, are using writing as exploration of the self and others—at least that was the sentiment in the essay I responded to. The Why I Write essay would probably not be considered "good" literary work, but obviously that's not the only value to be found in writing.

ArtSpring students also opened up further. One inside student (Student J) wrote:

> My initial "Why I Write" piece was the most difficult. Prisoners are guarded as a rule. To write that piece and not reveal much about my self turned out to be my biggest mistake because it gave the students a glimpse of the person they'd be corresponding with. After the initial exchange it was much easier to honestly reveal my thoughts.

ArtSpring participants are generally on guard when they meet community members because the motivation behind these visits varies widely. Said one inside student (Student K):

We have had visiting academics (unconnected to ArtSpring) come to Homestead to do seminars. Often they have some personal agenda that is not beneficial to us. Their attitude is sometimes condescending. And I am afraid of the sideshow. I fear people who think that prisoners and prison issues are entertainment on boring days. Any time I am submitting a paper to be read by people outside of prison, I envision the infamous clown painting of John Wayne Gracy. People are morbidly interested in his work because he was a notorious serial killer. I don't want people to be interested in what I write because they see me as a monstrous criminal.

Wendy's visit to the ArtSpring class early on helped relay the genuine intentions behind her students' and her engagement. Similarly, an ArtSpring student (Student J) noted that Kathie's visits to the university classroom allowed her to "pass on some impressions and thoughts that helped significantly in breaking barriers to the exchange." It helped build trust and reinforced the objective of the partnership exchange.

Because the number of outside students was exactly twice the number of inside students, outside students worked in pairs in their responses, sometimes writing collaboratively, sometimes separately. This enabled them to think through their inside partner's writing together, providing full and detailed responses. Similarly, the inside students shared the outside students' writing among themselves, circulating it within the group as a way of creating shared knowledge about their writing partners. Because writing pairs shifted with each exchange not everyone saw everyone else's work, but there was an effort to circulate and discuss their partnered writings with classmates, allowing students in both classes the opportunity to read and learn from writers with whom they were not paired.

As the classes progressed, close relationships formed in and between the two classrooms, so much so that at times we felt it necessary to hold back some of the things disclosed by both groups. One inside student, for example, revealed information about her crime, another gave information about an intimate relationship with a fellow inmate, yet another gave details about her family. These specifics were ultimately removed from the exchanges and were an opportunity for us to talk individually with the students about the necessary boundaries of our partnership. Our understandings of what we might need to hold back were evolving alongside of our students' connections to each other: we began with an understanding that disclosures of crimes could put the ArtSpring students at risk, but we hadn't thought about the other personal information that they might reveal, mostly because we couldn't anticipate the kinds of connections that were formed through the partnership. However, these moments of "over-sharing" indicated to us the level of trust we had helped to build between the two groups, and showed us how that trust was moving and changing students' writing on both sides of the prison walls.

Becoming Better Writers

All of the participants were deeply changed by the experience, particularly the outside students, who learned to question assumptions and rethink fundamental paradigms that had shaped their conceptions of justice, criminality and imprisonment. As one outside student (Student L) described:

> There is no doubt that I began my Rhetorics of Incarceration class at FAU with many preconceived notions of correctional institutions and the inmates that populated these facilities. Throughout our class correspondences with the participants of ArtSpring, many of my prejudices and negative expectations have been shattered. The ability to share my views, views that have been shaped by my upbringing in a family full of lawyers and judges, and my limited exposure to people that have been incarcerated, with a group of writers who are exposed to every aspect of prison life daily, and the chance to receive their feedback, has helped me to better understand the conditions and environment associated with prison life. It has also helped to enlighten me on the many struggles associated with imprisonment.

One inside student (Student K) wrote:

> It was scary writing the first essay. The responses were equally daunting. I didn't know what to comment on, so I chose to comment on how each piece made me feel and recount memories the writings brought up for me. I didn't want to be negative. After I got the first responses, I relaxed more. To me, the exchange of essays and comments feels like a conversation.

Such transformations are the goal of most prison-university partnerships engaged in a critical dialogue about the prison-industrial complex: outside students are changed by first-hand accounts of the prison system, and prisoners are changed by the opportunity to voice their accounts. Pompa aptly describes this "deeply transformative experience" for students in the Inside-Out project: "Assumptions are debunked . . . worldviews are shattered . . . and participants begin to look at themselves, their lives, and the world in whole new ways" (Pompa 2013, 132). Challenging their conception of what is even possible was part of our own, broader goal of bringing our classes together.

However, it's important to understand that our partnership did not just make our students better people by expanding their thinking—it also made them better writers. This was an intended consequence of the assigned readings and subsequent discussions and analysis but also, and perhaps more significantly, the feedback they received from their peers. Both groups of students were generous in their feedback, engaging their writing partners' ideas as well as their writing style. Outside students frequently offered responses twice as long as the original submission. It was particularly gratifying to watch these students, several in the last semester of their degree, grow as writers. For example, the student who had initially been unable to get beyond his writing partner's thirteen years of incarceration revised his response with a new appreciation of his responsibility as a reader to a writer: he complimented the writer on her use of imagery and offered organizational alternatives to make her piece stronger.

The ArtSpring students grew as writers as well: the attention and care they received in response to their writing was new to them, and helped them gain confidence as writers. Describing her reaction to the university students opening up through their exchanges, one ArtSpring student (Student M) wrote, "[They] encouraged me to go deeper and divulge more since their acceptance made me feel comfortable." Another inside student (N) reflected on her personal growth and growth as a writer during the course of the partnership:

> The honest and personal experiences really opened up doors to make everyone look inward and to gain from the experience. . . . The weeks were not enough for the transformations taking place. I've grown a lot just in the past five years but it meant everything to me to just be known by a nickname and let me talk about

things I've hidden deep within. I put myself, my life and my experiences on the line for self-growth and also for every other woman incarcerated to be a voice that we can change from traumatic events in our lives. . . . Sometimes an experience like this can make you look in the mirror and make a real change.

Another inside student (Student O) commented,

I began to relate to [my writing partners] as other human beings instead of words on pages. Their views and ideas became something that I either wanted to try to change or help evolve, or better yet take on myself.

As the course progressed, the question of safety in anonymity began to change organically. One outside student noted that writing is a "safe way to engage with the world, without the physical risk of engaging the world" (Student P). This very safety, however, was key in allowing the students to open up and let their guard down.

Writing exchanges grew longer and came faster: our initial plan had included one exchange per writing, but from the very first assignment, writers in both groups found themselves with more to say. The response guidelines seemed to place artificial ends to conversations that wanted to continue.

Traditionally ArtSpring hosts a graduation ceremony at the completion of a course, and often community guests and family from the outside are invited to attend a performance of their work. But this graduation was going to be different: we had begun our partnership from the safety of anonymity, with no requirement to meet face-to-face. In consultation with the DOC, we arranged for the outside students to travel to the prison to meet their writing partners and for the first time to place names and faces with stories and continue conversations that had been limited by the writing exchange. ArtSpring students decided unanimously to leave their badges face up, allowing their full names to be visible to the outside students. Was this because they trusted them not to look up their crimes, or was it because they trusted them with the choice?

The face-to-face meeting, which, for a variety of reasons included only half of the FAU students, was a final opportunity to identify the writing with the writer and be identified by their own writing. Remaining assumptions were shed as writers revealed themselves to be older or younger, taller or shorter, darker or lighter than their colleagues may have imagined them to be. It also made clear the risks in writing, even from within the safety of anonymity:

risks of discovery, of commitment, of feeling. Students in both groups learned to commit to and put themselves into their writing on new levels. As one graduate student (Student G) reflected:

> My first correspondence was with [Student O], and she started right out of the gate with a deeply compelling image from her childhood, one that encapsulated the mystery of words in her budding perceptions of the world in an emotionally resonant narrative. Despite the effect of that correspondence, my responses stayed on the surface because I was afraid to show that much of myself—not because of the communication between the two of us, but because I have always been afraid of that kind of exposure. The inhibited quality of my own nature, which I had before been unaware of, became a topic of conversation as I was defending my thesis, because this same issue with holding back what is felt and what is true was seeping into the characters I created—they were also guarded. Because my writing is almost always driven by a desire to have a character break away from a social inhibition or cultural expectation, I can't successfully free them. I would love to say that I have overcome this problem, but I know that it will take much time and much writing and much reflection. But I now know of the problem, and can stay on a course to resolve it, and cannot thank the women of ArtSpring enough for the revelation.

Another outside student (Student H) composed a letter to the ArtSpring students when he was unable to attend the final celebration, noting:

> I've always been ready to commit time, money, and brainpower to my college courses, but committing emotionally didn't come so naturally. Over these past few months, I've learned that just the mental commitment hasn't been enough for a course like this—I had to learn to care.

But he also described the important role that writing had played in his transformation, and recognized the value of their writing for his class and for the wider community:

> I could go on talking about me, and how I've been affected by this course, but that would be stupid and narcissistic. I'd rather simply close by urging each of you to continue writing. If there's one concrete fact this course has taught us, it's that your voice cannot be silenced. If you want to be heard, even in the prison system, and you can express your desire eloquently, there's nothing that can stop you. So write . . . write like you mean it!

This shift that he and other students experienced, from writing for themselves or for a class to writing for an outside audience, became complete in their recognition of the value of their writing beyond our class.

Conclusion

Our partnership began by bringing our students' writing across our two classrooms, but it eventually positioned all of us toward a wider, more public audience. We didn't anticipate this as part of our objectives in designing our partnership, but as communications between our two classes grew the need to connect to a wider public became obvious. We were on a trajectory that, to borrow from one of our texts, we "couldn't keep to ourselves." For inside students, their writing became an opportunity to encounter and affect the outside world they have been removed from. As one inside student (Student O) described:

> *The whole idea of doing this class was exciting because not only would my words be breaking through these barriers, but I would get to see inside your minds and to hear your thoughts, too. It enabled me to hear the voice of the future and take hope in the thought that each of you might have a positive influence on others and the community, as hopefully we have had on you.*

Another inside student (Student M) suggested:

> *This class was an experiment and the first of its kind for us in ArtSpring. I live in a place where mistakes slap me in the face on a daily basis but the experience was amazing because we saw changes in people's opinions about women in prison.*

Inside students were inspired to continue to seek outside audiences for their writing, and some of them ultimately submitted their writing to this and other publications.

Outside students became advocates for their inside partners, and for ArtSpring more broadly. The ArtSpring celebration offered them their first opportunity to speak publicly about their writing and the value of our partnership. Even as the correspondence mandatorily ended with the last class, some of the outside students continued to support ArtSpring as patrons by attending celebrations open to the public. One outside student collected art and writing by inside partners for publication in a zine she is starting. Another is hoping to become an ArtSpring facilitator.

As instructors, we were also moved to find ways to continue our partnership and build support for it at our respective institutions. We have found ways to continue partnering with larger undergraduate classes at the university, lowering the number of exchanges to make correspondence more manageable while preserving the heart of our partnership: the opportunity to connect inside and outside students through writing. We also sought ways to share our experience with our wider community. Kathie has done this through publication and speaking engagements. Together we have presented at the Conference on College Composition and Communication for teachers interested in pursuing their own prison partnerships. We hope to offer, as well as continue to develop, models for prison-university partnerships that can be sustained across distance and adapt to diverse institutional conditions.

References

Chevigny, Bell Gale. 1999. *Doing time: 25 years of prison writing—A PEN American Center Prize Anthology.* New York: Arcade.

Glenn, Cheryl. 2004. *Unspoken: A rhetoric of silence.* Carbondale: Southern Illinois University Press.

Kerr, Tom. 2004. Between ivy and razor wire: A case of correctional correspondence. *Reflections: A Journal of Public Rhetoric, Civic Writing, and Service Learning* 4 no. 1 (Winter): 62–75.

Lamb, Wally, and the Women of the York Correctional Facility. 2003. *Couldn't keep it to myself: Testimonies from our imprisoned sisters.* New York: HarperCollins/Regan Publishers, 2003.

Lawston, Jodie Michelle, and Ashley E. Lucas, Eds. 2011. *Razor wire women: Prisoners, activists, scholars and artists.* Albany: State University of New York Press.

Novey, Idra. 2012. *Exit, civilian.* Athens: University of Georgia Press.

Pompa, Lori. 2013. January. One brick at a time: The power and possibility of dialogue across the prison wall. *The Prison Journal* 93 no. 2: 127–34.

Mothers and Daughters

Meditations on Women's Prison Theater

JEAN TROUNSTINE

In 1989, three years after I began teaching at Framingham Women's prison, the most secure facility for women in Massachusetts, my mother died. At the time, I was directing a play, surrounded by women who know about that hollow place inside, a curved arc of loneliness. They ache even when their children are alive or their mothers come to visit.

When I came back from the funeral, they asked how I said good-bye. I thought of standing in the doorway of the funeral parlor, my mother's casket looming at me like a ship, her body rising out of it, enormous. I imagined her voice: "For God's sake, get rid of those hideous green drapes." The years of scotch, straight up, seemed less important than the image of the feisty tennis player, champion of the Ohio Valley, the mother who taught me chutzpah, to fight back. I reached into the coffin and took hold of my mother's hand.

I wanted to tell the prisoners that I couldn't imagine what it must feel like to be locked up and not to be able to go to your mother's funeral. Even when there was nothing but stoniness locked in her knuckles, I longed for my mother. The women too, had always come to my writing and theater classes with this longing, looking, I imagined, for a clean slate of comfort. They had written reams about their losses, their fears, and their loneliness, but they often cringed when we wrote about mothers. It is a paradox, this loving those that hurt us.

At the time I had worked only with women in prison, but now nearly twenty-five years later, I work with women on probation, and they too find themselves in stories. Sitting in a room with a judge and a probation officer, all who delve deeply into their lives, they find their daughters in Toni Morrison or their mothers in Tillie Olsen. We read books to find ourselves.

The women in prison could talk all day about their kids. "Hey," they told me, "that's what keeps us going." And when I learned that 80 percent of them were mothers, I got it. They wanted to make their kids proud. Hey, we all want reconciliation in spite of our crimes.

But after my mother died, they were what kept me going. I would enter my theater class, in the barely functioning gymnasium, ready to rehearse and there they were: women who knew about loss. I found myself able to laugh in a way I wasn't able to laugh in the outside world and I found myself comforted in their presence. Although the prison was always present, the bars disappeared. With every piece they read aloud and every step they took on stage, we were all just mothers and daughters doing time.

"Freeze," I yelled from the sidelines, catching Bertie off guard as she swung around a wooden bench, arm outstretched accusingly at the woman playing her mother. We were in the gym, our rehearsal space, with a basketball backboard at one end and a stage at the other, practicing improvisations to prepare for an adaptation of Nathaniel Hawthorne's *The Scarlet Letter*. It was February, 1991, and wind whipped against the windows. Winter jackets were strewn on the wood floor, hats and gloves in piles. A few prisoners sat in a semicircle on bright blue aerobics mats, all in sweaters or heavy shirts, notebooks open. Some were looking over their scripts. Some rereading notes from writing exercises invented on the spur of the moment, questions about character or theme. Others huddled near the volleyball net, watching the action onstage. The heater was broken and inside the gym, we were hit with gusts of chilled air.

Bertie's outstretched arm ended in bright coral nails. "They're dramatic, Jean," she announced when I first met her four years before. She sauntered into class wearing anything but prison clothes—a bright orange shirt, a hat even though she had nowhere to go, and earrings that jangled when she walked. These were the days before high tech scanners and jumpsuits that spelled the names of your unit on the back. This was before someone's false teeth could be taken away for "being a possible weapon." Bertie, only twenty-one, was far from her family in Jamaica, and had already done two years. I loved her swagger, the way she told someone off with her whole body. Bertie never talked about her crime and when the subject came up, she averted her eyes.

Earlier in the evening, while we were exploring mother-daughter relationships, Bertie sat studiously on an aerobics mat, discussing her outline for an improvisation about a prison visit. I had asked them each to write down what I thought would help them get into the play at a deeper level. I often used writing this way, as a prerehearsal tool. I told them, "Create an improvisation around a scene from the play, something that could take place today." I didn't expect a complete idea, just scribblings, something that might be flushed out in talking, and something I might garner into a scene to help them understand a character or a theme. Journals were a class tool in acting. They analyzed characters; they wrote about their reactions to what they read; they often went off the text and talked about themselves. I never expected much.

Rhonda, one of Bertie's scene partners, had been halfway involved all evening, up and down, at the bathroom, getting water. She stood by the gym door, preoccupied with her new girlfriend waiting outside. Statuesque, with jet black eyes, Rhonda was "stylin'" in a silky warm-up suit, ready for volleyball that she played feverishly when she wasn't cruising the halls, looking for a hustle. "Meet me after class," she had whispered to the closed door.

Samantha, a fiery thirty-year-old who mouthed off at the guards, was the only one besides Bertie interested in the exercise. Samantha was sexy, "stacked," we would've said in high school, about five feet four with wild, nappy hair and big hoop bracelets that seemed out of place with jeans and an old sweater. She hadn't done the assignment—something that didn't surprise me with Samantha, who mostly came to class to complain about her mother, who stole money from her for booze and got her arrested. Samantha's thick plait of hair rested on another prisoner's leg, the length of her ample torso extending across the mat.

Bertie had crossed over to Samantha, smoothing out creases in her teal blue leggings. "Let's go, girl," she coaxed, prodding Samantha to her feet. She read out loud from her notebook:

The war in Iraq is on and her husband is at war. Her daughter is in trouble. It's damp outside and cold. She has stood in line, been processed and searched, and escorted to a visiting room to see her 15-year-old who is in D.Y.S. [because she was] caught drinking and driving a stolen car for the second time. The daughter is upset. She really doesn't want to hear her mother lecture now. She wants her dad to come see her. But as usual, he is not there. So she too is disappointed.

"I'll play the daughter. You're the mother."

They'd gone to work, turning the proscenium into a prison visiting room, setting up chairs and pushing a bench to center stage. Samantha found a Bible in a box backstage and made a list of what she'd bring to her daughter, locked in the Department of Youth facility (D.Y.S.). She decided to play the character as Jamaican so that she'd seem more like Bertie's real mother, to arrive with Rastafarian music and Caribbean rice and beans flavored with spices.

But Rhonda, who always one-upped Samantha, reminded her that D.Y.S. was a locked facility and that gifts weren't allowed. "Besides, your daughter was arrested. Don't bring her presents."

Samantha had stomped across the proscenium and in a rush, fitfully torn up the list. "You play the damn mother, then," she hissed at Rhonda, tossing her the Bible.

"Fine," I'd interjected. I was used to these cracks, having mediated my way through *The Merchant of Venice* and *Lysistrata*, having placed myself between women when they were about to go at it, and having seen prisoners struggle with themselves whenever they dug deep inside. But I disliked the tension all the same. Rushing toward the stage, I spoke too loudly for the room, "Rhonda, you're up." Rhonda rolled her eyes.

Samantha, pouting, hopped off the platform and flopped down on the mat, her face, a dark cloud. "Bitch," she spat under her breath. I motioned for Bertie and Rhonda to take their places. If I ignored Samantha, she usually calmed down.

It was at that moment that the most infamous prisoner at Framingham, Evelyn Cagliano, first walked into our rehearsal. And frankly, it had been a relief. I flashed back to a few months before in the greenroom, where couches lined walls and a TV on a stand was shoved into a corner near a lamp. It was Christmas and this tiny woman with a strained face and bright red lips, was making a card, cutting a heart out of construction paper at the table across from the coffee pot. Her neck was etched with lines, extending gracefully into the tight bun of white hair, and she wore a starched blouse with a Peter Pan collar, too girlish for her seventyish years. I watched her spread glue on the back of her construction heart, filling it with lumpy dollops. I crossed to the table.

"She loves to use the glue, makes her high," said the table-mate, a tall horsy-looking woman whose hair fell in a sheet across her back. "I can talk like that. She's my mother."

The mother took a fistful of glitter and scattered it over the heart. "I'm Evelyn Cagliano." She spoke with a faint Boston accent. "I'd shake your hand but I'm indisposed. This is my daughter, Laura."

"Nice to meet you." Headlines flashed into my head. A mother, her daughter and son in a horrific case that polarized a working class town on the outskirts of Boston. Accusations of Satanic cult rituals at their day care center. Pictures of Evelyn turning to the court with fury. I glanced away, trying to shield my discomfort.

"I'm thinking of taking your class this spring," Evelyn announced. From the corner of my eye I saw her hold up the glittered heart to Laura who nodded approvingly.

I took in as much air as possible. "Oh, really?"

"Mother's had a lot of experience in community theater. We also produced some plays at our school." Laura spoke as though she thought I'd heard all about the Caglianos.

Evelyn pushed back her chair and rose, carefully putting on the black cardigan that was draped over its metal frame. She was ninety-five pounds at most, and her slight build, A-line skirt and little heels made her look more like a porcelain doll than a prisoner. There was something off-putting about her, cold and distant, but fascinating, too. I wondered why Laura seemed protective of her mother, keeping an eye on Evelyn as she walked gingerly across the room to get coffee. Laura had already ripped up several art attempts and sat with the dime-store scissors, trimming edges on a green paper tree.

"I hope my brother likes this card. It's taken me long enough to make it."

When Evelyn returned and sat, sipping coffee, scowling at Laura's art work, she said lightly, "We're aiming for prerelease but not until summer. In fact, my lawyer has an entire new trial proposed. We didn't get to see our accusers, you know." By "accusers" I knew that she meant the children who charged Evelyn, her daughter and son, of sexually molesting them. "What is the next production you're planning?"

"*The Scarlet Letter.*"

"I read that in school." Laura jumped in. "That awful Roger something-or-other who tormented Hester. And standing all day with an 'A' sewn on your dress in front of a crowd? Mother, you could play her." She reached across the table and placed her hand on Evelyn's. The mother's hand darted away like a skittish bird, lighting on her lap, neck, bun. Laura looked at her mother curiously. Evelyn tossed the tree on the table.

That gesture, that tossing off of her daughter's work, eventually made me draw back when Evelyn walked primly through the gym door and without words, pulled a chair into our circle. "I'm just observing, dear," she whispered to me.

I tried to be fair and smiled tentatively at our guest. After our initial meeting in the Greenroom, I had worked feverishly with my students and with an outside playwright to get a script for our production. We always adapted classic texts for my prison productions, something I had begun with *The Merchant of Venice*, the women sitting in a circle, putting the playwright's words into their own. But this was different. We had to commission a play but even with a script, the women still suggested changes and created their own adaptation. I'd imagined Evelyn as Hester, the "A" standing for "abuse," instead of "adultery." Evelyn as Hester, perceived as a bad mother, maybe even a witch scorned by the community. "A's" swirled around in my head, "adultery," "abuse," and "AIDS." How Hester redeemed herself in the community with good works, and how her crime affected her daughter's development seemed what might matter most.

Now I wondered what I was in for. Samantha sulked and the others stared at Evelyn as if she had three heads. On stage, Bertie and Rhonda stopped hassling and Bertie came over to the stage apron and curtseyed toward Evelyn, graciously welcoming "Mrs. Cagliano."

Bertie was the only one who was pleased when I first mentioned that Evelyn might join the class. Those accused of sexual abuse are usually shunned in prison, but Bertie snapped at students who groaned when I brought up Evelyn's interest in the play. "No one here has a right to judge."

On stage, Bertie had paced the room, involved in the improv. She harangued her mother, Rhonda, who sat, Bible in lap.

"Why didn't Papi come? Don't tell me. I know." Bertie rattled off something in what sounded like gibberish, throwing herself into the scene. "I know. He's overseas. He can't visit." Bertie circled Rhonda who was silent, eyes downcast. "You had to tell him I was arrested, booked even. You had to be tellin'." Bertie's voice grew louder and more shrill.

"Honey, he's your father."

"I didn't mean to get in no accident. It wasn't my fault."

"It's not the first time you've been in trouble. I don't know what to do with you any more."

"Papi would know what's up."

"Well, Papi's not here now, is he?"

It was after this exchange that I yelled, "Freeze," at Bertie playing the young girl visited by her mother. I looked over at Evelyn who seemed slightly intrigued. I called from the sidelines to Bertie, "Hold that pose, as though you're a statue." Bertie stood, her arm still outstretched, angrily pointing at Rhonda. Evelyn leaned in. "Rhonda," I continued, "imagine you are saying things to your daughter that are deep inside. Imagine you're speaking to her soul. Call her 'Pearl.' Go."

Rhonda looked up, at first startled, but then, seeming to understand, tilted her head and spoke into the emptiness of the gym. "You've always been wild, Pearl, cut off from the world, never had friends. From the time you were a child, you accused me." Rhonda paused, running her hand over the Bible's binding, as though it could give her answers. Evelyn stared with interest, and the other onlookers seemed equally engaged, their eyes on the actors.

Rhonda's voice trailed off into the smoothness of memory. "I remember writing once, on a slip of paper, 'she knows I am guilty.' But for what, Lord, I didn't know then. I don't know now." She placed the Bible near her on the bench and looked over at Bertie. "I wonder what's wrong with you Pearl. You're only a child. Am I the problem?" Rhonda was shaking her head sadly.

"Freeze," I yelled again, this time at Rhonda. I moved closer to the stage. Evelyn was still leaning in, her hands folded neatly in her lap. "OK now Bertie, what do you want to say to your mother about being in D.Y.S. What do you want her to know that you've never told her? Imagine you can speak to the deepest parts of her. Go."

Bertie's arms dropped to her side, and her neck arched longingly. She began circling again, only now in slow motion, as if she was trying to feel out what she was thinking. She took her time, developing some innate sense of Pearl, drifting away, looking out over all of us, and then slowly speaking. "I lost you a long time ago, Mother. I always thought you were the perfect mother, too perfect really." Bertie wrapped her arms around herself, forcing the words out in clipped speech. "You never complained about anything in our house. You took care of your children as if you had been born for that task. I dreamed every night that you would love me, but every day . . . every day, you took away my dreams."

Bertie had angled herself away from Rhonda, avoiding her eyes. I imagined how complicated and painful it must be for her to be away from her mother in Jamaica, and then flashed on the short story she wrote years before—Bertie running in fields with her goat, "my childhood best friend. I loved that goat with all my heart," Bertie confessed. "One night my mother had a party, and I feel strange, something is happening. I go out behind the house and there it is, in tall grass, my goat's head in a pot." Her mother had slaughtered the goat and served it to her guests for dinner.

I shuddered. What other dark secrets lay in the hearts of these women who stood before me? For that matter, in any of us?

Evelyn was shifting in her seat, fiddling first with her bun and then with wisps of hair around her face. Bertie turned toward her. Her voice was faltering, hushed. She took a few more steps away from Rhonda, ending up at the edge of the stage. "I know I can never be like you Mother, so silent, so strong. Women come to you for advice, for knowledge. I want my own place in the world, but I don't know how to get it." Bertie turned toward Rhonda, still holding herself as tight as ever. "I've hurt a lot of people. I don't want to hurt you." Rhonda looked away. Whatever memory Bertie is summoning to play her role was working. I began to see Pearl grown up, suffering, without Hester.

Bertie paused, and broke into sobs. Immediately, Evelyn rushed onto the stage to comfort her, soothing her with touches, with cooing sounds; stroking her hair like a good mother, like the mother Bertie had always wanted. We all watched without moving as Bertie threw herself into Evelyn's lap, crying like a lost child, looking up every now and again to make sure Evelyn was still there.

Evelyn was standing on the newly constructed set, a scaffold in the middle of the gym for theater-in-the-round, while prisoner townspeople circled the platform. It was mid-March and the heat had been turned back on, so we were all in shirtsleeves. The Puritan leader reeled off accusations of witchcraft at Evelyn as Hester. She grinned toothlessly up at Hester, waving a script in the air. Evelyn stood stoically, her long white hair held in place by a headband, facing her accusers.

We were refining Joyce Van Dyke's play that had three Hesters and interwove scenes from three separate centuries: the original Hester from 1642, condemned to wear a scarlet "A" because of her sin of adultery; Hester number two, mystic and outcast, taken as a slave from the West Indies in the mid-1800s and now out West, a single mother oppressed by her master; and Hester number three, a woman with AIDS in prison in 1991, abandoned by her husband, hoping for custody of her daughter. Since scenes with each Hester emphasized her relationship with her daughter, Pearl, our early read-throughs draw painful sighs. Several women in class had lost their children to foster care. Others suffered because, in spite of safe homes with relatives, their children were growing up without them. And all of us were daughters with complicated memories of our mothers.

Evelyn, playing the Hester from the 1600s, swayed above us, her eyes aimed somewhere over our heads. Other inmates formed a sort of judgmental chorus, a band scorning Hester for her sin of adultery. They yelled, "Hang her! Hang her!" at Evelyn, and jeered at teen-aged Pearl, the child out of wed-lock, who in our version, was held from Hester's arms and kept offstage by the governor, Samantha. The Puritans moved in different directions, first this way and then that, a crowd more than individuals, voices swelling, "Where is the bitch? Show us your sin!"

One woman stomped around the platform in boots. "God keep her filth from vilifying our congregation."

"Amen," came the chorus.

"Make her show the mark of her shame," another cried out gleefully.

"Shame! Shame!" echoed the women, encircling the platform. "Show the mark of your shame!" Offstage, Bertie, who played one of our Pearls, clutched her script, and watched, turning her head from side to side as if to shake off some kind of trouble. I knew she would come on soon and tear at us with her rendition of Pearl abandoned by mother Rhonda, the slave gone West in the 1850s. But now, Bertie looked forlorn.

"Hussy," a Puritan was snarling at Evelyn. "Look what she's done. She's decorated it, made an ornament of it." She took her script and pointed at Evelyn's breast where the "A" would be. "The hussy! The hussy! Oh!"

I wondered if the parallel between denouncing the witch and the woman accused of sex abuse was as clear to the cast as it was to me. I felt my own willingness to condemn, heard myself sneering "abuser." I also felt sympathy for Evelyn alone on the scaffold, branded in the play as in life as "unforgivable." I was glad she would have her day when she turned to the audience triumphantly in the last scene: "And now there are many who come to me for help. Women do—women who have been wounded or wronged, women whose lives have been wasted. . . . I tell them there are more guilty ones out there than criminals in here." Evelyn reminded me that truth is not always so clear, and that theater had the power to unleash it.

The intensity of underlying issues had crept into prisoners' daily routines. They snapped at each other in their units and not just at rehearsals. Some couldn't handle it. A woman, cast as the Hester who has AIDS in prison, quit the class, saying she couldn't deal with the idea that inmates might think she had the virus.

Evelyn had thrown herself into the witch aspects of the script, particularly at the end in the closing monologue where she turned on her scaffold to the audience, in defiance. Like a bird trapped, she whirled around, hauntingly crying out, "The dream of a 'normal' life is a hoax perpetrated by the Devil to drive us all to despair." It was chilling to see Evelyn play Hester Prynne. But now, as I heard the Puritan chorus taunt and whisper, pointing at Evelyn, I couldn't take my eyes off Bertie waiting in the wings.

She looked as if she was trying to leave the room. She had taken steps backward toward the door to the gym, away from the area by the stage steps where her Pearl was to enter. "They should have branded her forehead with a hot iron! That would have made her wince," a Puritan hooted up at Evelyn, then crossed her arms and leaned in. "What does 'wince' mean?" the actress whispered to me while others kept on. I made a face, to show her how to wince.

"Whore," someone screamed. "Tramp! You're polluting the town."

"Those words aren't in the script."

"I'm improvising," came the scornful answer. "Wicked wicked woman." The others followed, spewing hate up at the figure on the scaffold. Before I knew it, the room was filled with improvised shouts and insults, all in the name of acting. The danger of art hit me hard as stone.

In a second, Bertie was out the door. We all turned and watched her go. "Rehearsal's over," Rhonda announced and threw down her script. We had opened Pandora's box.

The next time we met, Bertie came in all smiles. She had her lines memorized. She agreed to lead the audience discussion after the play, since she was a veteran of four productions, and at the end of rehearsal, she handed me her acting class journal. "The assignments you asked for are all there, Jean, but you'll be proud of me. I've begun to talk about it."

"Talk about what?" I asked the recreation officer, following her around the gym after the women had gone down to their units. She carried a long metal pole with a hook on its end, and she crossed over to the tall windows and opened one.

"I like to have a little air in here when I start my shift in the morning." I nodded, and watched impatiently as she put down the pole, checked doors, and turned off lights with her key. We pushed the scaffold to the end of the gym where it wouldn't be in the way for basketball. The officer and I stood together outside the gym door, in the familiar glare of the overhead lights.

I repeated my question. "What's Bertie pleased she's talking about?"

"After all these years, nobody's told you about Bertie?"

Talking about someone's crime was against the prisoners' unspoken code and also a Department of Correction violation of privacy. I weighed my words carefully. "I know her mother is in Jamaica, and a son is here."

The officer pulled a piece of gum out of her pocket, unwrapped it and popped it into her mouth. "Bertie's in prison for murder. She killed her daughter. I'm sure she assumes you know. Everybody does."

Later that night, standing outside the prison, I stood with journals I had collected. They were filled with writing from the class, exercises and some reactions to the rehearsal process. Leaning against my car, I read Bertie's journal:

When I first came here, the inmates called me names because of my crime, and I had to fight my way to prove myself to them. I felt like her standing up on that stage, with people calling her all those names, and there was no one there to help her. I did have people that stood up for me, because they know me, the person, and not my crime. But I still felt alone. I did not wear an "A" for adultery, but something even more devastating, "B. K." for baby killer. I know this is only a play, but I have been there. And I know what it is like to be judged and chastised by other people.

No, I am not excusing what I did. I don't walk around boasting about it, and I never talk about it. I have to live with this terrible crime for the rest of my life. . . . I relive it every day and I will continue to until I find some kind of peace with

myself. I am not asking people to love, or even to accept me, they shouldn't have
to. I just want them to accept that I am a person. My sin was taking a life, not
just any life, but the life of a four-month old baby who was helpless and couldn't
help herself from my hurting her.

Yes I am mad, because no one was here to say, "Leave that woman alone and
let God judge her." This is just a little note to let you know why I reacted the way
I did to the rehearsal at last class.

The prison audience was hushed when women dressed in Puritan black
with white bonnets and aprons rushed in, encircling Hester. They watched
in awe as a prisoner, playing a guard, wearing plastic gloves, brought in
our modern day Hester with AIDS to the scaffold, in fake handcuffs. They
occasionally glanced at Evelyn's daughter, Laura, who sat in the front row
watching her mother's every move, head down when Pearl was forcibly kept
away from Hester. A few even looked at me, my face wet with tears, as each
Hester talked lovingly about her daughter. They cheered when Evelyn told
off Samantha, the town magistrate who wanted to imprison Pearl. And they
whispered their approval when Pearl stood up for herself. Much of the play
drew a stunned silence. But the audience seemed most moved by Bertie, who
slid gracefully on stage in a bright red satin dress, her skirt touching the floor.
"I'm looking for my mother," Bertie told them, moving into the circle. Seating
herself on the edge of the scaffold, she took a silver hairbrush from her traveling suitcase and brushed her hair, telling the story of how she lost her mother,
long ago, lines that she had adapted from the original script:

My mother was the perfect woman. Always working, always helping others,
never taking anything for herself. Once the life had been drummed out of her,
they began to think better of her. They came from miles around, almost as if
what she made with her sinful hands was specially valuable and desirable . . .
it was the fashion. . . . I never saw my mother fight back. I never heard her
complain. She would sit there sewing. The only ornament she ever wore was the
scarlet letter.

Townswomen entered, one by one, on their way to the market, to the
church, ignoring Pearl. Bertie rose, followed them from step to scaffold, an
embroidered hanky in her hand. "Has anybody seen her?" she plaintively
asked. The townspeople, shrouded in cloaks, hurried by, ignoring her. Look-

ing at the audience, Bertie darted from face to face. She whispered into our eyes, shaking her head "no" and then, she tried again. "Are you my mother? Are you?"

It is Rhonda who first told me that Evelyn was out, up for a new trial, and that Bertie gave birth a year after she left Framingham. "It's got to be healing," Rhonda said to me on the phone, calling from her new job at a busy health care clinic. "I miss the girls," she confessed. "Those plays were family."

I knew what she meant. Evelyn rushed on stage to comfort Bertie. Rhonda protected her friend by calling an end to rehearsal. Bertie defended Evelyn to those who scorned her. There, within the confines of prison came comfort, a place to temper some of the ache, a communion. Theater is redemptive; the line between the woman and her crime was not so clear.

My mother was a study in contrasts. Standing by her side in memory, I am grateful for the drama she brought to my life. I hear Bertie in the prison gym, singing an old refrain: "Sometimes I feel like a motherless child." And I know I could sing it with her. I recall reading about Evelyn's funeral, her casket covered with flowers, and Laura in black, distraught, by her side. In spite of the wounds, we want our mothers to live.

The prisoners come to me now when I'm in my car, alone at home, watching a movie. I see their struggles in the women on probation who have freedom to shelter them. The prisoners are a comfort to me as I was to them, as they were to each other. I am one of the few who knew them as good people. Even though they were each immersed in pain, I saw them love each other, re-mother each other through small acts. Through words, I brought them some solace and challenge. They responded to my spirit, the kind of spirit that my mother raised me to have.

14

As Others Stand By and Ask Questions

ROSHANDA MELTON

I write to squeeze emotion from stone hearts
To show pedophiles that I did not break
To make my doubters eat their words.
I write to absorb tears (yours and mine)
To make up for lost time
To fight when I feel as if all the fight is out of me
To shatter mirrors that distort who I am.
I write to prolong my life; to live forever
To give to those who've had their dream taken away.
I write because what else am I supposed to do with
These hands, stuck at the size of a teenager's
Stained fingers walking over lined paper
Leaving trails of memories needing release.
I write to find peace for this chaos in my mind
To give a voice to those who are too afraid to speak
To provide evidence of my love to those who seek it
To express my heart's contents to a small child.
I write to bring forth smiles that are hard to find
When I'm too blind to see, my words guide me
When forgetfulness kicks in, my words allow me to remember again.
I write to define myself, as others stand by and ask questions.
I write because I have a story to tell and only I can tell it.

Poetry, Audience, and Leaving Prison

HETTIE JONES

This is the first time I've written *about* my prison work. My purpose in going in has always been—or *was* (more about that later)—to bring other voices out.

Although I'd worked with various community/educational projects, when I began teaching at Bedford Hills Correctional Facility in September 1989, I wasn't on a mission. I was just cobbling together adjunct teaching jobs, and at that point had been to one prison only—Sing Sing—and only because the estimable Janine Pommy Vega had convinced me to take over her class, where I'd briefly earned $50 a session. Then I met a woman who got me a grant to work at Bedford, which hadn't had a writing workshop since the mid-70s. I like teaching groups of women, who usually do their homework, at least for me, and this one at first seemed no different.

But it *was* different, of course; how could it not be? Perhaps *because* the possibilities were limited, I wanted the results to be as good as those produced by my university classes. Does that make sense? I taught the same lessons. I brought student work from the university to the prison, and vice versa. I had no expectations beyond getting the point across to anyone who'd listen, but I believe that everyone who wants to write has a right to learn the *craft* of writing. Some of my students at Bedford had as much education as those on the outside. Others had never written a poem before. The main difference was that at Bedford we did most of the writing in-class, after examples were read. Everyone thinks prisoners have lots of time on their hands, but no, they're programmed, everything they do is circumscribed. If they have any free time it's for phone calls, letters, cooking, anything to maintain—to *defend*—a personal existence. By 6 p.m., they're *tired*. My students came to write because for them writing was, as they used to say, "like getting out of Bedford for a while."

There were challenges of course, the first being that I had to be supervised, and no one was interested, at least at first. Mine was the only non-church-affiliated or addiction-recovery mandated program, a puzzle, a bother. We took up space; officers had to be nearby. But when it became clear (to me and to the prison) that I wasn't going to quit arriving every Wednesday evening, the staff warmed up (though one night my *Art against Apartheid* anthology was denied entry as "Incendiary!").

"She taught us how to think about ourselves," one woman said recently. That's flattery! I just brought them poetry to read, and encouraged them to express their feelings in plain English with a little metaphor for kicks. I accepted whatever they wrote and, maybe this is important, I didn't push them to write about their crimes. That I sat in a room every week with some women who had killed another person was not of interest to me; I'm always wary of the prurience in such investigations. Besides, my students were all suffering under the moral burden of those crimes as well as the burden of their punishment, and who was I to worry them further? They were alive; they *had* to live, and to write about life.

In 1992 we got together a little chapbook anthology, *More In Than Out*, which the women in the workshop designed and printed in the prison print shop, and I duly copyrighted in their names. Public response was a startled, "Why, these women can *write!*" Success fuels ambition: These women needed a wider audience. I managed to get permission to bring in a tape recorder one night, and thus was able to take their voices to a radio program. With the great help and largesse of a printer friend of one of the women in the workshop, in 1997 I published *Aliens at the Border,* and got it around through Small Press Distribution. Amazingly, the prison allowed me to organize a reading—first ever, with guests from outside—and even permitted a video of it (courtesy of a friend, gratis), which I was then able to have edited professionally (gratis, another friend), and showed at colleges and elsewhere. I may not have had money, but I had real, committed help. All this was accomplished on the watch of a Deputy Superintendent of Programs who happened to have been an English Lit major in college. After he retired things got dicier.

On the inside, these achievements were noticed, the poets admired and congratulated. Bedford's nascent but ambitious college program featured big blowups of some of the poems at a benefit to attract wealthy donors from all over pricey, exclusive Westchester County. When I subsequently volunteered to offer a poetry class for credit in that program, it was overenrolled.

On the outside, by focusing attention on prison issues, the women's writing proved effective. But it also was good *writing*—a couple of poems from *Aliens* were published in *The New Yorker*. Because I was concurrently the chair of PEN's Prison Writing Committee, I was able to include some of the Bedford video footage as part of the Committee's annual award ceremony. Some of my students, postrelease, have participated in radio performances for the Committee. From my casual, limited observation of them and other former prisoners, learning to write and being required to read aloud seems to matter when women get out; they have a more practiced persona behind which they can sort themselves out in their own good time. The PEN Prison Writing Program now has a few postrelease workshops, though none specifically for women. Any workshop is a good idea; money's the barrier, of course.

I don't seem to have an opinion about gender stereotypes; I think the poems I've read—from workshops I've taught as well as my work with PEN—are all over the place, like the work of many women who are in some control of themselves, even if someone or something else is apparently controlling them.

Dealing with prisons, though, you're dealing with control. In January 2002, planning to take a few months off to write a book, I went into Bedford one evening with the woman who would take over the workshop. I'd been having difficulty finding a meeting room but had arranged one with the help of a prison employee. My replacement and I were met at the location by a deputy who escorted us to the front gate: no workshop, no room. Several weeks later I got a Dear John letter thanking me for my years of service and reiterating that there was no longer any room for me. By this time a well-known, well-connected playwright had discovered my students and begun her workshop with them, so I figured I had been replaced without my even knowing it.

But the important thing is that incarcerated people be helped to *leave* prison. I don't begrudge the women in Bedford any opportunity, especially a wider access than I could provide. Recently they held a successful poetry slam.

Slams are not my readings of choice, but a slam beats a blank and does keep language moving in the mind and mouth. It'd be nice if someone were to go to work in there and bring it to the rest of us, on a CD, say. That might get the poets out of Bedford for a while, and perhaps prepare them for their eventual real time out. Last I heard, this was called rehabilitation.

SECTION III

Writing, Resistance, and the
Material Realities of U.S. Prisons
and Jails

16

"... *to speak in one's own voice*"[1]

The Power of Women's Prison Writing

JUDITH SCHEFFLER

Hidden for centuries in a shadowy margin of women's literature, whose own acceptance into the literary canon is only a few decades old, writing by women prisoners currently commands interest. Some of this interest arises from its literary merit, some from its sociological insight, and some from its potential as a rich source of ongoing, critically engaged writing.

Readers approaching women's prison writing from any of these perspectives may choose to consider only the writing at hand, in isolation from any other works emerging from women's current or historical experience of imprisonment. Indeed, because the writing of incarcerated women is being created in the present and because it carries the potential to spark controversy or even conjure a strange sort of glamour, the tendency is to gloss over its larger context or to ignore the work of those prisoners who write in obscurity. This tendency to miss the big picture ends up shortchanging all women prisoners who write or have ever written; they are part of a larger tradition, which needs to be acknowledged in order fully to appreciate the writing being done by imprisoned women today.

The Early Period of Prison Writing: Distinguishing History from Biography

Before writing workshops began to appear in North American women's prisons in the 1970s, female prisoners worldwide had been writing about their individual experiences for over 1700 years. The profile of the early imprisoned writer may be generalized as follows: she was relatively well educated, often elite or economically advantaged, and incarcerated for her conscience or beliefs. Many women who wrote about their prison experiences, such as Vera Figner (1968), Emma Goldman (1931), and Rosa Luxemburg (1978), were politically active. Others were condemned as heretics by the religious establishment, as was the case with early Christian martyrs and Quaker reformers. Mme. Roland (1798, 1998) and young Queen Elizabeth I (2000) are examples of prisoners who, through parentage or marriage, had angered or threatened those in power.

Because many of these early prisoners were very conscious of their audience as they wrote, their works carried a persuasive agenda, though the writer sometimes knew that her argument's triumph might be posthumous. In letters, memoirs, and political and religious tracts, the writer advocated for her cause and sometimes attempted to justify her own reputation as a decent woman who subscribed to the definition of "femininity" acceptable to her culture. In some cases, as with Mme. Roland during the French Revolution, vindicating herself involved writing disparagingly of other women the writer encountered in prison.[2] To record their experiences these writers overwhelmingly chose forms of life writing as opposed to poetry or fiction.

Only a few early writings by prisoners from the general population survive, mostly in the form of letters. A very few women convicted of high profile crimes published their accounts, such as the nineteenth-century prison memoirs of Florence Maybrick (1905), an American imprisoned in England for poisoning her husband's meat juice, and those of Mme. Marie Lafarge (1841), imprisoned in the 1840s in France for a similar crime.

The writing from this early period has generally been read for its biographical or historical insight and has rarely been considered as literature. Reading prison texts in relation to each other, however, offers new insight into each work. Writings by authors from the same religious or political movement, for example, share a common context that enriches our understanding of a woman's perspective on her prison experience. This is demonstrated by the seventeenth-century Quaker literature of "sufferings," those accounts witnessing to religious persecution and intended to encourage others in the Religious Society of Friends and to spread their message. Similarly, British suffragettes of the early twentieth century vividly described their personal experiences, which, when read together, offer a deeper, more comprehensive appreciation of their achievement.

Grounding the Early Years: Prison Writing after the 1970s

Reading prison texts as small, specialized collections helps to foreground the historical writing of women prisoners as a body of texts with noteworthy characteristics that reward investigation. Since the 1970s, prisoners of conscience, such as Assata Shakur (1987) and Nawal El Sadaawi (1994), have continued to produce individual works testifying to their prison experience, in the century-old tradition of women's prison writing. Simultaneously, however, women's prison literature has taken new directions that broaden and energize the entire corpus of writing by imprisoned women. Reading these more recent works as texts that are firmly grounded in the earlier tradition fosters respect for and deeper understanding of their significance.

Three notable, related changes dramatically transformed women's prison writing in the 1970s in the United States. First and undoubtedly most significant was the emergence of writing by women from the general prison population. Although they might have been sentenced for nonpolitical crimes, some of these women, such as Diane Hamill Metzger (1999) and Barbara Saunders (1999), were well-educated, talented writers. Others, like Judee Norton (1999), were motivated to express their responses to imprisonment and became writers while in prison. Still other women, like Patricia McConnel (1995), wrote extensively about their prison experiences after their release, motivated by a desire to inform society of the injustices and abuse they had witnessed.

The 1970s saw a second change in women's prison writing: an expanded range of genres made life writing only one among many choices available to authors. Poetry and fiction began to appear, and today they are often the preferred modes to communicate a woman's life experience. In a third change, which incorporates both of the other changes, the implementation of writing workshops as organized forms of programming in women's prisons, gave a distinctive new direction and character to writing produced by imprisoned women. These workshops, encouraging a broad range of imprisoned women to write and supporting their efforts to create in a variety of forms, capitalized on the emerging interest among the general population of women to use the written word as a powerful form of self expression.

Prison Writing Workshops in the 1970s and 1980s

The writing workshops of the 1970s and early 1980s arose to a large extent through the activist work of recognized writers and the sponsorship of universities. Some, in fact, were programs that granted college credits and degrees to prisoners. In the early 1970s poet Carol Muske (n.d.) led the Free Space Writing Project of the N.Y.C. Correctional Institution for Women at Rikers Island and activist Karlene Faith (1993) was very involved with the Santa Cruz Women's Prison Project at the California Institution for Women. Poet Rosanna Warren (1995) led a poetry-writing group at the Massachusetts Correctional Institute in Framingham in the1990s. Most recently Hettie Jones (The Writing Workshop 1997) and Eve Ensler have worked with women at the Bedford Hills Correctional Facility in New York, and Wally Lamb has led a writing group at York Correctional Facility in Connecticut. Workshop participants are usually diverse in educational background and writing experience, as well as in length of sentence and reason for incarceration. Established, well-published poets and writers, such as Judith Clark at Bedford Hills and Kathy Boudin, formerly at Bedford Hills, are among participants in some of these programs. These are often educated women, who are sentenced for politically related crimes and whose profile tends to fit the earlier description of an imprisoned female writer. These recent, accomplished writers, however, differ in that they write individually but also *collectively*, as part of their writing group.

Just as some women from the general prison population began to emerge individually as writers after the 1970s, workshops often fostered a similar discovery and development of talent among participants. Norma Stafford, for example, began to write her moving poetry in Karlene Faith's workshop at Santa Cruz (1975); she went on after her release to support women writers at the Santa Cruz Women's Prison Project. Precious Bedell (1997), a former drug abuser convicted of the 1979 second-degree murder of her daughter, also began to write in prison, an experience that contributed to her rehabilitation and widely-publicized early release. But most workshop participants are women whose convictions as well as writing will doubtless never command much individual notice. Their writing nevertheless contributes to the overall workshop collaborative production and therefore functions as an essential component of the work that defines the group.

The writing produced by prison writing workshops shares the following characteristics:

- It extends the definition of "writer" to include women of all classes and races.
- It emphasizes poetry, along with life writing, fiction, and creative nonfiction.
- It is essentially collaborative in nature. It supports the development of individual talent as well as generating collaborative work. Writing together is part of the point, part of the artistic process.
- It exploits the therapeutic and rehabilitative potential of writing.
- It questions authority; it is art as resistance.

Expanding the Literary Tradition: "Hyperinvisibility," Activists and Celebrities

The concept of "hyperinvisibility" illuminates how workshops have transformed women prisoners' writing experience while simultaneously maintaining the tradition of women's prison literature. Activist Angela Davis, who wrote about her own experience as a political prisoner, uses the term "hyperinvisibility" to describe the "twice-marginalized" status of imprisoned women: "invisible in the 'free' world by virtue of their incarceration, and largely overlooked even by prison activists by virtue of their gender." She explains, "Challenging the hyperinvisibility of women prisoners is central to effective activist and academic work around issues of imprisonment, and it guides the work of many people on the outside who provide a range of advocacy, aid, and support services to women in prison" (Davis 1999, xi).

Written accounts of women's incarceration undermine hyperinvisibility, disrupting stereotypes of female "criminals" through firsthand, literate testimony and art. A certain celebrity mystique serves to publicize some writing, not unlike the process by which Norman Mailer's association with Jack Henry Abbott's case made that prisoner a literary phenomenon of the early 1980s (Abbott 1981). Indeed, celebrity-led writing workshops may be viewed in this respect as literary descendants of earlier celebrated female prisoners' accounts, which exposed prison abuses and highlighted the plight of the invisible poor they encountered behind bars. Early social activists, like Kate Richards O'Hare, imprisoned for her protests against World War I, turned prison sentences into prison advocacy. O'Hare's letters to family and supporters exposed the prison's mixing of healthy with syphilitic women, and following her release she gave her report on prison conditions to Congress (O'Hare [1923] 1976). As witnesses for silenced inmates, celebrities like Glenn Close and Whoopi Goldberg endorse the voice of imprisoned women.

This method of contesting hyperinvisibility raises some questions, however. In media releases such as the recent PBS documentary "What I Want My Words to Do to You" (Gavin, Katz, and Sunshine 2004) or Wally Lamb's collection of prison workshop writing, *Couldn't Keep It to Myself* (2003), one might reasonably question the names that figure prominently in the credits. Whose work or talent is noticed and remembered when celebrities offer readings of works written by prisoners—the words of the imprisoned writer or the performance by the celebrity reader?

Activists and celebrities outside the bars can be powerful allies in communicating women prisoners' messages to the public and raising awareness generally about a social institution that affects increasing numbers of citizens but ironically is so ignored. But they are joined now by the active, often angry voices of the women they support as sisters. Since the opening of women's prison writing to the general prison population in the 1970s, writers increasingly speak for themselves, in their own voices. No longer writing mainly to justify themselves and preserve their reputations, they write with increased confidence against the forces seeking to render them hyperinvisible. They write in protest, and even if they express only their personal stories and witness to their individual truths, their writing opposes the prison industrial complex. In the tradition of slave narratives, these female writers assert their right to literacy and exercise its potential power.

Women's Prison Writing: Critical Resistance and Collectivity

This potential of prison writing to serve as an instrument of resistance is, of course, centuries old, but recent writing from women's workshops amplifies that potential through the power of collectivity. Critic Barbara Harlow's comments on the memoirs of international political prisoners are relevant here: "The prison memoirs of political detainees are not written for the sake of a 'book of one's own,' rather they are collective documents, testimonies written by individuals to their common struggle" (Harlow 1987, 120).

The acquisition of literacy is an event both individual and communal in its potential to give testimony about women's experience of imprisonment. The words that a woman writes about her life history, crime, and responses to prison may serve as therapy for her own personal situation, but a workshop environment extends their reach. Women prison writers today are becoming aware of the complex social issues that share complicity in their crimes. In the context of a writing workshop, they work to defeat those negative forces as they take responsibility for themselves and for each other.

In his study of autobiography, Paul John Eakin explains the importance of "relational identity" to autobiographical writing: "The myth of autonomy dies hard, and autobiography criticism has not yet fully addressed the extent to which the self is defined by—and lives in terms of—its relations with others."(Eakin 1998, 63). He continues, "All autobiography is collaborative, figuratively speaking, for any autobiographer is obliged to negotiate the terms of his or her sense of selfhood by drawing on the discourse of the person in the ambient culture; culture is the silent partner in the transaction" (Eakin 1998, 72).

Ironically, prison may empower women as they contemplate and then articulate their life experience, when they practice literacy and collective communication in the supportive culture of a writing workshop. Again, current writing workshop productions suggest links with the history of women's prison literature. The older paradigm of an imprisoned woman's written production was a traditional form of life writing—letters, memoir, diary or journal. These life-writing forms, as Eakin argues above, are "relational" genres that consider the autobiographical subject in the context of her world of human associations and interaction. Similarly, women prisoners' current predilection for collective (relational) writing situations expands their world of experience and its potential for communication beyond the narrow confines of an individual prison cell. Thus, minority and working class women find voice, support, and motivation to write collectively in prison writing workshops.

Imprisoned Sisters: Programs for Female Prisoners

Collaborative or collective works by imprisoned women include a broad range of genres, beyond those of fiction, poetry, and life writing. Some of these writings function practically by addressing an immediate need for information among imprisoned sisters. Several excellent examples come from the innovative programs at Bedford Hills. Judith Clark, sentenced to seventy-five years to life for her political activism, conducted an "'insider's' ethnographic study of mothers incarcerated at Bedford Hills." In particular she examined the potential of Bedford Hills's progressive programs to counter institutional forces working against women incarcerated in prisons today. She explains:

> Infantilization and the push toward conformity undermine women's efforts to
> take responsibility as adults, mothers, and citizens. . . . The repressive atmo-
> sphere in prison and the impact of multiple losses reinforce women's tendency
> to deny their emotions. Women turn their grief and anger against themselves,

sinking into depression or getting swept up into petty fights and trouble. It is far easier to seek relief in quick fixes through medication or prepackaged therapeutic answers than it is to undertake the difficult process of coming to terms with themselves and their children. (Clark 2001, p. 326)

Bedford Hills's model programs combat the infantilization of female inmates, and many incorporate opportunities for participants to reflect in writing upon the responsibility they assume for themselves and each other. These writing opportunities serve as change agents on two levels: on a more abstract, individual level, they combat the internalized dependency that erodes women's self-esteem; and on a more objective level they support programming such as literacy classes and AIDS education, which empower women by encouraging them to acquire and share information.

Kathy Boudin, recently released from a twenty-years-to-life sentence at Bedford Hills, worked with sister prisoners in a literacy education class in the late 1980s (Boudin 1999). She engaged the women's interest and encouraged group cohesion by applying Paulo Freire's literacy theory to the class, which used the participants' great desire for AIDS information as a vehicle for literacy instruction that related directly to students' lives. The class united in writing and performing a play about AIDS, entitled *Our Play*. The literacy education of these women, with its focus upon AIDS, was the genesis of the innovative AIDS Counseling and Education (ACE) Program at Bedford Hills. The women approached Superintendent Elaine Lorde with their request to implement an inmate-designed and led AIDS education program—a self-help approach to combating the fear of AIDS that threatened health and alienated women living in this unnatural, closed society.

Breaking the Walls of Silence: AIDS and Women in a New York State Maximum-Security Prison (The Women of the ACE Program 1998) illustrates how the communal approach to writing transformed attitudes and lives of women at Bedford Hills. Their great success with the program led to publication of their collective book, a compilation of program history and rationale, brief writings by some program participants, and program lesson plans. The explanation of the women's process of writing *Breaking the Walls of Silence*, which cites The Women of the ACE Program of the Bedford Hills Correctional Facility as author on the cover, indicates their unorthodox, collective approach to authority:

Our definition of "writer" is not the usual one. Everyone here counts. There
was intense debate during the writing process. Those who could write with
ease tended to do much of the writing, while others resented this because they
felt left out. Some didn't feel confident; some felt there were more important
priorities than writing. Some just didn't want to write. We learned through our
mistakes how to involve more people. Some women like to write in a narrative style; others wrote analytically. Some were more at ease telling their own
experiences in their own voice; others preferred to talk while another woman
wrote it down. This resulted in a unique end product. Like ACE, this book is a
collaboration. Many voices come together as one, but the individual voices also
come through. (The Women of the ACE Program 1998, 27)

The ACE program's collective work in education and dissemination of
information is an effective application of critical literacy. It stands, as well,
in the tradition of intellectual activism that inspired earlier prison writing
by women who fiercely retained their self-respect, often in the face of severe
institutional restrictions.

Yet another example of collaborative writing addressing an essential, practical need is the Parenting from a Distance program at Bedford Hills. Kathy
Boudin explains,

When a woman goes to prison, her relationship to her children is a central
emotional focus; she is torn by guilt, anxiety and a sense of failure, yet, at the
same time, her child continues to be a source of hope, a connection to a part
of herself, a motivation for her to change. This crisis is potentially an opportunity for enormous growth if it is faced, growth in a woman's ability to develop
emotionally and growth in her ability to parent her child. (Boudin 1998, 104–5)

Drawing upon "feminist consciousness-raising," "group psychotherapy,"
and "trauma recovery" methods (108–9), intensive group meetings over a
three-month period led to "collective empowerment" (113). As with the ACE
program, incarcerated women acted as both participants and facilitators in
the group. They met to tell their stories and to help each other to grow in their
understanding of how those stories impacted their experiences with their
own children. Written communication was an integral part of their program,
with the women's life stories serving as the "primary material." (108) Writes
Boudin,

[W]e had as a goal that the group experience would lead to a final product—out of their own experience they would write something to help others, either for their children, for other mothers, or caretakers of their children. In addition, the fact that the group would be facilitated by inmates and function totally as an inmate group we felt would play some role in creating the sense of self-reliance and autonomy. (Boudin 1998, 107–8)

Over a period of two and a half years, additional groups formed, using as a resource the book created by the first group. The Parenting from a Distance group supported individual women in their goals to improve relations with their own children, while it acted collectively in solidarity with other incarcerated mothers in Bedford Hills through the written account of its participants' experience.

Preserving the Tradition: Challenging Oppression through Writing

Prison writing is all about power. Whether historical or contemporary, written individually or collaboratively, women prisoners' words usually center on the major themes of desire for release and ability to cope, assertion of rights and of identity, belief in a cause, and concern for loved ones. In the role of writer, a woman claims, perhaps for the first time in her life, a degree of power over an aspect of her intellectual life, a power that may dramatically defy her physical, restricted condition. That power may continue to inform her writing after she leaves prison.

Some of the most compelling works by and about women in prison are written by women after their release and after great pain and introspection. Judee Norton (1999) and Patricia McConnel (1995), for example, assume the time-honored prison writer's duty to expose brutal realities of the prison institution and awaken a complacent and uninformed public. But, as McConnel explains, this grim message is balanced by the writer's celebration of the power and will to survive exhibited by imprisoned women: "I am impressed, all these years afterwards, at the resiliency of the spirits of the women I knew. . . . My stories are about women struggling to preserve their wills, their self-respect in a system intent on destroying them" (McConnel 1995).

When a woman is incarcerated, oppressive forces render her hyperinvisible to her family and to the public. For centuries and in many languages, the written word has dared to give her a voice and a face. Women prisoners today write within the confines of a dehumanizing institution, but they also perpetuate a legacy of dignity and self-respect through the power of communication.

References

Abbott, Jack Henry. [1981] 1991. *In the belly of the beast: Letters from prison.* Reprint, New York: Vintage.

Bedell, Precious. 1997. Poems. In The Writing Workshop, Bedford Hills Correctional Facility, *Aliens at the border*. Edited by Hettie Jones. New York: Segue Books, 42–47.

Boudin, Kathy. 1998. Lessons from a mother's program in prison: A psychosocial approach supports women and their children. In *Breaking the rules: Women in prison and feminist therapy*. Edited by Judy Harden and Marcia Hill. New York: Harrington Park Press, 103–25.

———. 1999. Participatory literacy education behind bars: AIDS opens the door. In *Critical literacy in action: Writing words, changing worlds*. Edited by Ira Shor and Caroline Pari. Portsmouth, NH: Boynton, 182–210.

Clark, Judith. [1995] 2001. The impact of the prison environment on mothers. *Prison Journal* 75 no. 3: 306–329. 24 pp. 13 June 2001. EBSCOhost.

Davis, Angela. 1999. Foreword. In Jacobson-Hardy, Michael, *Behind the razor wire: Portrait of a contemporary American prison system*. New York: New York University Press.

Eakin, Paul John. 1998. Relational selves, relational lives: The story of the story. In *True relations: Essays on autobiography and the postmodern*. Edited by G. Thomas Couser and Joseph Fichtelberg. Westport, CT: Greenwood. 63–81.

Elizabeth I. 2000. *Collected works*. Marcus, Leah S., Janel Mueller, and Mary Beth Rose, Eds. Chicago, IL: University of Chicago Press.

El Sadaawi, Nawal. 1986. *Memoirs from the women's prison*. Marilyn Booth, Trans. Berkeley: University of California Press.

Faith, Karlene. 2000. Reflections on inside/out organizing. *Social Justice* 27 no. 3: 158–67.

——. 1993. *Unruly women: The politics of confinement and resistance*. Vancouver, BC: Press Gang.

Figner, Vera. [1927] 1968. *Memoirs of a revolutionist*. Camilla Chapin Daniels et al., Trans. Reprint, Westport, CT: Greenwood.

Gavin, Madeleine, Judith Katz, and Gary Sunshine, Dirs. 2003. *What I want my words to do to you*. PBS Home Video.

Goldman, Emma. [1931] 1970. *Living my life*. Reprint, New York: Dover.

Harlow, Barbara.1987. *Resistance literature*. New York: Methuen.

Lafarge, Marie Cappelle. 1841. *Memoirs of Madame Lafarge; written by herself*. Trans. from the French. Philadelphia, PA: Carey & Hart.

Lamb, Wally, and the Women of York Correctional Institution. 2003. *Couldn't keep it to myself: Testimonies from our imprisoned sisters*. New York: ReganBooks.

Luxemburg, Rosa. 1978. *The letters of Rosa Luxemburg*. Stephen E. Bronner, Ed. Boulder, CO: Westview.

Maybrick, Florence Elizabeth. 1905. *Mrs. Maybrick's own story: My fifteen lost years*. New York: Funk & Wagnall's.

McConnel, Patricia. Letters to Judith Scheffler. 1 April 1983; 6 July 1983; 2 March 1985.

——. *Sing soft, sing loud*. 1995. Flagstaff, AZ: Logoria.

Metzger, Diane Hamill. 1999. Writings. In *Doing time: 25 years of prison writing—A PEN American Center Prize anthology*. Edited by Bell Gale Chevigny. New York: Arcade, 35–37, 220–21.

Muske, Carol, and Gail Rosenblum, Eds. n.d. *Songs from a free space: Writings by women in prison*. New York: Free Space Writing Project of the N.Y.C. Correctional Institution for Women.

Norton, Judee. 1999. Norton #59900. In *Doing time: 25 years of prison writing—A PEN American Center Prize anthology*. Edited by Bell Gale Chevigny. New York: Arcade, 228–35.

O'Hare, Kate Richards. [1923] 1976. *In prison*. American Library, no. 30. Reprint, Seattle: University of Washington Press.

———. *Selected writings and speeches*. 1982. Philip S. Foner and Sally M. Miller, Eds. Baton Rouge: Louisiana State University Press.

Roland de la Platière, Marie-Jeanne Phlipon. [1798] 1998. *An appeal to impartial posterity: By Madame Roland*. Reprint, New York: AMS Press.

Saunders, Barbara. "The red dress" and "After lights out." 1999. In *Doing time: 25 years of prison writing—A PEN American Center Prize anthology*. Edited by Bell Gale Chevigny. New York: Arcade, 52–53, 221–22.

Shakur, Assata. 1987. *Assata: An autobiography*. Chicago, IL: Lawrence Hill.

Stafford, Norma. 1975. *Dear somebody: The prison poetry of Norma Stafford*. Seaside, CA: Academy of Arts and Humanities.

Warren, Rosanna, and Teresa Iverson, Eds. 1995. *In time: Women's poetry from prison*. Boston, MA: Boston University.

The Women of the ACE Program of the Bedford Hills Correctional Facility. 1998. *Breaking the walls of silence: AIDS and women in a New York State maximum-security prison*. Woodstock, NY: Overlook Press.

The Writing Workshop, Bedford Hills Correctional Facility. 1997. *Aliens at the border*. Hettie Jones, Ed. New York: Segue Books.

Notes

1. The source of the title is Karlene Faith (2000), "Reflections," 160: Lesson #1. The first human right is to speak in one's own voice.

2. For a discussion of the writing of French women prisoners and their attempts to affirm their respectable "femininity," see Elissa Gelfand, 1983, *Imagination in confinement: Women's writings from French prisons* (Ithaca, NY: Cornell University Press).

17

Writing is My Way of Sledgehammering these Walls

TAYLOR HUEY

Why write? To bear witness, to stay sane, to keep our hearts pumping, to not be eaten up by the rage or the despair, to figure out how we got here, or to discover what truly matters.

I'm Taylor and I write because I cannot fly. I am doing close to twenty-five years in prison. I'm on my fourth year, and writing is my way of sledgehammering these walls.

To be able to say what you mean, to put in words what you perceive as the truth, to impose form on the formless, this is a way to reconstruct life, to restore one's sense of meaning, of responsibility to oneself and others.

Writing forces me to remain conscious of the suffering around me and to resist getting numb to it. I write to keep my heart open, to keep pumping fresh, red blood.

There are so many things I want to do with the knowledge I've obtained while being incarcerated. I want to write. I want to travel and show everyone that I am the exception to what society calls "criminalistic." I would like to be the one to change minds and open eyes to what society has been blind to. And with this, here's my story.

I'm in prison doing close to twenty-five years. I am working to try to stabilize myself and be at peace while doing my time. I was nineteen when I got locked up and now I'm older and have come far in this "world" I live in.

Most of us in prison have taken the initiative and are motivated, despite our tribulations past and present, to make ourselves into better people.

People from the established society could learn so much from women in prison. We have so much to teach, so much to tell. I only wish people would listen.

For me, prison hasn't been the end of the world. It has been a beginning—a chance to stand aside and look. When I tell you I have grown in the short time I've been in, I mean it. Not because of any programs, but rather the women I've lived with and the bed I've slept in. I'm beginning to live with myself and accept myself. I know I am more of a woman, a valuable soul, than I would have been, had I not come here. Though no one can go back and make a brand new start, always remember anyone can start from now and make a brand new end.

Prison, with its rigid conformity and structured regularity, has taught me that time is cyclical, not linear. The world, I have realized, allows for second chances, but only if you create them.

Quite honestly, some of the most thoughtful, mature, compassionate people I have ever met are people in prison doing life or long-term sentences. Many have murdered. Many committed their crimes several years ago and have used their time to grapple with their actions, the impact of their actions, their feelings, and have appropriated their remorse properly. Out of a difficult past, they have recreated themselves into women of great depth and compassion.

Ironically, in a place where the freedom and power to make a hundred practical decisions a day is stripped away, you can discover the true meaning of freedom and power. No matter what is going on around you, you can experience some control over your destiny.

I readily confess that my life on the streets was undisciplined, unfocused, and out of control. And I accept that I am in prison for being a threat to society and a threat to myself.

Not only do I have remorse for the wasted years of my youth, I have remorse for the lives I put at stake while committing my crimes. And for every year I've been in, I have been sustained by the hope that I might one day earn my release.

I now look at those times as one chapter closing in my life and a new chapter beginning. Since I was taken away from my environment that I'd been so accustomed to, I was forced to face change. I resisted change as much as I possibly could, and resistance brought nothing but exhaustion and misery.

Like many others, I am simply trying to show that I am worth a second chance. Now is the time to take charge of my life, to start the impossible, a journey to the limit of my aspirations, and for the first time, step forward toward my loveliest dreams. If I had only known then what I know now, but now I know enough to begin.

There is only so much I can do sitting behind this fence. I need resources, I need support. I want to help women, as well as society as a whole, to understand that prison is not a joke, nor is it something to be taken lightly. If I can help to bring society back into the light that for so long has been snuffed out, I want to be there.

Writing began for me as a desire to be heard, to be accepted, but soon moved into a form of self-discovery that eventually became mind opening.

Because prison is a mechanism to repress and control people, I write to maintain my voice and to encourage others to lay claim, or hold on, to their own voices—to scream, if necessary. My words do not come from books or textual formulas, but from a deep faith in the voice of my heart.

To close, I write about it all—about people I have loved or hated, about the brutalities and ecstasies of my life. And for the first time, the child in me who witnessed and endured unspeakable terrors, cried out, not just in impotent despair, but also with all the power of writing. Suddenly, through writing, my grief and joy could be shared with anyone who would listen. And I can do this all alone. I could do it anywhere. I was no longer captive of the demons eating away at me, no longer a victim of other people's mockery and loathing that made me clench my fist white with rage and grit my teeth to silence. Words now pleaded back with the bleak lucidity of hurt. They were wrong, those others, and now I could say it.

Through writing I am free. I can respond, escape, indulge, embrace or reject earth or the cosmos. I have been launched on an endless journey without boundaries or rules, in which I salvage the floating fragments of my past, or am born anew in the spontaneous ignition of understanding some heretofore-concealed aspect of myself. Each word I write steams with the lava juices of my primordial making, and I crawled out of stanzas from the chaos of my life.

18

She Bore the Lyrical Name of Velmarine Szabo

CLARINDA HARRISS

If a person is interested in creative writing by female inmates of U.S. prisons (fiction, poetry, nonfiction, whatever), word gets around. Many may share this interest, but not many actually pursue it. It isn't an easy thing to do. Having worked with inmates at the Maryland House of Correction for Men (MHC) for decades (when it was Maryland's highest security men's facility), I felt it my duty as a woman writer and a feminist to devote the same energy to incarcerated women, but I found my efforts foiled at almost every turn. There were a number of reasons why.

For one thing, the women's prisons I approached offered fewer educational and therapeutic programs than MHC, and these could not boast a solid core of "regulars." The accepted wisdom of the time, the late 1980s and early 1990s, as expressed in both anecdote, for example, what I was actually told by authorities at the Maryland Correctional Institute for Women (MCIW), and published statistics from the State of Maryland Department of Correction, was simple: women tended to serve shorter sentences than men. I assumed that this explained why women's prison writing was less extensive; a few, short, school-type compositions or a few poems were likely to constitute a female prisoner's entire oeuvre.

I was soon to learn that women prisoners who write were (and are) often viewed with suspicion and outright hostility by both prison workers and prison inmates. Writerly honesty was actively discouraged. Jean Harris's famous prison memoir, *They Always Call Us Ladies* (1988), speaks eloquently to a fact I ran up against constantly in my efforts to get hold of substantial writings from female inmates: a woman in prison is expected to "uphold the image of the institution," a phrase that appeared in every issue of the women's "literary magazine" put out during my years of effort to penetrate the minds and writings of women in the Maryland Correctional Institution for Women. The mimeographed publication, printed monthly, opened with page upon page of announcements, regulations, and warnings issued by the MCIW authorities. Contents submitted by the women themselves ran to short, "uplifting" poems and essays, followed by pages of quotations from the women's children and, sometimes, the children's elementary school report cards. The majority of women incarcerated in Maryland have dependent children, and not "upholding the image of the institution" could cost them their phone privileges, which, for many, would prevent them from piecing together child care. Comparing the title of the MCIW magazine, *This Is It: The Last Stop*, with the titles of the two magazines emanating from MHC for Men—*The Iconoclast* and *The Conqueror*—is telling.

Some years ago, I gave an informal talk at Towson University, where I am professor emerita, about my comparative experiences with male and female prison writers. In attendance was feminist sociologist Dr. Natalie Sokoloff, of the John Jay School of Criminal Justice. She put me in touch with Dr. Leanne Alarid, a scholar of criminology, now at University of Texas–San Antonio who, as part of a research project, was receiving in handwritten installments, one old-fashioned, black-and-white, cardboard-covered notebook at a time, a memoir by a female inmate of the notorious Gatesville, Texas, prison system. She bore the lyrical name of Velmarine Szabo.

Dr. Sokoloff told me the memoir was extensive; I had no idea, then, that it was passing the five-hundred-page mark. Dr. Alarid secured permission from Ms. Szabo to share the memoir with me. I had worked previously with an extremely well-written, thought-provoking memoir by a then-inmate of a Salisbury, Maryland, prison, Carol Dryden Leef, and thought it a goldmine at close to one hundred pages. Thanks to Ms. Szabo—her writings and our mail conversations about it—I learned what tremendous courage and stamina it took for a woman to become a writer in prison. It was the hostility to writing and fear of reprisal, not "shorter sentences," that curtailed women's efforts. In point of fact, not only did Velmarine point out to me that, in Texas at least, women often receive much longer sentences than males for the same offense, but Carol Dryden Leef had received a fifteen-year sentence for a drug possession charge that her keepers themselves told her would probably have resulted in probation had she not been the kind of "girl" the judge wanted to make an example of.

It took me only one reading of one early Szabo notebook to realize that the contents were not only brilliantly written but also, unmistakably, of potential importance to social scientists, behavioral scientists, cognitive theorists, and psychologists. And, as I read on—over several years—I realized I was watching a writer finding her true content in the very process of writing it. She was gradually learning the meanings of her life by writing her life. Seeing a writer actively engaged in this process—watching it *while* it happened, and recognizing the courage it took to make it happen—may well have been the single most thrilling experience of my life as a writer and teacher. In what follows, the reader will witness on a small scale the intersections between Ms. Szabo's "outside" life, her prison life, and her understandings of both.

Reference

Harris, Jean. 1988. *They always call us ladies: Stories from prison.* New York: Charles Scribner's Sons.

"You Just Threatened My Life"

Struggling to Write and Remember in Prison

VELMARINE O. SZABO

Author's Note: In 1996, in order to make visible who I really am to future readers and very possibly help my children who I feared might have been suffering from abuse, I began the undertaking of "writing my life." I'd been forewarned that I would most likely suffer some ostracism from fellow prison inmates because of my decision. However, that warning did not even begin to foreshadow the three-and-one-half-year wave of scorn and ridicule that I received from my fellow women prisoners, prison guards, prison staff in the system's education department and elsewhere. The essay that follows is a compilation of excerpts from that larger work and my current reflections on writing in prison.

I have included graphic excerpts of the molestation that I experienced as a child, which kept me in a drunken tailspin of feelings of worthlessness as an adult—thus, the birth of self-victimization that became a very real aspect of my life. I want to include these excerpts because they reveal my biggest battle during the time that that the original essay was written.

It was near the year's end of 1997 that a female officer walked up to my waist-high cubicle where I wrote an average of eight to ten hours a day and said, "You know, I don't think *inmates* should be allowed to write."

At that moment, I was caught off guard. I had been focusing on my personal life. I had not yet reached Part III, the final section of my memoirs, which were chapters that focused on the U.S. penal system and my life within it. I simply said nothing, shrugged my shoulders, and went back to transcribing the rough draft. I did a lot of impromptu writing—waking up from bad dreams in the middle of the night, or simply waking up to an inspired memory. Thus, I spent a great portion of my days editing and transcribing this work.

Our mother had moved. Going up the rickety stairs that were practically rotted through, we walked all the way back to apartment number 22. It was the very last apartment upon exiting the stairs. After knocking on the door and identifying who I was, my mother came to the window, peered out, and began laughing, a wild sound that resembled a cross between an embarrassed child, and the cackle of a lunatic. My mother refused to open the door or come out. I'm not really sure that she believed who I was, or that I'd come with the sole intent of visiting her. Growing frustrated, I begged her to let me see her, while telling her that I'd been worried about her. Nonetheless, for the paranoid, delusional moment, she refused to trust me enough to open the door to me or to come out herself. I even offered to wait until she got dressed, but she refused. Stubbornly, I promised her that I would return on another day.

A few days later, I returned by bus. This time my mother let me in while expressing much joy upon seeing me. I'd spilled some beer on my thin, light-colored summer pants. I asked my mother to allow me to rinse the spot (to avoid staining) and blot it with a towel. When she actually saw the size and shapeliness of my legs, she let out a loud whoop of joy. Not only did the sound startle me, it unnerved me a bit. Embarrassed, I put my pants back on only half-cleaned.

I was more than happy to run to the store to buy her some green onions and a box of baking soda—the only things that she said she needed. The apartment looked decidedly worse on the inside than it did on the outside. At least the outside of the building sported sunlight. The inside of the apartment was dark and cluttered. My mother looked so emaciated (worse than a severe anorexic case) that tears stung my eyes as I took in her squalid surroundings. After I made her store purchases, I gave her the few dollars and change that I had left. Knowing that such a small amount of money wasn't enough to really do anything for her, and feeling guilty for having splurged on a beer, I caught the bus back home.

Two weeks later the same officer antagonistically wrote a major "Out of Place" disciplinary report against me and I was on restriction (a normal retaliation for grieving a prison situation or guard). I'd left the restroom area by a two-cubicle distance—approximately 20 feet—to return a hand-held mirror to another offender. Unsolicited, the offender had brought me her hand-held mirror so that I could practice makeup applications for work. As applying makeup was not a normal activity for me while imprisoned, I was grateful for the loan. After the officer yelled at me to come to her in the dayroom area, she made fun of my makeup by calling me a "drag queen." There is nothing masculine about my facial features, and I told her as much. Glaring at my response, the officer asked why I had walked up to the cubicle wall near the restrooms. Daring not to mention having returned the mirror (another major offense implicating not only myself, but the other offender, through "Trafficking and Trading"), I said, "I don't know."

After telling me to return to my cubicle, the officer laughed and yelled to my retreating figure that she'd written me "another major case." Frustrated, but realizing that this officer was out to get me, I decided to lay low and work on my memoirs. Unfortunately, as I unlocked my locker box, the string that I'd tied on to the lid and the catch, broke and my lid crashed to the floor. Not missing a beat, the guard yelled for me to bring her my I.D., she was writing me another major case—"Creating a Disturbance." Angry, I took her my I.D., and tried to explain that the string on my locker box broke, which only gave her reason to write a "Possession of Contraband" (minor) offense report. Furious, I told her that the judge sentenced me to the "TDC" (Texas Department of Criminal Justice) and it was not her job to try to keep me there with unnecessary cases and her personal prejudices. Of course, she only laughed at me. In a full rage, I sputtered, "You know, you're the kind of person that they can't give a job at Jack in the Box, or you think you own the place!"

This sparked anger in the guard. She quit laughing, and yelled, "You're going over in J-2 before the day is over." J-2 was the building that housed closed-custody inmates. Turning away from me, the guard walked over to the second dorm guard who was sitting in the inside picket and said loud enough to reverberate throughout the then quiet, 100-woman dorm, "You just threatened my life." Turning to the picket guard, she said, "Didn't you just hear Inmate Szabo threaten me? I need you to write a back-up statement and call Command for rank! We need an escort to take her to segregation!" This was my first personal encounter with falsified offense reports in prison, and one of many obstacles geared toward stopping me from writing my memoirs.

When we went to the Beach Boys Bicentennial Concert, all of us were equally excited. Theresa, Linda, Janet, and I all carried marijuana cigarettes in our cigarette packs. Although we couldn't buy beer, we could pass "weed" cigarettes (lit of course) off into the crowd—a custom at rock concerts in the 1970s. I wore the white jumpsuit that Helen had helped me to sew for my Home Economics class. As a part of the ensemble, I wore a straw, wide-brimmed, Budweiser hat. While feeling euphoric and proudly prancing ahead of our little group in haste to get to our seating area, I was stopped by a white, male, city police officer in order to search my purse. At first, I was a bit surprised, and then I became angry at having being singled out of the throngs of white people entering the stadium. In the next moment, I experienced panic as I remembered the marijuana cigarettes in my cigarette pack. I looked around at Helen and John, our house parents, and the other girls in our group who had all stopped where the policeman and I stood.

Knowing or believing that we were all carrying marijuana, John cheerfully looked at the officer and said, "Is there a problem, Officer?"

I didn't really fully comprehend the embarrassed blush of the officer as he responded, "Oh, is she with y'all?"

John replied, "Yes, she is. I'm a houseparent with the Hobbitt Center for Youth Program and we're just bringing some of our girls out to enjoy a bit of the Beach Boys."

The officer assured us that all was fine by saying, "No. No, there's no problem at all."

Handing my purse back without searching it, the officer ended his initiation of my arrest by cheerfully saying, "Enjoy the concert."

All I knew on that day was I'd come awfully close to going to jail, and had John not intervened, I would have. Today, I know that I'd simply experienced for the first time, the selective power of arrest and imprisonment given to police officers. Although I was one of four teenage girls carrying marijuana cigarettes, I was the only black, and the only person in a throng of people subjected to arrest and imprisonment.

Using a bit of desperate ingenuity and the prison psychiatric department, I managed to side-step that guard's false allegations, but I was emotionally devastated as I began to understand my precarious situation. At this point, I had to take a stand with the work that had become of a great personal importance to me—the completed writing of my memoirs. Something was happening as I cried, laughed, and pondered my way through my life. The thousands of pages I wrote left me drained on a daily basis. The intense feelings of anger, fear, and emotional pain that I gave to pen and paper daily somehow left me lighter in spite of the daily stress of prison life. The intense moments of joy and hope I felt every time I received a letter of encouragement from Clarinda Harriss made me realize that I was not alone in my isolation. This encouragement also helped me carry on with what I felt at times was an extremely long and laborious birth. Little did I realize that this would prove to be truer than I could have ever imagined.

After a few weeks, on a Thursday, Helen received a call from my sister Barbara, announcing that my mother was in the hospital. Not surprised by the news, I asked Helen, "Which Funny Farm is it this time?"

Helen replied, "No, it's different this time, Velma. Barbara says she's real sick and seems to think that we ought to take you to see her right away."

Upon arriving at the hospital, I was in no manner prepared for what I saw. Mama was in an intensive care unit, wearing an oxygen mask and could only speak with great difficulty. After I introduced Helen to her, my mother called to Helen who had remained seated in a nearby chair, and her words embarrassed me thoroughly because I hadn't understood their full meanings.

She said, "Miss Helen, you've been taking care of my baby, and I thank you. . . . Miss Helen, are you still there?"

Helen politely answered, "Yes."

My mother continued, "Please keep taking of her, Miss Helen. I want you to keep taking good care of her, Miss Helen?"

Helen answered softly, "Of course I will." . . .

Friday night, on our second visit, my mother was hooked up to a respirator, and although she was unable to talk, she could see. As I made small talk, she grabbed my left hand and began fingering the cheap, gold engagement band from Gene with a frown on her face and a questioning look in her eyes. Feeling embarrassed, I explained that although this was an engagement ring from Gene, I had no intention of seriously considering marriage until well after I'd finished high school. . . .

On the following evening (Saturday night) and our third visit, my mother no longer opened her eyes and was hooked up to other life-support systems along with the respirator. The intravenous feedings, the tubes in her nose, and the big tube going down her throat, as well as the EKG hook up, all signified life support to me. At this point, I began to think that maybe, somehow, it was all a mistake; maybe she'd pull through anyway. As I stood over her bed, I began a soliloquy of promises. I began telling her how we would do things together that we'd never had the chance to do in the past, once she got well again. Things like berry picking. During my formative years, she'd always promised to take me "once I got bigger," and going for walks in a nice, big park, "just to talk and be close." I told her about how I was still going to "join the Army real soon and buy her a nice, brick home—just like the one I'd promised her when I was three years old. . . ."

At this point, my mother's life-support system went off (beeping like crazy!) signifying that her heart had stopped beating. Helen and I were literally thrown out of the ICU amid yells of "cardiac arrest" from hospital technicians. However, we could still see through the massive glass windows.

As the doctor snatched the covers off of my mother's body, I could see that she looked more like a human skeleton than I had imagined. I could see that she was only wearing a diaper as the doctor began beating her chest with both fists while calling and yelling for the technicians to bring more equipment. Finally, he was handed something that he placed upon her chest that caused her to convulse while trying to get her heart beating again. I didn't want to watch this, didn't want Helen to see it, but I couldn't move. As if reading my mind and emotions, Helen gently pulled me away from the huge window while saying that we needed to call John and let him know what was happening. . . .

After they got her heart restarted, the doctor in ICU attendance came to have a talk with Helen and me—basically, me. He caught my wrath, filled with an anger that I didn't understand when he said, "Honey, mama is real sick. Mama might not make it."

I interrupted with, "Wait a minute! Now whose mama are we talking about?!! Mine or yours?!"

Shocked momentarily, the doctor quickly recovered his composure and went on to explain the rapid deterioration of my mother's condition. He explained that all of her major organs (including her brain) had stopped functioning at least once during various stages of her hospital stay. The problem was that they could not afford to take my mother off the respirator long enough to run needed tests because they would surely lose her—extra oxygen alone would not keep her breathing. The doctor went on to explain that even if by some miracle they could save her, she would be a complete mental and physical vegetable living inside of an iron lung for the rest of her few remaining days.

Even after listening to the doctor's detailed speech, I couldn't accept having heard that my mother was rapidly dying. Although I knew that she'd always said that she never wanted to be bedridden for years before death (like her mother and aunt had been) I was selfishly happy with even the thought of her being around a bit longer in an iron lung. So in my own mind, I altered the doctor's speech. I loved my mother; thus, I reasoned, "God wouldn't take her from me yet." . . .

On Thursday, as I walked in the front door of what I then considered my home, intent upon spending what was left of my school lunch break with Helen, the phone was ringing. It was Barbara calling. After Barbara hemmed and hawed around for a while without saying much of anything, I asked her if our mother was dead. She said yes. . . .

For hours I cried. I cried for the joy-filled moments that my mother and I never shared. I cried for the unhappy childhood that she'd known, for the beatings that she recounted for me, suffered at the hand of my stepfather in her young adult life. I cried for the sadness she'd expressed feeling when her childhood beau had returned from the military with a small nest egg and dreams for the two of them, to find her deserted by my stepfather and a mother of four. I cried for the longings that she had for my biological father for so many years after his demise. But most of all, I cried because I knew there was no God. If such a Being had existed, surely He would have at least allowed me to get old enough to provide a little happiness for my mother before her death.

As the years wore on, and I continued to write my life, I realized one day (via gentle questioning and prompting from Clarinda) exactly what caused my downward spiral within society. The spiral began with social drinking, escalating to uncontrollable drinking, and ended with a small, but dangerous sprinkling of drugs. Without the help of A.A. or N.A., I experienced an awakening, and on that day I understood that under no circumstances could I ever drink or drug again, recreationally or otherwise.

With this realization, I lost all desire to drink or use drugs. Even to this day, while facing many obstacles, which include 14-hour days bouncing around on city buses, doggedly applying for jobs (sometimes not even stopping to eat my first meal until after 5:00 p.m.), ironing sometimes for as long as 12 continuous hours to earn enough money to finance a trip with my 12-year-old son to the park and zoo for a picnic (while managing to stay within the guidelines of my electronic monitor), and being faced with seemingly insurmountable obstacles and rigorous demands of the facility that I must live in for now, I still feel no desire to touch an alcoholic beverage or drug. This is only one of many miracles that became manifest as a direct result of writing my memoirs. The further back I explored, the more I understood who I was.

At the beginning of my fifth-grade year, my mother was sent to a mental institution in Austin, Texas and I was shuffled back to my sister Barbara's house. . . .

Gloria and Paula, my nieces, were initiating a kissing game on the concrete porch steps while their daddy, my brother-in-law Ben, sat on the porch drinking Fitz beer with Mike's daddy. Crowded into the small area of the steps were Anthony, Gregg, Mike, my nieces and me. Gloria gave Gregg a quick, dry peck on the lips; Paula in turn gave Anthony a similar quick kiss on the mouth. Mike looked at me expectantly; I hesitated and Gloria said loudly in her excitement, "Aunt Bamm-Bamm, it's your turn to kiss Mike!"

Ben swiveled around from where he sat on the porch, eyes blazing, and ordered the three of us into the house and told us to have a belt ready for him when he came in.

When all was said and done (in spite of my protests), Ben accused me of teaching his daughters bad habits. Not only had I not thought up the kissing game, I hadn't actually participated in any way other than observing what was happening. My nieces were simply ordered to go to their room while I was beaten in the kitchen. Later that day when Barbara returned and heard the details of the incident from Ben, she actually laughed when he told her that he'd broken his leather belt on me. On that day, I recognized and felt my first sting of injustice.

On the following day, a Sunday, again drinking beer, Ben sat in the room where his two daughters slept in twin beds. Seconding as a family room, the room held a floor-model color television, a couch, and a large chair. My nieces had gone to sleep watching television. I was sitting on the big chair as far away from Ben and his belt as I could get and remain in the same room. Calling to me in his typical quiet, low voice, Ben asked me where I'd learned how to kiss. I was startled by the question and filled with awe by the smile on his face. Averting my eyes and face away from his smile (not wanting to allow myself to believe that I was actually being smiled at by him) and looking down at my dirty, jagged fingernails, I mumbled, "I don't know."

Then while patting a space on the other side of where he sat on the couch he said, "Come over here and show me how you kiss."

Even though I didn't allow those words to fully register in my mind (it was sort of like I was in shock; like I'd entered a dream state), I knew that something was awfully wrong. As I looked at Ben's smile, I thought about the beating that I'd received on the day before and the broken leather belt. Dumbfounded and somewhat fearfully, my legs somehow found their way over to the couch. I stiffly sat down next to Ben, turned my attention to the television and dared not take my eyes off it. He allowed me to sit there a few minutes before saying anything else about a kiss. When he questioned me a second time, I began a timid explanation, "Just pucker your lips and give someone a peck on the lips and—"

Ben interrupted, "No, I said show me how you kiss."

Full awareness dawned on me and there was no way that I could deny in my mind what I was being told to do. I thought about the pros and cons (so to speak) and finally in my childish mind, I reasoned that my obedience and cooperation would give me ease of beatings, scorn, and being blamed for everything. I visualized for a brief moment a scene wherein Ben was stopping my sister from using scornful of disdainful words against me; Ben refusing to beat me for the tears that my nieces would sometimes bring forth. . . . Filled with hopeful fantasy, although somewhat afraid and doubt-filled, I leaned forward with my lips puckered, he touched his lips to mine and I let loose with a resounding smack.

Sitting back, relieved that it was all over, I watched for Ben's reaction via my peripheral vision as I stared at the television. Ben drained his Fitz beer, took a long drag on his cigarette, stubbed it out in the ashtray, turned to me and said,

"Now let me show you what a real kiss is."

I looked all of seven years old at the time. . . .

Hours later, I was awakened to the sound of Ben's voice as he fussed and scolded Barbara without truly raising his voice much. A few seconds later, I heard what sounded like his fist hitting her over and over again between her muffled cries. These sounds in the night only served to increase my fear of Ben and drive home the fact that my sister was in no position to help me, no matter what her husband did to me.

Again, with gentle prompting from Professor Harriss via my writings, I realized that due to victimizations I'd endured as a child, I'd developed a sick acceptance of sorts that led to my own vicious cycle of sabotage and victimization throughout my adult life. Alcohol and other mind-altering chemicals contributed greatly to this self-perpetuated cycle of destruction, another of the many realizations and personal growth spurts that the writing of my memoirs enabled.

Standing by the refrigerator, Ben pulled up my shirt and . . . a warm, tickly feeling spread over my chest, and down to my hips and groin area that created a throbbing sensation between my legs. Ben mumbled some nonsense about us falling in love and running away together (hell, in my own eyes I was just a skinny, barely-nine-year-old kid). Hearing Ben's words brought me all the way back to reality and feelings of fear and guilt overrode those new, physical sensations.

Taking me by the hand, Ben led me down the short hallway to my sister's king-sized bed. As he laid me back on the bed, I took a long look at my dirty, bare feet that I soon forgot. . . . Then he pulled my pants down. Once again, I looked at my dirty feet. . . . As I screamed out in pain, he slapped his hand over my mouth. After trying unsuccessfully and repeatedly, . . . Ben gave up trying to penetrate me. Ben showed me the true meaning of the word "torture" without beating me with a belt. . . .

When I asked if I could go back outside, he said "yeah," but told me not to say anything about what had happened. Apparently not feeling too comfortable with my lack of response, before I made it to the back door, Ben overtook me and I received my first series of threats from him—not that I wasn't already scared witless.

"Listen, do you love your sister?"

Nodding, I said, "Yeah."

"I know you love your little nieces."

Again nodding, I said, "Yeah."

"Well, if you tell what we did last week or today, I'll have to leave your sister all alone, and they'll all be on welfare because of you! Do you understand what that means?"

Feeling as if I was carrying the weight of the entire world upon my small shoulders, I simply nodded in response. I understood all too well what he meant because Barbara was always saying that she didn't know what she would have done if it hadn't been for Ben. (Not only had he married her when he got her pregnant, but in doing so, she believed that Ben also rescued her from her home life of poverty with our mother.) I also knew well the stigma that being on welfare and poverty carried.

My sister's husband began unending, almost nightly trips to the bed in which I slept, in his effort to have vaginal sex with me without causing noticeable injury. Without a known reason, I began peeing in the bed at night. . . .

Ben added threats of physical violence to his threats of the severe hurt and hardship I would create for other family members if I told anyone what he was doing to me. One night he told me that he would simply tell Barbara that he busted my mouth because he was tired of me ruining his kid's mattresses. Of course, I simply whimpered and tried harder to allow him to penetrate me with his finger. My school grades (for the first and only period of my life) dropped from straight A's to B's, C's and a D.

Encouragement from my writing mentors helped to unlock my barred, mental doors; although I was told that I that I had an innate gift for writing, I needed education beyond the 7th grade and a GED to shine a good light on those capabilities. Those doors had been long shut to me in my low assessment of my self-worth, in spite of my having been pronounced a child prodigy and genius in my youth. Today, I continue my academic climb in hopes of realizing my long-term goal of becoming a professor of Sociology and Criminal Justice Studies. At one university, I maintain a 4.0 GPA and still am an "A" student after all of these years.

I came to know well and dread the sight of the white t-shirt and cotton boxer shorts slowly (while seeming to glow in the dark) making their way to the bed that I slept on, in the middle of the night. I used to close my eyes tight hoping that it was a ghost or that I was dreaming, but in a matter of moments, I would feel Ben's hands on me shaking me fully awake. I became a near insomniac. On the nights that I would fall asleep from sheer exhaustion, I would usually awaken to a wet bed. One such night, while exhibiting extreme anger, Ben told me that Barbara was out with her girlfriend, Lydia again.

"Git up! You done pissed in the bed agin!"

Whimpering in fear and embarrassment, most of the actual sound caught in my throat, I scrambled out of the bed.

"Shut up! You don't want to wake up Gloria and Paula. Git out of those wet clothes!"

When I peeled out of the old wet slip (which Barbara had given me to sleep in) and panties, Ben grabbed my small, bony frame. Pulling me close to his body with one hand holding my buttocks, he tried to force something inside of me. . . . I cried out in fear and pain. Halting what he was doing and in between clenched teeth, Ben hissed, "Shut up! If you make one more sound, I'm going to bust yo' mouth open with my fist! And if anybody asks why I did it I'll just say because I lost control, I got tired of your pissing in the bed every night—ruining my kids' beds. Your ole sister ain't gon' say nuthin'."

Realizing what he was saying was probably true, I steeled myself against the pain. . . . Tears of frustration clouded my eyes. . . . I wondered if it would ever end. As usual, I could smell the beer on Ben's breath. With no hope of a reprieve or interventional help, I went to the restroom to clean the urine off me as Ben had ordered. . . .

Ben told me to get dressed and get back into bed before my sister got home. After finding some dry, clean panties and a gown, I crawled back into the twin bed while trying to miss the big wet spot (an impossibility).

Later that night, or in the wee hours of the morning, I once again heard the sound of Ben's low, scolding voice as he hit my sister. I listened to her muffled cries between punches as she pleaded for him to stop while promising that she wouldn't stay out late with her girlfriend again.

This time, I crept out of the wet bed, out into the hallway, and squatted on the floor by the kitchen table. After freezing in place, listening to those frightening sounds coming from my sister's bedroom, my only thought was to get as far away as possible from those sounds and the signified hopelessness of my position.

Easing up into a crouching position, I tiptoed to the back kitchen door. Easing the deadbolt lock open, I unhooked the screen door and slipped outside while pulling the door closed behind me. Once completely outside, I ran all the way down to Walnut Drive. I reached the edge of the field where Anthony and Gregg's father kept his 18-wheeler parked, and I squatted on the ground against one of the big wheels and gazed out at the lodge across the intersecting freeway entrance that was Walnut Drive.

No cars were on the road. Staring at the deserted freeways intersecting, it seemed that I was the only living person in the whole world. Suddenly I seemed *and felt really small. As I listened to the still, quiet night, I became aware of the cold chill of the air. Leaning my head against one of the big tires, I began to cry in gut-wrenching spasms. There was no place to go. I had no place and no one to run away to; besides, I wasn't even wearing clothes. As I cried my last tears of destitution, the sky began to show traces of pink. With the beginning of dawn, I realized that at the very least, I would receive a beating for having left the back door unlocked. Holding my arms close around the cotton gown, I hurried back across the field, diagonally crossed the two streets, rushed up the gravel driveway and much to my relief, found the screen unhooked and back door still open. Carefully easing myself back inside, I realized that the house was quiet and Barbara was no longer being hit. As stealthily as possible, I hooked the screen and locked the door. Pausing to still my breath and racing heartbeat, I listened to the sounds within the house again. Hearing only light snores mixed with the gentle breathing of light sleep, I tiptoed to the bathroom and wiped my feet on a towel from the dirty clothes hamper before crawling back into my wet bed.*

I'd just drifted into a light sleep when I heard my sister using the bathroom. A short while later, my nieces got up. It didn't take them long to discover and announce my wet bed. Ben came into the room snorting while my nieces mocked me, and ordered me to take the sheets off the bed. After the bed was stripped, he took the mattress outside to air in the sun. I hated this because this remedy made the whole neighborhood aware of the urine-soiled mattress.

Later that day while Barbara was in the kitchen cooking (I wanted so badly to confide in her!), I mentioned that I was out under Anthony's dad's trailer truck by myself during the night. Barbara looked up from what she was doing and scowled while scolding me, "What were you doing outside in the night by yourself? Don't tell me that you're fixing to start acting up!"

I got scared and told her that it was just a bad dream that had seemed real. So much for confiding in good ole sis.

A successful hunger strike marked my exit from prison as a response to a final retaliatory falsified offense report, which was eventually deleted from the prison computer system. That falsified report would have voided my earned parole and increased my prison stay by three to four years. The fact that I'd not been charged with a major/minor offense report for several years helped to tilt the scales in my favor in eradicating that false report and the freedom that my earned parole granted. Until the day that I was released from prison,

I upheld my right to write—even grievances concerning injustices. I had not come this far to drop the ball. Writing is my love, as are the rights of all women and children in this nation.

During my last eight years of imprisonment, I saw women successfully hang themselves to death to prevent the additional prison stay that the commonly used retaliatory lie of "she threatened my life" was about to cause, just after having earned parole on extremely long sentences. At times, I saw female prisoners stand up under the guns of a lying officer (as an inmate is powerless to dispute an officer's word) only to later act out and earn their way into a closed-custody or administrative segregation status. Fortunately, I was able to stop myself and use the system to climb up from the degradation and disparaging treatment of the medium-custody level offender. Prison is dehumanizing; moreover, disparaging circumstances become greater for those female prisoners who are unable to remain at the general population level.

Having seen, and having known how the prison guard retaliation system works, and having realized a great amount of retaliatory punishment for my struggles to write and grow, I do not believe that any woman bearing any semblance of intelligence will ever be encouraged by prison staff to freely express themselves on paper while in prison without the enlistment of a writer's club or workshop. In addition, for less literate women prisoners, the guidance that a writers' club may provide could prove invaluable. Not to say that many offenders would not attempt to misuse a writing workshop (as a meeting place to focus on things other than writing), but I believe that enough women would grow and benefit to give the word "rehabilitation" a new face.

Women and minorities face untold biases or disparities when they are channeled through our penal system (on misdemeanor as well as the felony level). According to Professor Harriss, people such as sociologists, psychologists, writers, and so on, have benefited in some way from my memoirs. Thus, my efforts have proved valuable to someone other than myself (as was my initial intent). Hopefully, the work will see paper publication someday to reach a wider audience. All in all, these memoirs were born in prison—the desperate works of a woman who was struggling to find her self-worth and acceptance.

20

Out at the Swamp and Back

Reflections on Prison and Release

GRETCHEN SCHUMACHER

We write in prison because we are not allowed to express ourselves freely. In prison we have to watch our language and watch what we do. And so I wrote the first section of this essay, originally named "Out at the Swamp." I wrote it to convey the things I feel and the truths about America's Department of Corrections. Why did I write in prison? Because the one thing our "Corrections" Department fears the most is regular people finding out the truths behind bars. Now that I have been released, I write my truth online.

1. On the Swamp

I live in a place that is basically built on top of a swamp. They call it wetlands. They say we are to preserve these lands, and yet they built a building on top of this swamp. I don't understand the concept of what's right anymore. Common sense is not something used here, at least as far as I know of common sense.

In life there have always been things that just didn't make much sense. In the end, it scares me. I live in a world where I must perform in certain ways. In this world of cement and closed doors, I am unsure that I am performing up to that standard of what is expected. However, my behavior will be monitored and measured by the very same people who would close down schools. I am confused because I value education, and I hate prison.

We all have heroes. I have developed my list of heroes. This list starts with my mother, who is a woman able to overcome all hardships, able to leap tall buildings and all that. There's the woman in prison, she sits beside me, she holds her head high, and she is one of the wrongfully convicted. Of course, Jodie Foster, and sometimes Cher. My heroes are women, because I can relate to them. In my relating to women, I found Angela Davis.

Most people know about Rosa Parks, but most people don't know about Angela Davis. I hope that one day many will know of her. She was convicted of murder, kidnapping and conspiracy, but later acquitted of all. She spent time in prison. She knows what it is like to be on the inside of nothing. I am on the inside of nothing.

Angela Davis is out there still speaking up for prisoners. Her voice is becoming heard, and I hope that one day, my voice will be heard. I have many things to say, and only walls to listen.

I am in prison. I have been incarcerated for nearly all of my adult life. I am subjected to physiological evaluations that measure my stability, my sanity, my insanity.

My last evaluation measured nothing. There's no more insanity, and how can that be? Yet they did say that I am "antisocial." When I looked that up, I discovered that 2–3 percent of the world's population is "antisocial," and they are scheming politicians or successful business executives. I guess I don't mind being in that class. Further reading revealed to me that, "research on the etiology of this disorder has implicated genetic vulnerability, inadequate socialization, and observed learning" (Weiten, Lloyd, and Lashley 1990, 449–50).

My sanity is questioned by people who say I could benefit from being in prison. How sane is that?

Here, out at the swamp, I remain a prisoner. Here I am genetically vulnerable, have inadequate socialization, and I observe things that make me question my very own sense of right and wrong. They say these wetlands are to be protected and cared for, and yet they build a prison.

11. The Dream of Water Under the Bridge

Water Under the Bridge is about the past being the past. "It's water under the bridge." Over the years a lot of women have made their way through prison.

We have our experiences in common. Many have been beaten, sexually abused, neglected and treated like garbage. So before we made it to prison, we most likely have suffered from some traumatic event. We are hurt, scared, confused, and feel like no one wants us unless they can hurt us, use us, abuse us and sexually assault us. Then we were thrown away into prisons and fed food not fit for human consumption, and given substandard medical care. In truth, we are damaged.

When you get out of prison you are expected to be loving, kind, responsible, independent, and good. For a parole officer you have to be taking classes that "teach" you how to get a job, or you have to have a job. You might be required to go into drug treatment or simply do the NA/AA meetings where you will meet friends to do drugs and alcohol with. For your family, you have to be overjoyed to be out of prison and just loving every minute of it. All the while they are expecting you to be mom, daughter, lover, maid, and whatever else they thought you used to be, instantly. For your friends still incarcerated you have to be sad to have left them, but you are also expected to be experiencing a new wonderful life where everything works out for the best and the sun always shines. If you go to church, you are expected to show gratefulness to the congregation and God for . . . I don't know exactly what.

In truth, you are out. It feels good not to be in. Yet, you still suffer from the fallout of your life! PTSD does not just go away because you are now free. You still have it. The difference is that now you have PTSD because you have spent half your life in prison. It is now worse than it ever was but you can't afford counseling, nor do you know where to get it.

You are supposed to get a job, but you can't get a job because you have a criminal record. So you eventually get something to at least appease your parole officer and the job you got is physically demanding, as well as it being one that has no benefits, and pays very little money. If you do get that job, your boss treats you like you need to kiss his butt in order to keep the job, as if you owe them for doing you this huge favor.

It will all come at you like that. Even if people don't treat you like you are subhuman, you'll feel like they are, because you suffer from out-of-prison paranoia, which is different from the usual paranoia, and it is compounded by PTSD.

Suddenly, you are on a new playing field, and no one is really there to help you. Water Under the Bridge is going to address those issues and more.

The goal of Water Under the Bridge is to meet people where they are and to help them in areas that they most need help. A lot of organizations claim that they "want to help" but in truth, they want to do it their way. Has "their" way worked yet? Well, I suppose for some people, but prisons are still full and there is still a problem.

The matter becomes, "Who do you feel most comfortable to be real with?" If you are not "real," how can you advance in the striving for freedom? Most likely you can finally open up with someone who has experienced life like you have. Someone you hope won't judge you. Someone who is very careful about what they say to you because they won't want to offend you.

At the very core of what Water Under the Bridge is designed to do, it might resemble something like the AA model first introduced by Bill W. We don't have steps, we will never believe that a cup could be or should be anyone's "god," and there can never be a belief that you can fake it to make it. As survivors of abuse and neglect, we have already faked many things. This is about what a woman wants her life to look like after prison.

For example, I want to become someone who is respected, heard, and cherished. What does all that look like for me? *Respected* means that I finally get the job for which I am qualified and it is not just peeling potatoes in some restaurant. *Heard* means that someone is going to hear what I am saying without thinking that they know ahead of time exactly what I am saying. *Cherished* is to be loved with a love that doesn't try to change who I am. I am going to change all by myself. I might need some help, but I will be asking for that help as I need it. It is not helpful to me if I ask for a sandwich and you give me a drink of water.

The people I want to reach are the people who have been doing time since 1972 or half their lives. The ones who are worn out and just don't want to do that anymore, yet they don't really know anything else.

The plan is to contact women I know who are out of prison, to create a network of friends. We are able to communicate through Facebook, e-mails, and phone. My beginning expenses will be building a web page, hiring a grant writer, and small expenses of ink for printing my plan to present to various audiences that will help me see this dream come to reality.

I have resources, and will use them. It really ought to be an interesting journey.

111. From Water Under the Bridge's Facebook Page

Water Under the Bridge is a non-profit organization started May 15, 2013. We are a small organization and our goal is to help women coming out of prison. The women we are focusing on to help are the ones that served five years or more. That is what our by-laws say. I prefer to help women who have served 7 years or more. But it only takes 90 days for a McDonald's to be built and a road to be changed. Although it takes 10 years to improve a highway or fix a bridge.

Anyway, the point is, things change in this world quickly and adjusting to those changes might be scary and difficult. We want to help.

I figure within the next 2 years Water Under the Bridge will be fully up and functioning. Until then, we will do everything we can do to help.

Still we are new at this and still we are working on this. One day it will all be just water under a bridge. The past will not hold us down!

Often times, even though it was messed up to be in prison, I just want to go home. I remember feeling like I just wanted to go home when I was in the county jail. I felt it in prison, and I feel it out here.

I just want to go home.

Then I was working with someone with Alzheimer's and discovered that often they start getting this feeling like they are not at home, and they will pack their bags, or cry that they want to go home.

They are at home, and they just keep saying they want to go home.

I wonder just where it is that I now think home is? Wherever it is, my heart aches to be there. I just want to go home.

I have a warm fire going, and it feels nice. I remember being in prison and one channel would play a video of a fireplace, at midnight Christmas Eve. We would stay up just to watch the fire on TV.

Amazing that discrimination is the law and everyone just goes along with it. Are you convicted of a crime? Some crimes no one cares about and others, forget it, you will not get a job with a lot of companies. But do not give up! I am here to tell you, you will get a job. There are people out there that do want to see how well you will work for them. Those are the jobs I find. I can get a job, so you can get one too. I don't give up, so you can't give up either. And I have a crime involving a death. I have what they call "forever crimes." Meaning forever they can hold it against me. But if they were really in charge, we would all be in a world of hurt.

Your stories need to be told, too.

Reference

Weiten, Wayne, Margaret A. Lloyd, and Robin L. Lashley. 1990. *Psychology applied to modern life adjustment in the 90s*, 3rd Ed. Pacific Grove, CA: Brooks Cole Publishing Company.

21

I am Antarctica

I Shriek, I Accuse, I Write

BOUDICCA BURNING

Writing is my official job in prison. I am a law clerk—someone who files collateral review motions in state and federal appellate court for indigent inmates unable to afford representation. This position requires a lot of writing every single day. At this moment, I am in my communal office that I share with five other law clerks. The stench of dying books assaults me every time I enter the room, though my eyes have long since ceased to water and my nose has become impervious to all but the rankest of odors.

Mold-encrusted, khaki-colored legal tomes cling to steel shelves like sickly lichens. Crammed into this space are small desks—the kind you expect to see tossed in the corner of some forgotten government basement. They are paired up like old-fashioned partner's desks with one clerk seated on either side.

I have an executive model, too large to match with the other desks so I am in a corner, a continent unto myself. I am Antarctica. From here, I write inquiries searching for children who are lost in the labyrinthine bureaucracy of Florida's Department of Children and Families; I write pleas on behalf of fellow inmates begging for a reduced sentence; I write motions claiming that civil and constitutional rights have been violated. I write to plead for medical treatment for the elderly, clemency for the mentally ill, and even for people who I don't particularly like. I take on all comers. It is adversarial, it is competitive, it is . . . war.

A person's entire future can hang by the thin thread of my words. A warrior has to prepare mentally before combat. I often put Wagner on my MP-3 player so that when I am writing a defense motion I become a Valkyrie riding into battle. I wield my sharpened pencil like a drawn sword as I research a barrage of arguments. In particular, I enjoy taking apart cases of youthful offenders and the mentally ill who are being railroaded by the system. Many times a case is technically legal but results in morally repugnant sentencing, sentences that don't take into account mental health, abuse, or addictions. Prison should not be a tool for incarcerating the mentally ill as an alternative to providing treatment. Prison must be a punishment for willful criminal activity.

I know that I cannot win most of these cases, but even when I am writing a motion I know is hopeless, I try to argue so that the State's Attorney has to respond with an answer brief and the judge is forced to publish a written opinion. In this way, some of my most vulnerable clients will have the details of their lives and cases permanently recorded in case laws. My hope is that one hundred years from now, historians and researchers will look at these cases and be horrified by the intransigence of the law in the face of the abuse of the young, the suffering of the mentally ill, and the warehousing of the elderly that masquerades under the guise of doling out justice in America.

I shriek, I accuse, I write.

Writing gives me an easy life with soft hands. Before this job I was doing hard labor or confined in the dormitory performing mindless drone work. Awaiting trial, I spent two years without seeing the sun. I have to see the sun every day. My office has a large picture window that looks out on a sunny flower garden. Being confined with no sun was far more difficult than working on the roofing crew in furnace-like conditions, in the sweatshop conditions of the laundry, in the poorly ventilated prison kitchen cooking unrecognizable foodstuffs, in the yard with my bare hands because of a lack of tools. It was more torturous than swinging a pickax to break up hard ground or performing the backbreaking labor of harvesting food crops by hand in the failed experimental farms. I have also been forced to sweep and mop the same patch of hallway over and over again for hours every day. My ability to write has saved me in prison.

I write letters to friends and family. Since I have been locked up for fifteen years, I feel I am drifting further away from the outside world every day. I never tell anyone what really happens here. When I am abused, injured, or just feeling sad, I barely reference it. Nothing good would come of that. Either it would cause my family and loved ones pain and sorrow, or it would cause me pain and sorrow to have them think I was exaggerating or lying, as the staff would surely insist. Or even worse, I couldn't bear to think they might become inured to my complaints of our callous everyday treatment. I have been assaulted more than once by staff. If I had reported this, chances are I'd be in solitary or transferred to a facility even worse than the one I'm in now.

The bottom line is that there is nothing anyone can do to help me. No call to the warden will affect what happens here. No complaint to Tallahassee will change my treatment. In most cases, when an outside person complains, the usual result is worse treatment or solitary. The bureaucrats who run prisons are happy to tell you that all inmates are liars, so I've learned it's best to be silent and endure. I write to keep in touch with those who love me because I still need people. Antarctica may be a remote continent, but fortunately some people still want to visit me.

Meanwhile I live in constant fear of committing the smallest infraction and drawing attention to myself. I never know when the thread will unravel and a sword will fall on my head. I have been under investigation for the most minor infractions: having one too many pencils, leaving dust in a corner of my cell, wearing my crew socks folded down. Each staff has a different pet peeve or personal interpretation of the rules. It is much worse to be investigated than disciplined—one time I was confined without a bathroom for more than seventy-two hours.

In this camp, I put my head down in humiliation and accept whatever treatment is meted out. To resist is to gain punishment. To speak out is to gain punishment. I hate the Department of Corrections. I despise everyone who works here. Not all DOC employees and officers are malicious or spiteful, but I still despise them for working here. They see and do nothing. They hear and do nothing. They witness and do nothing. The State pays them for silence.

Political theorist Hanna Arendt said all sorrows can be borne if you put them into a story or tell a story about them. Why do I write? I write to tell my story in hopes that I move people to feel compassion. I write so people will see me as human. I write to engage the heart and mind of all who read my words.

I must write.

I will write.

I write.

No Stopping Them

Women Writers at York Correctional

BELL GALE CHEVIGNY

It started with a cry for help. When a rash of suicides and suicide attempts had plunged the prisoners at York Correctional Institution into despair, Wally Lamb, the best-selling novelist who lives nearby, was invited to talk with a group of incarcerated women about writing as a way to cope. When he was leaving the Niantic, Connecticut, prison, one woman asked, "You coming back?"

Four years later, in 2003, Harper Collins published *Couldn't Keep It To Myself: Testimonies from Our Imprisoned Sisters* by Lamb and the women in his York writing group. The pieces are about the women's lives, not about their crimes. An enlightened criminal justice system would take pride in such shining evidence of prisoners' rehabilitation. But, before the authors received their first checks, Connecticut's Attorney General Richard Blumenthal invoked the state's vaguely worded and very selectively applied cost-of-incarceration law and billed the contributors at the rate of $117 a day. One, who has three dollars in her prison account, received a bill for $913,777. Another contributor, now free, remarked recently, "If I'd known it was so expensive, I wouldn't have stayed so long!"

The American Center of PEN, the international writers' association to which I belong, protested the law and Blumenthal's action in May, 2003. After months of silence, I encouraged Wally Lamb to nominate a contributor for the 2004 PEN Newman's Own First Amendment Award, a prestigious prize granted to an individual who has courageously defended the right of free expression. It was a long shot. Lamb nominated Barbara Parsons Lane, "a hard-working middle-class mom with no criminal past," who shot and killed her husband "in a moment of frenzy when he taunted her with the knowledge that he had sexually abused her granddaughter." Lamb's eloquent case for Lane, for her own growth and achievement and as representative of others active in the group, won her the honor and $25,000.

The York administration reacted by barring Lamb from the prison, confiscating the students' floppy disks and—in a remarkably foolish provocation to a writers' organization—erasing their work from computer hard drives. But, by the time "Sixty Minutes" interviewed Corrections Commissioner Theresa Lantz, she had ordered experts to retrieve the erased material, and Blumenthal had dropped the suit.

Meanwhile, opposition had sharpened the women's determination to write. When the workshop was suspended, the women took the initiative to exchange and critique each other's work. Denied access to computers, they wrote longhand. There was no stopping them.

In May, 2004, I visited the writing group at York, which Lamb cofacilitates with prison teacher Dale Griffith. I wanted both to meet Barbara Lane and to encourage participation in the PEN Prison Writing Program's annual literary competition. The fifteen women were friendly and sharply engaged. Their ages and backgrounds—in education, class and race—are widely diverse; three are African American, two West Indian, two Latina, and eight white.

At their previous session, Lamb had discussed the seven deadly sins and their contrary seven virtues. "Wally!" one woman cried before he sat down at the table, "I couldn't do my assignment. I tried to write about greed, but it kept changing to deceit!"

Another had the same problem. "I chose gluttony—and abstinence, too. They're really the same eating disorder. But my writing kept going somewhere else."

"Hey!" Lamb protested. "You're the boss! The sins were just suggestions to get you started. *You* decide what you want to write."

Lamb's respectful and enabling approach shapes this workshop's process. Kathy read her piece, which described a blissful childhood and her popularity at school: "I surrounded myself with people who were as interested in me as I was." She learned to manipulate others to get her way and only later realized that hers was the sin of pride.

"Wow!" someone exclaimed. Lamb explained the drill to Kathy, a relatively new student: she would simply listen while the others offered her positive comments and suggestions for improvement. The women jumped in. They admired Kathy's perspective, her honesty, and the humor with which she delivered it. But they urged her to delve more deeply into her story. Kathy nodded and took notes.

Lamb commended her vigorous verbs, and suggested she must have done a few bad things as a child.

"No," Kathy insisted. "I was perfect—except for the pride!"

At one point, I asked the women if they would talk about why they write and what writing means to them.

"It's simple," Brenda offered. "I write to keep my sanity." As a girl, she'd locked herself in her room to write, and in prison, she rediscovered that writing could take her to other places. Chasity put it succinctly, in an apparent contradiction: "Writing is an escape. It helps me to stay grounded." For such prisoners, writing helps them elude the maddening stress of their environment and get closer to their inner selves.

"When I first arrived," Kathy said, "I was so angry. I wrote a letter to my brother, full of spite and anger. Luckily, I didn't send it, and the next day I felt so much better."

"I started writing because I liked the feel of a pen in my hand," Stacey volunteered. "When I didn't have school, I copied books." The workshop changed that, she said. "I can put meaning behind what I write instead of just copying. And I discover I have a very interesting story, so writing is fun." Pam, a Trinidadian who is constantly writing to plead for her right to remain in the States, remarked, "The hopelessness with which I live makes it hard to write fun things."

"I write to find out who I am," Melissa said. "I write things I am afraid to say—and didn't even know. Writing helps me face things." As it turned out, she spoke for several who write to understand and make sense of their lives.

Many testified to emotional growth. Creating characters makes Chasity more compassionate. "Writing gives me peace," Michelle said. "It's a way to close my past and open the door to the future."

Lamb's workshop emboldened Lynn to write about something she had never confided in anyone. In prison, where misplaced trust can be disastrous, the achievement of trust is as precious as it is rare. The women described the workshop as a safe haven.

The trusting atmosphere surely helped Bonnie, she told us, to purge herself of secrets—about incest, abuse, and her dysfunctional family. "Writing helped me to forgive, if not to forget. It taught me to respect the truth of reality; it helped me to heal."

Barbara Lane's experience illuminates that of many: writing has meant breaking out of the prison of silence that had bound her all her life. Growing up, she told me, she learned that children should be seen, not heard. Though she was unaware of her mother's schizophrenia, she knew that something was wrong. "I didn't trust my own experience. I thought maybe that some of the terrible things had not really happened. Because my mother was ill, I wondered whether I imagined things. I feared that I too was paranoid. I wouldn't ask questions, I dismissed troubles."

The terrible things that did happen to Lane include her grandfather's sexual abuse and her husband's terrifying behavior. After killing her husband, Lane suffered post-traumatic stress and entered prison on a suicide watch. "I found my voice by writing," she told me. Lane couldn't weep when she wrote, Lamb said, but she broke down when she heard her work read aloud. Now her writing is much more moving. "My goal with my piece," Lane told me, "if it helps just one woman not end up here, it's worth it."

When I met her, Lane was writing about nature at York, on the ways the sight and sound of seagulls, for instance, help her to survive prison. She also wrote daily to a childhood friend, a letter-journal. And she tried to compensate for all she misses in the lives of her children and grandchildren. "When my son Arthur was married, everyone sent me photographs. So I wrote a story about Arthur's wedding as if I were there." Was it accurate? "Well, Arthur had to tell me about some of the hors-d'oeuvres."

Lane was fifty-six years old then and had served eight years of her ten-year sentence. Four grandchildren had been born during her incarceration. Until she was granted parole and released in April 2005, she continued to imagine and write herself into their lives.

23

"Dear Shelly . . ."

Reflections on the Politics of Teaching Inside

Tsehaye G. Hèbert

—ibaye ibaye tonu

—Yoruba blessing for souls of the deceased

Dear Shelly:

The old ways are not working. Of course you already knew that and you took care of it your own way, but I want you to know that I finally got it. When I would no longer cry at the mention of your name, and saw my way clear, I finally made it to Cook County Jail, as I promised you I would. After a number of sessions, somewhere between *The Bluest Eye* and *Sula*, a woman raised her hand.

"What's your testimonial?" she asked.

Testimonial? Something that religious sounding made me feel awkward and unprepared. What if they expect me to quote from "the book"? I'm not one who came to the jail full of spiritual clarity. A "questioning Thomas" since birth, I worry if God can really love a "wretch like me." I'm not a preacher, just a believer, a seeker and a teacher. Try as I might to conform, truth is, I never did. Taking ecumenism seriously, I openly admitted to questioning Catholicism. Not just Catholicism, but southern Louisiana pre-Vatican II-mass-in-Latin-2nd Sunday Sodality-Tuesday Novena-rosary every night-Queen of the May-flower petal kissing-dressed in white veils and blue capes-ash wearing the day after Mardi Gras French-church every day-Creole Catholicism, to explore Yoga, meditation, Buddhism, Yoruba, Islam, Judaism. I want to know exactly what it meant to be Methodist, Baptist, or COGIC.

"Testimonial?!"

The women leaned forward. I hesitated.

"Tsehaye, why are you here? That's your testimonial."

"OK, so you love the book, but why did you really come here?"

So Shell, I told them that I came because I was afraid.

"*Afraid of us?*" one of the women asked.

I was afraid that I wasn't up to the task and that I would break the promise I made with God. No matter how hard I'd tried and no matter how many times I saw *Cabin in the Sky,* it was the scary stern-faced blonde staring down at us from the ceiling of Sacred Heart church, where just the side of his furrowed brow was visible from the colored section. Shelly, I made both you and God a promise and I was afraid of falling flat on my face.

I remember your face that fall day when you refused to get into the limousine unless I went with you. Your father's funeral is a blur, I was only six or seven, but that day I was just beginning to understand that a world without my Uncle Tap would be a bleak one. It wasn't until later that I was able to appreciate the magnitude of that loss, when Mom recalled him leaning out the car window yelling "You the prettiest, blackest woman I have ever seen in my life." He made real his unconditional love of the Black self.

Shell, don't you remember? They were on a mission to make us feel, no—to know—that we Black girls were all right just the way we were. Even in our color-addled world. Despite the cross burning on our front lawn. Despite the neighborhood kids greeting the first Black kids on the block with dogs that chewed the innocence out of our ankles and bit our feet into a kicking rage even as we lay broken in a heap on our toppled bikes. Despite the bomb detonated in your bathroom and breaking the window. Despite all that, we knew that we were OK and nothing on the face of this earth could deter that. So I thought. Then we tripped on the reality of what happens to uppity and magnificent, smart, wonderfully beautiful Black girls. Maybe one is OK, but certainly not some. They would prefer the pathologically broken and tragically flawed stereotypes they have of us, rather than us.

I am here because I made a promise to a little girl, who wouldn't get in the limousine without me and whose outstretched hand locked onto mine in one of those iconic moments lasered into the soul. The adults who had no more fight left, relented and we sat, a knot of pure grief. Years later, I stand in a line and file into another church. This time it is I, bent with grief walking behind your coffin. When you could no longer fight with your demons, when life at Black and forty was too much, you decided to end it. Ashamed that I hadn't cried in seven years, I cried every day for seven months, wagered with God, if I could just stop the crying, that I would promise to do something real nice. I didn't make it here until I felt I could get past the guilt of having my own freedom and the luxury of my innocence about the prison system.

So Shelly, I am here at the jail because I find the hypocrisy difficult to withstand in a world that talks compassion, transformation, and change, yet dissolves into collective amnesia when it has to deal with the impact of race, poverty, and gender on corrections and the death penalty. I am here because I need to help create a just and equitable system out of one that imprisons a twelve-year-old for life. I must do this even if it's in a creative writing and performance class.

I am here because someone called me *Mother-Teacher*. I am here because I can no longer read statistics about poor Black and Latina, sexually abused, single-mother high school dropouts who underwrite this system. I coax intellectual wings out of a good argument. I celebrate when the light bulb goes off. I am ecstatic when one woman confides, *"This the first book I ever read!"* Or, when another who's shy because she *"doesn't know all the words"* finally reads aloud for the first time.

I am here because I have to learn how to teach the woman who keeps jumping up to be the first to answer the question, the first to read her poem, and the first to give feedback, but who doesn't have a language for the "me first" white privilege she manages to negotiate, even behind these bars. Or, how to respectfully handle the Bible student who fought to be in our workshop, but who can't help but blurt out in the middle of a lesson on Black female stereotypes in *The Bluest Eye, "I'm not white! I'm Canadian!"* How can I shift and return to the flow of their work without letting the focus of the class being broken?

How do I earn my nickname of Mother-Teacher, come to terms with my own fractured mothering, and model the difficult discussion about ill-equipped or absent parents?

"I wish you were my mommy. If you were . . . maybe I wouldn't have ended up here," says a newly twenty-year-old who faces a twelve-year sentence and the loss of the six-month-old she leaves behind.

Dear God, please tell us how to heal this thing spinning out of control and devouring the next Ida B., Malcolm or King. I am here because just when I think I've figured it out, it grows a new Hydra-like tentacle. I've learned to find compassion where I thought I had none and courage where I know I had none. Chicago police have beaten and killed inmates, shot out the windows in Black folks' cars and chased them down the interstate in a drunken rage. Yet, I've learned that not all police officers are monsters. Despite the spectacular headlines, most are just regular people who want to do a good job and bring professionalism and caring to their work. There are bad eggs everywhere. They all don't come in one skin color, one profession, one uniform, nor are they housed in one building. I've learned that officers, like the rest of us, have to be taken on an individual basis. That's the least I expect from another human being, so I must apply those same humanistic principles to both inmates and officers alike.

"Where are you when we get out? We would've never met you on the outside."

"When I was tricking, you could've passed me a thousand times on the street and you probably would have crossed the street."

"You think it's my karma to be here?" another inmate asks.

The old ways are not working, Shelly. So we talk about Malcolm, how he learned to read on his spiritual and intellectual odyssey in prison. We discuss the *Middle Passage* and how incarceration recreates slavery both experientially and emotionally. We write about how prison can either be a womb to grow a new person with a new perspective or it can be a tomb to house a dead soul.

We sharpen the already acute sensibilities that being here creates. We argue about a little Black girl named Pecola Breedlove as she slips into insanity fueled by incest, internalized oppression and abuse in a world that preferred its girls blonde and blue-eyed. We analyze the dyad that is Sula and Nel's friendship. We note Sula's betrayal foreshadowed by her mama's admission that she loves Sula, but she doesn't like her. We discuss revenge at the Days' settling of the score. We ponder Milkman Dead's search for himself that would steer him away from the cancerous materialism that destroyed his father's soul and rendered him contemptuous of poor Blacks. We try to understand Milkman's spiritual quest for his own wings. Or, the irony of Sethe being sent to jail when the murder-suicide intended to free herself and her children from slavery goes awry. After Sethe serves a prison sentence, not for killing her own children, but for destroying the slave master's *property*, she serves an unending one as an exiled member of her community.[1]

"What are you gonna do with our writings?"

Poor and female, Black, Latina, white and Native women struggle to find their tongues and grow their wings. Articulating the breadth of this experience is so overwhelming, so chaotic, and so nerve-rubbing raw that words defy any description of it. I live in a space where I own my own tongue and where I have several platforms to own my own work. So, I have chosen not to perform any of the work that I have been privileged to witness. I do not own the experiences that have brought the women to prison; I have chosen to wait until we can stand on the same stage and do them together.

"Tell us about that left-brain, right-brain stuff."

"Tell us about the Middle Path and the Middle Passage again."

"Remember what you said about the grain of sand . . . and the oyster?"

"I wasn't gonna talk about rape, until you broke the ice and talked about your own."

"Say that word again . . . axiology, the study of values."

The curriculum is interrupted again and again, so that the real learning and teaching can happen. We work through, not around, the big questions and we prod each other, no holds barred.

"I hate rules!"

"So do I," I respond. "But who wants to live in a world with no stoplights and stop signs?"

We discuss the *guidelines* for our workshop and maneuver through the complexities of life outside, on the street, where following the rules is of even greater consequence for ex-offenders.

"The system is unfair!" as someone points out an obvious discrepancy, but it cannot be used as an excuse for failure.

"Being here, has made me really want to try to understand law. The way my trial went was so wrong, even the judge said so. My lawyer didn't even have a license. He skipped off to Poland with all our money. I think I want to be a lawyer. Do you think that can happen?"

"No I don't think that you can. I know you can. It will be hard work. You'll have many battles to fight, but you won't know until you try."

"But we can't borrow money for college and don't the laws prevent us from being lawyers?"

"We can't find jobs. We can't rent apartments. They say we paid our debt, but we don't start to pay until we get out of here."

And so it goes for over two million U.S. citizens who are imprisoned across the country. Each week as the jail's series of interlocking doors slam shut behind me, I have one thought: "There but for the grace of God go I." It is rarely of comfort, and cannot numb the pain of knowing what I leave behind me. Seventy percent are survivors of rape, incest, and physical abuse, and illiteracy continues to be the norm. Their net worth is primarily negative, as are most of their zip codes. Most will never know what it is like to go on a vacation, nor will they be able to amass enough money in either an IRA or a 401K to comfortably retire. What IRA and 401K? Most have never worked a job that pays above minimum wage or one that provides adequate benefits. Many are the latest link in a seemingly unbreakable chain of mind-bending, generational poverty. Most have never had enough of anything, let alone a surplus of anything.

Society has already discarded my students. Most of the time they can't rent apartments or work for the same corporations that employ them inside the penitentiary. It is then that they learn that the Christian value of forgiveness stops at the doorsteps of ex-offenders. We would rather have amnesia and turn our collective heads, because changing a desperately flawed system is equivalent to turning the other cheek.

It is the same system that endorses corporate welfare and feeds money into a war machine, yet requires more and more of its most vulnerable, its women and children, back home. Women and children bear the brunt of social malaise and prison. Most women here are single parents who do not have adequate childcare. Most will send their children into foster care. Inadequate medical care both inside and outside of the correctional system is a fact. Sadly, the most consistent medical care many get is when they're incarcerated. On the outside, these women are required to do more with fewer resources, and the outcome of those practices continues to feed the exponential growth of the female prison population. What little safety net that existed for poor families on the edge becomes increasingly tattered. Former president George W. Bush chose Chicago to announce an initiative where women moving from welfare to work are now required to work more hours per week, with no additional money for child care. The irony is that the American tax dollar is purportedly assuring that women in Afghanistan and Iraq acquire adequate health and childcare resources for women.

Programs that address these issues exist. They are underfunded and cannot keep up with demand. Along with economic crime, the largest number of inmates have a history of substance abuse. For every available bed in a facility that provides services for substance abusers, there's a line going out of the door of folks waiting to get in. Solving the drug problem will not happen by incarcerating abusers. It will happen when we stop the flow of cocaine and heroin entering this country and when drug abuse is treated effectively.

"What of the victims of crime?" An irate, white male confronted me at a conference.

The question itself is a well-aimed knife. Double-edged and sharp, it confronts me at every turn. I am both a victim of and a survivor of rape. A casual acquaintance offered to walk me home from a party, but wanted to grab his coat first. He raped me at knifepoint and gunpoint, threatening to throw me out the window. I fought back with every bone in my body. After the rape, I was made to take a shower to erase every trace. I went to court, but I lost the case and was raped a second time by a legal system that held me responsible, the judge said, for not knowing any better. I later found four other women who were raped by the same man.

I live in a world that sees me, a middle-class African American woman, as either an unprincipled, immoral, sexually licentious being on the one hand or, as a pathological, deviant, out-of-control, welfare queen breeder of criminals on the other. I do not, nor have I ever, condoned crime. Nor will I, under any circumstances. It has taken me nearly thirty years and hours of therapy to be able to speak about this without dissolving into a puddle on the floor. But having that experience allows me the gift of being able to relate to women who struggle with these same issues.

It places me in a unique position to address those who confront me as being soft on crime. I am compelled to do my best to make the world a safe place for all of us. Regardless of our political affiliation, our class status, our educational level, our addresses, and all that defines us, we all pay for our ability or inability to effectively deal with the causes of crime. We must make hard choices and do the right thing. Those who are ready to flip the electric chair's on switch must recognize that in Illinois alone, nearly twenty individuals—all male and predominantly African American—have been released from death row based on DNA evidence.

People often compare the plight of poor Blacks to that of immigrants who thrive in this country. I'd be rich if I had a dollar for every time I've been asked, why can't Blacks do it?

Comparing Blacks and immigrant groups doesn't allow us to correctly analyze the problem. We share radically different social histories. I. W. Charny's A Proposed Definitional Matrix for Crimes of Genocide (1999) asserts that Americans of African descent have been targeted, both consciously and not, for insurmountable race hatred and bear the twin yoke of being the victims and the survivors of ongoing genocide in most of its permutations, including ethnocide—religious, political, social and economic and linguistic ethnocide. Until we squarely face the racial issues that confront us at every turn and acknowledge a hidden history told through the lens of those who suffered through it, we'll never heal this thing. For the record, this argument does not absolve those who commit crime.

Until we address poverty issues from the perspective of those American men, women and children who continue to suffer in a "land of plenty," prisons will continue to grow and we will continue to place society's failure on the backs of victims. What I see from my work is the outcome of every failed social program imaginable. I've heard so many excuses; you may pick the one of your choice: The "they don't want to work" excuse, "which is why they turn to crime." "They are baby-making machines and should be sterilized rather than create another criminal mouth to feed." Or, how about "they just don't want to learn"?

Between 70 percent and 90 percent of the prison population has learning disabilities, which were inadequately diagnosed and treated, or not even treated at all. As long as schools are funded based on property taxes, schools in poor neighborhoods will remain inferior. Underresourced, they lack the ability to attract the best teachers. Oh, they'll get those firebrands who are willing to "do time" long enough to get catapulted to other more prestigious schools or perhaps even cushy jobs that attempt to put a Band-Aid on the problems. Or, forgive me, Shelly, those who will collect enough field notes for a book deal.

Maybe it's too much to hold onto the notion that the money, the educators, and the programs that substantively address poverty, family and other issues impacting poor children will end up in the neighborhoods that most need them. It takes a village, y'all, and no, Hillary did not coin the phrase. Square that with a world where a whole city will rally to save a baby whale from dying, but we tell the welfare mom who is on the emotional and financial edge to buck up, suck up, shut up, and work harder. Whole communities shun her, and they will not come together to assure her survival. We will complain at having to hear her explain that she's trying to keep a family together by the threads, and we will blame her for not achieving her potential in the meritocracy in which we live.

In our post-9/11 angst, the nation's attention has been riveted outward at the expense of the domestic agenda, and ex-felons are at the bottom of that list. Over two million citizens are the survivors of domestic policy terrorism. It does not matter how hard they try to make amends for their crimes, nor how long they've spent in jail. They will pay for the remainder of their lives. What are we to do with them? Return them to the same community settings that landed them in jail in the first place? In Chicago, communities like Lawndale are home to 60–80 percent of returning felons. Where will dedicating more money to prisons and less to aggressive antirecidivism get us?

Shelly, I came here because I thought I had something to teach, yet I am the one who gained an education here.

Dear Shelly, I am here because the old ways are not working.

Reference

Charny, I. W. 1999. A proposed definitional matrix for crimes of genocide. In *Encyclopedia of Genocide*, Vol. 1. Edited by I. W. Charny. Santa Barbara, CA: ABC-CLIO.

Note

1. Morrison, Toni. 1970. *The Bluest Eye*. New York: Knopf; 1987. *Beloved*. New York: Random House; 1977. *Song of Solomon*. New York: Plume.

24

All with the Stroke of a Pen

Joyce Cohen

Why I choose to write is a question I've asked myself many times as I do not enjoy the mechanics of writing. I have half-jokingly said I write to get off Inside Grounds work crew, but it is so much more than that. As cliché as it sounds, words do not come easily to me, yet I continue to struggle to explain myself.

There are times during the day or the long nights when a thought, a feeling or an idea comes to me and something in me wants to capture it, hold on to it, pursue it, reflect on it or just examine it at another time. Writing allows me to do that.

Being behind prison walls takes away your freedom, and yet I can erase these walls and soar through reality and fantasy. I can get lost in make-believe or perhaps someday write something of great magnitude or sound importance.

Maybe I can even help change a system that is corrupt, flawed and broken—all with the stroke of a pen.

25

The Prisoner's Lament

SAMSARA

At the end of the day, when I lay in my cell,
under the constant fluorescent lights,
the memories invade my mind,
what's been done, what I've done, who cares, who doesn't,
every painful experience, every soft touch, every not so soft.
How can I forgive, even myself and God please let me
forget.

Numbers, labels, statistic, convict, what have I become?
This is not who I wanted to be, so how'd I become me?
I lay here and wish the lights would go out, so dark,
please cuz I don't like what I see.
Shackles and chains, off to court again.
What will the verdict be?

The sad, worried look on my mother's face,
Where did her baby go?
The one with all those hopes and dreams,
the little blonde girl who screamed about dresses,
t-shirts and overalls, that's me.
Daddy's little girl, he had high expectations for the

little baby girl that he still sees,
behind the prisoner shuffle.
They don't want to see the oranges, the shackles and the chains,
they see their baby through glass, talk while the tape records,
never get to touch her, hug her, kiss her, love her.

How much I'm missing with this unfortunate life,
look at the scars left from years of pain,
secret thoughts, tearful sighs and wailing cries.
I close my eyes and try to block it all out,
it's all there constantly, the people I love, their faces,
seems to be torturing me.

Never wanted it to get to this point, unfazed,
didn't want the time to become easy.
Like this is how I learn a lesson, should be!
Razor wire in my eyes, number on my chest,
what my future seems to be, unknown,
scary as hell.
So much life to live, want to know how to live it.

Hope Is There

CREE

We tend to look at the ugly
and miss all the beauty.
Hope is everywhere
We just have to open our eyes
a little wider stop looking
so hard and just ease back.
Hope is there, Hope is today.
Hope was yesterday
Hope is for tomorrow.
Hope is always there for the taking.
Believe in your heart
for a new start
Hope.
Pass it on.
          Hope.

Speaking Out for Social Justice

Institutional Challenges and Uncertain Solidarities

TOBI JACOBI

I have walked that long road to freedom. I have tried not to falter; I have made missteps along the way. But I have discovered the secret that after climbing a great hill, one only finds that there are many more hills to climb. I have taken a moment here to rest, to steal a view of the glorious vista that surrounds me, to look back on the distance I have come. But I can only rest for a moment, for with freedom come responsibilities, and I dare not linger, for my long walk is not ended.

—Nelson Mandela, *Long Walk to Freedom*, 1995, 625

Many people assume that prison is the end of the road, a holding space for those who have committed wrongs. Yet as the iconic Nelson Mandela reminds us, the long road to freedom has no permanent destination. The writers featured in this book and in the many prison writing programs across the world reside along many points on that road of personal and public freedom. Many of the writers we have written with struggle with substance and relational addictions, systemic poverty, and the lack of healthy models for social and familial structures. They love those who hurt them. They hurt themselves and those they want to love. They slip and slide between the social expectations of work, family, body, place, and the will to find a temporary haven, a break, to suspend the challenge and trauma of daily living. Sometimes writing becomes that haven, both painful and fulfilling.

241

Historically, there is a strong tradition of writing and language activism within U.S. jails and prisons with roots in revolutionary and social justice movements. While women's voices have been less visible than their male counterparts, there is much to celebrate. Consider the increase in available print, performance (music, film, theater) and digital texts focused on women in prison over the last twenty-five years. A selected list of resources is found at table 26.1.

Table 26.1 Selected Resources for Writing and Expressive Arts Programs in Prisons

Selected Print Resources	Selected Audio, Film, and Theater Resources	Selected Digital Collaborations
• *Wall Tappings: An International Anthology of Women's Prison Writing 200 to the Present* edited by Judith Scheffler • *Razor Wire Women: Prisoners, Activists, Scholars, and Artists* edited by Jodie Michelle Lawston and Ashley Lucas (2011) • *Interrupted Life: Experiences of Incarcerated Women in the United States* edited by Rickie Solinger et. al. (2010) • *Inside This Place, Not of It: Narratives from Women's Prisons* by Robin Levi and Ayelet Waldman (2011)	• *The We that Sets Us Free* (audio) (Valle 2008) • *Mothers of Bedford* (film) • *The Grey Area* (film) • *What I Want My Words to Do to You* (film) • *Freedom Road* (film) • *Assata: A One-Page Comic*[1] by Rachel Crane Williams • *Juvenile Justice Zine Project*[2] by Rachel Marie-Crane Williams • *Well Contested Sites* community theater project[3] • *The Medea Project* theatre project[4]	• Justice Now's advocacy for women prisoners http://www.jnow.org/ • Women and Prison: A Site for Resistance (community writings) http://womenandprison.org/ • Prison Public Memory Project (historical archiving project) http://prisonpublicmemory.org/blog/ • California Coalition of Women Prisoners http://womenprisoners.org/wp/ • Women's Prison Association http://www.wpaonline.org/

1. See Assata Teach-In at http://assatateachin.com/comic/.
2. See "Juvenile Justice Zine Project" at http://www.uic.edu/jaddams/hull/hull_house.html.
3. See https://www.facebook.com/WellContestedSites.
4. See http://themedeaproject.weebly.com/.

Social justice projects such as these offer alternative ways for prisoners and outsiders to interact with each other, to find humanity within each other's experiences and serve as collective gathering points for multivoiced stories and experiences from across the globe. Even a brief sampling would reveal how consistently these prison narratives and representations often center on visceral experience. The slam of doors. The orange and gray blur of bodies.

The corrosive exchanges that pass for communication. The worn instep of year-round flip flops that have paced a twenty-yard hallway thousands of times. As the writers in this collection demonstrate, prisoners both embody and transcend these physical realities as they pen their lives onto pages and send them out into the world.

The work in this collection attests that there is power in their narrative actions. To effectively walk along roads in the proactive ways that Mandela suggests, however, we must move beyond vivid descriptions of material, physical, and affective violence. We must recognize collective selves as road builders—and acknowledge the risks that come with such work.

Embracing Community, Recognizing Road Signs

As the writings and projects highlighted in this volume demonstrate, each year women are producing enough writing from behind bars to circle the earth many times over. Community and shared time to write and explore voice often lies at the heart of what we sometimes read as a collective endeavor. As Adrienne Rich suggests,

> Most often someone writing a poem believes in, depends on, a delicate, vibrating range of difference, that an "I" can become a "we" without extinguishing others, that a partly common language exists to which strangers can bring their own heartbeat, memories, images. A language that itself has learned from the heartbeat, memories, images of strangers. (1993, 85)

Writing behind razor wire, we shift from a community of strangers into a gathering of women through the language, heartbeat, and memory that Rich invokes, a lineage that has never felt clearer to us than in the moments we spend with women in prisons. We sit in tight circles after weaving our way down elevators, past intake and visitation rooms, through the threshold of the men's wing of the jail where the scent notably changes, grows heavy like the stories we may or may not tell. We look each other in the eye after pacing down the moments to get out of the housing unit, after indulging a mild curiosity about what a writing workshop might hold, after banking on the promise of paper and a cheap plastic pen.

Like so many of the women whose work motivated, inspired, and influenced the work within these pages, we cling to the possibilities of change. We maintain hope that our words will resonate with someone, some bodies who will embrace the horror of the system that warehouses hundreds of thousands—as we do when we enter for workshops, respond to writing partners, analyze the statistics we create or are given. We cling to the notion that a confluence of hope and horror might result in change that results in more community writing groups that women join before or after imprisonment because they have more beautiful than horrifying experiences to share, because they have joys that must get out. As poetry therapist Geri Chavis argues, writing as healing can lead to both affirmation of the "heroic aspect of one's own life journey and . . . relief from suffering due to loss, trauma or the shame of a dark secret" (2011, 155). Together we both create and revise anew common languages for understanding what (in)justice is.

Yet as Sadie Reynolds (chapter 9) so astutely points out, there are limitations to what writing inside can accomplish; there are risks that no quickening of the heart after a poem well received can temper. As an institution, the criminal justice system both enables and disables the impulse to circulate one's words and ideas by both allowing and constricting educational programs. Many programs have witnessed serious consequences for encouraging conversations and writings that empower individuals and/or groups. Risks to writers manifest themselves in unexpected ways. A simple writing prompt takes on the weight of a heavy discussion, perhaps resulting in the loss of privilege or the ability to attend the very workshop that led to euphoria, depression, anger, even humor. An encouragement to assert one's right for humane treatment (or even justice) is later met with silence, sarcasm, or worse. A workshop disclosure is violated and stories travel and morph into loneliness, guilt, shame, or fear. The perils of writing and circulating narratives then might include any of the following:

- Being locked in a cell for a defined or undefined period of time,
- Having your written narratives physically confiscated,
- Having your own voice used against you as a legal tool,
- Losing your sense of self,

- Losing your social standing within the social structure of the prison,
- Losing your good time,
- Risking violence by those who have been included in written disclosures (e.g., male partners, work associates),
- Losing positive (or what remains of) relationships with family and friends due to written disclosures,
- Feeling silenced or afraid to writing further.

The raw truth is that outside teachers and activists can never understand or even recognize all of the actions and interactions we set in motion by bringing texts, writing exercises, literary and creative craft, and ourselves into carceral settings. The reality is that most writing teachers, activists, and scholars leave after sixty or ninety minutes, however meaningful the conversation or beautiful, traumatic, or banal the words penned. Yet, if we embrace the will to narrate, to take up Muriel Rukeyser's call for a universe comprised of stories rather than atoms, we must continue to look in every place for contributions to that collective enterprise.

Roadblocks, Detours, and Solidarity

One of the writers asked me if I needed to take a deep breath the other night. The truth is that I did, and often do. Educators and activists working inside prisons and jails put a lot of pressure on the time spent inside. It must often stand in for so many things: activism, scholarly progress, teaching, personal writing time, middle class-white-heterosexual guilt. In hallways and at academic conferences, those of us who work inside often discuss the limitations of writing groups in jails and prisons, and envision workshops and classes in writing for formerly incarcerated women in the community. And there are times when the institutional structures seem insurmountable when we cling to an abstract notion of solidarity to sustain our work.

Though we often hear about provocative writings or confiscated notebooks, it isn't only written words and their circulation that spark controversy. Often writing programs themselves clash with institutional regulations and even facilitators' expectations and assumptions. Two brief examples focused on pens and farewells illustrate this tension.

The Power of Pens

A few years ago our program weathered the "great pen incident," a moment that is difficult to relate without a bit of irony. The late-night television headline is all too clear: *Writing teacher kicked out of jail for failure to control pen.* The truth lies not far from there.

Our weekly program was jeopardized and reprimanded for failing to collect pens that had been left for us to distribute, as was our usual practice. These pens, however, were slightly different in design and, although still black-inked and clear, were somehow in violation of code and the source of much consternation and anxiety over a weekend. Women were locked down. Pens were confiscated and consequences were doled out to both prisoners and staff. The result was several months of pen regulation, despite the reality that the same pens were for sale through the commissary.

Even as the details of the moment fade, my frustration lingers with an institution so determined to control how language and communication circulate, as well as my own self-reflective dismay at the privilege that permits me to critique the larger institution. Who, exactly, am I to prod the regulations in ways that may risk the presence of a much-loved program? Who am I to buck a system whose internal organs and appetite I have never fed? Who am I to wear the badge of "volunteer facilitator" so lightly? In the end the great pen incident wasn't about pens. Instead the plastic vessels represented not freedom of expression but rather a thinly veiled reminder of who was in charge, who limited the number of sheets of paper one can possess, who designates the staple as a deadly weapon. We bend our heads and pose penitent; we promise to let no pens loose. We nod and go on. This is not the language Adrienne Rich asked us to make common.

The Force of Farewells

Many writers have experienced the rush of anxiety and joy that comes with seeing writing transform into print. Our program publishes a biannual journal that is celebrated through a "reading and journal launch party," a rare jail event where male and female writers may interact. Recently, one writer commented happily that the end of the reading was the only time when it was okay to say goodbye to another prisoner without being written up. She and others waved goodbye to the men's writing group and they parted ways without physical contact or disturbance. Yet a few moments later, the reprimand came as the women returned to their housing unit and were confronted with "evidence" from the control room of their gestures.

The reading is a much-anticipated event in our program. It is a chance for writers to stand before their peers and own their words, to counter the myriad stereotypes that lock their life experiences into narrow boxes. They spent a collective hour or two naming alternatives and driving, as Anne Lamott (1994, 226) might say, "straight into the emotional center of things." As facilitators, we transform from program writers and teachers into jail volunteers as soon as we step from the auditoriaum into the sterile hallway. We corral the writers into straight lines for the silent shuffle back to their housing units. We witnessed the events of that evening and experienced both pride in their courage to speak to a crowd and dismay as we received staff scowls and the wave of dismissal as the guards bustled the offending women into a conference room for reprimand. We didn't try to intervene or defend their actions or plead with them not to crush the pizza-chocolate-cake-poetry-reading high that would carry the writers through the next few hours or days. We didn't stop because this was not how we could make a difference. We wouldn't be able to stop the lockdown for these four women or others in other housing units who were likely facing similar consequences. The best we could do at that moment was keep walking, head forward, pushing our way out into the winter air that the writers wouldn't breathe. We might stew upon the incident and transform it into motivation to return the next week and the next and the next. We could attempt to alleviate our guilt by e-mailing the programming staff, asking for lenience while recalling how well the reading event had gone. But it wouldn't matter. The punishment would likely be over by then. Control reasserted. The confidence and adrenaline inspired by our journal contained, perhaps morphed, into another poem of sadness or anger or shame.

There is little doubt that teachers, researchers, activists—even former prisoners—reside in a world very different from those on the inside. To claim solidarity is a dangerous proposition heightened by the availability of media representations and facades that offer viewers and potential allies that lure of understanding that masks the reality of life inside the U.S. correctional system. Well documented is the longing for solidarity and alliance that often germinates within a white, heterosexual, middle-class impulse to make change. Our experiences suggest that while a more diverse range of people are interested in developing and teaching literacy/writing programs for women inside, the majority fit well into these identity boxes. While those fitting this profile do enjoy a certain amount of power within American social structures, they are also ill suited to speak for the women of color who populate the majority of U.S. correctional facilities.[1] *What does it mean, then, to speak of solidarity and alliance with women writers in prison? Where might we channel our dismay at events like those noted above—whether temporal or material—so that we can see through the laws, the sentences, even our own programs in order to envision a world without so many women in prison?*

As he reflected upon his prison and life experiences, Nelson Mandela argued that "to be free is not merely to cast off one's chains, but to live in a way that respects and enhances the freedom of others" (1995, 751). When we don labels like "activist researcher" or "community literacy teacher" we must do so with the active knowledge that those labels may fail us—and that even when they do we must strive for programs that will work to both respect and press community writers to know themselves as they explore new roads. It is likely that the women knew they were taking a risk by keeping the pens and waving goodbye. They asserted their right to human communication by chancing institutional consequences. They were transforming the power of the workshop and reading event into moments of autonomy. They might reflect that it was worth the risk. And their actions forced us to reconsider our own freedoms and actions more deliberately than we otherwise have.

Reclaiming Roads

Just before the completion of this book, the tables were turned on me as a privileged, white, middle-class woman who had long constructed a relationship to prison through terms like "program director," "workshop facilitator," and "writer." I became—and fought becoming—a victim. As I stared through a smashed car window at the empty place where a partially concealed bag of valuables had been, at the faces of my stunned small children, at the tears of disbelief pouring from my sister's face, I felt helpless. I couldn't protect them—or myself—from the flood of outrage, anxiety, despair that would follow. After the hours spent brushing glass shards away from my children's hands and feet and outfitting the car with duct tape, after failed attempts to still the uncontrollable shaking of my sister's hands, shoulders, and heart as she worked through the loss of two years of research, after the rise and fall of innumerable trivial thoughts (*what about the dog 150 miles away, what about the inscription on her missing iPod, how to answer my toddler's constant queries about the shattered window*), a road remained. Stretching on and on. And it took me a couple of months to feel capable of moving along it again—and longer still to face a complicated jumble of feelings toward people in prison, people my activist-self was desperate to see as more than crime, more than single or even repeated events, even as my victim-self struggled to step back inside jail walls.

I don't pretend this confusion is unique; it might, in fact, align my own experience more fully with the women I write with each Wednesday evening since this loss, this betrayal of humanity, feels raw and unpredictable. It would be foolish to deny that pain is primal in much prison writing. Few women experience life behind bars without feeling or causing pain at some point, at many points. As critical race and prison scholar, Joy James argues, "When writing is a painful endeavor, marked by political struggle and despair as well as determination and courage, it is potentially transformative" (2003, 4). It was only by writing through this relatively contained trauma (*We were physically safe. The items were mostly replaceable. We had the tools to process the event and move forward.*), that I have been able to understand again why prison reform and abolition work is such a pressing issue for the United States—and how tactical literacy work might contribute to the reclamation of so many radically repressed and suppressed voices.

The other night at our workshop one woman introduced herself as Henry and gripped her four-inch pencil into submission again and again over ninety minutes. Purple hair tangling into her eyes, she read with an unexpected blur of street slang and buoyancy after each of our three or four writing exercises. Afterward she thanked me for the opportunity to join and talked hopefully about her release date. Henry, Mary, Greeneyes, Bama, Clarity, and Giggles— and myriad other women who have written with us—all have claimed the mantle of writer with varying degrees of comfort. All are women who have stories, histories, and futures imagined beyond bars, beyond even the roads they imagine walking. Samsara (in this volume) demands our participation, longs for the space and ability to envision alternatives:

> Razor wire in my eyes, number on my chest,
> what my future seems to be, unknown, scary as hell.
> So much life to live, want to know how to live it.

The transformations we've charted in this collection won't reform a centuries-old political system in our lifetimes, but they might spark small changes. When asked about coping, longtime political prisoner Marilyn Buck (2005, 266) replied, "What I do is that I write." As activist Angela Davis argues in her monograph *Are Prisons Obsolete?*, "The contemporary disestablishment of writing and other prison educational programs is indicative of the official disregard today for rehabilitative strategies, particularly those that encourage individual prisoners to acquire autonomy of the mind" (2003, 57).

This volume is an effort to intervene, to offer space to the writers, activists, and scholars who recognize and encourage the need for profound changes in our system of establishing and regulating justice. We celebrate different voices weighing in on how individual and institutional actions might be influenced by people with a diverse set of life experiences. This is a long road we must dismantle and rebuild together. Like Cree, we believe hope is there.

References

Buck, Marilyn, and Laura Whitehorn with Susie Day. 2005. Cruel but not unusual— The punishment of women in U.S. prisons. In *The new abolitionists: (Neo)slave narratives and contemporary prison writings*. Edited by Joy James. Albany: State University of New York Press. 259–73.

Chavis, Geri Giebel. 2011. *Poetry and story therapy: The healing power of creative expression*. London: Jessica Kingsley Publishers.

Davis, Angela. 2003. *Are prisons obsolete?* New York: Seven Stories Press.

hooks, bell. 1990. *Yearning: Race, gender, and cultural politics.* Boston, MA: South End.

James, Joy. 2003. *Imprisoned intellectuals: America's political prisoners writing on life, liberation, and rebellion.* Lanham, MD: Rowman and Littlefield Publishers.

Lamott, Anne. 1994. *Bird by bird: Some instructions on writing and life.* New York: Anchor/Random House.

Lawston, Jodie Michelle, and Ashley Lucas. 2011. *Razor wire women: Prisoners, activists, scholars, and artists.* Albany: State University of New York Press.

Levi, Robin, and Ayelet Waldman. 2011. *Inside this place, not of it: Narratives from women's prisons.* San Francisco: McSweeney's/Voice of Witness.

Mandela, Nelson. 1995. *Long walk to freedom: The autobiography of Nelson Mandela.* Boston, MA: Back Bay Books.

Rich, Adrienne. 1993. "Someone is writing a poem." *What is found there: Notebooks on poetry and politics.* New York: W. W. Norton and Co.

Solinger, Rickie, et al., Eds. 2010. *Interrupted life: Experiences of incarcerated women in the United States.* Berkeley: University of California Press.

Valle, Alice Do. 2008. The we that sets us free: Imagining a world without prisons. In *Telling stories to change the world: Global voices on the power of narrative to build community and make social justice claims.* Edited by Rickie Solinger, Madeline Fox and Kayham Irani. New York: Routledge Press. 161–71.

Note

1. As bell hooks so aptly reminds us, the risk of colonization is ever-present: "No need to hear your voice when I can talk about you better than you can speak about yourself. . . . Re-writing you I write myself anew. I am still author, authority" (1990, 152).

About the Authors

Irene C. Baird is an affiliate assistant professor of Education and director of the Penn State Harrisburg Women's Enrichment Center, an institute focused on learning programs for incarcerated women and men as well as other un/ underserved urban women. She is author of *Unlocking the Cell* and "Education, Incarceration, and the Marginalization of Women."

Nancy Birkla is a Disability Resource Manager at KCTCS at Jefferson Community College in Louisville, Kentucky. Her essay, "Three Steps Past the Monkeys" was included in Wally Lamb's 2003 *Couldn't Keep it to Myself: Testimonies from Our Imprisoned Sisters.*

Boudicca Burning is the pen name for this part-time student at Louisiana State University, a performance artist with ArtSpring who considers herself a slave of the Florida Department of Corrections. She enjoys practicing the craft of writing, reading *The New Yorker* and playing the dulcimer. Her work includes the plays *Evidentiary Hearing: The Musical!* and *Clemency Board Tango*. This is her first published essay.

Bell Gale Chevigny is professor emeritus of literature at Purchase College, SUNY, and editor of *Doing Time: 25 Years of Prison Writing—A PEN American Center Prize Anthology.* Her published works include *The Woman and the Myth: Margaret Fuller's Life and Writings* (rev. ed., 1994), *Reinventing the Americas: Comparative Studies of Literature of the United States and Spanish America* (1986), and the novel *Chloe and Olivia* (1990).

Judith Clark is a writer held at Bedford Hills Federal Correctional Institution in Bedford Hills, New York. Clark is a longtime participant in prison writing workshops and has published widely, winning PEN poetry prizes in 1993 and 1995. Her poems have appeared in *The New Yorker, IKON, Global City Review,* and *Aliens at the Border.* Clark also teaches prenatal and parenting classes at Bedford and has published essays on the subject in the *Prison Journal* and *Zero to Three.*

Joyce Cohen has been incarcerated since 1989. She is an enthusiastic supporter of the ArtSpring and AVP (1 to Violence) Programs. She believes they help keep her balanced while allowing her the opportunity to mentor younger women coming into the Florida prison system. She is an avid reader and often escapes the harsh reality of prison life through books. Joyce is parole eligible and continues to fight for her freedom.

Cree is a writer in northern Colorado. She is deeply committed to using writing and her voice as a tool for empowering the women (particularly Native women) to reclaim their experiences and cultural histories.

Crista Decker is a writer in Florida. She sees writing as a strategy for opening doors and seeing hope in the lives of everyone around her.

Dionna Griffin is a performer, writer, playwright, and the director of outreach and diversity at Second City Improvisation Troupe in Chicago, Illinois. She is also the founder of DMG Freedom. She weaves her experiences with prison with her current activism in creative performance.

Clarinda Harriss is professor emerita of English at Towson University, where she was chair of the department and taught "Literature and Prisons," a course for both English and sociology majors that included frequent visits to the Maryland House of Correction for Men. She has worked one-to-one with female prison writers for the past decade; currently she is excerpting *Velmarine's Story,* a 600-page memoir written in prison by Velmarine Szabo, for web publication as "Velmarine's Page."

Tsehaye G. Hèbert is a ritual artist, educator, and cultural activist. She is the founder of Prison, Arts and the Humanities (PATH), and teaches creative writing in its Women Writers Workshop at Cook County Jail and through a distance-learning module at prisons throughout the state of Illinois.

Jessica Hill is an advocate for children and teens of abuse. She is passionate about the journeys she embarks on and is a lover of love.

Wendy W. Hinshaw is an assistant professor in the English Department at Florida Atlantic University. Her articles on the rhetoric of trauma, teaching testimonial literature, and pedagogical approaches to student resistance have appeared in *JAC* and *Transformations*, as well as the collection *Silence and Listening as Rhetorical Arts*. Her current work investigates how prisoner art and writing shapes and is shaped by the historical, institutional and cultural contexts in which it circulates, and part of this work appears in the collection *Practicing Research in Writing Studies*. Currently she serves as the Director of Writing Programs for FAU.

Taylor Huey is a writer held at the Carswell Federal Medical Center in Ft. Worth, Texas.

Tobi Jacobi is an associate professor of English at Colorado State University where she teaches writing and literacy classes. Her research focuses on understanding the problems and possibilities of situating women's prison writing workshops as alternative literacy training. She has taught life writing at a county prison in Upstate New York and currently facilitates a women's prison writing project in Fort Collins, Colorado.

Hettie Jones is the author of sixteen books including *All Told* (2003); *How I Became Hettie Jones* (1990); *Big Star Fallin' Mama: Five Women in Black Music* (1974); and several books for children. Her fiction, poems, and prose have appeared in *Essence, Frontier: A Journal of Women Studies, Hanging Loose, Heresies, IKON, Ploughshares, Village Voice Literary Supplement, The Washington Post*, and other periodicals. Her first collection of poems, *Drive* (1997), received the Norma Farber First Book Award from the Poetry Society of America. She coauthored a booklet on facilitated prison writing workshops for the PEN American Center and ran writing workshops at the New York State Correctional Facility for Women at Bedford Hills.

Tom Kerr is an associate professor of writing at Ithaca College in Ithaca, New York. His areas of research include rhetorical theory, composition studies, and cultural studies. His advanced writing course initiated his prison letter-writing project in spring 2003. He is currently working on a book project titled *America's Most Maligned: The Rhetorical Foundations of the Prison Industrial Complex.*

Kathie Klarreich is an author and career journalist who spent half of the last twenty-five years living in and covering Haiti for radio, television, and print, including NPR, ABC, NBC, *TIME* and *The Christian Science Monitor.* She has found unparalleled satisfaction, however, as a writing facilitator in Homestead Correctional Institution, where she has been teaching for the past several years through the prison arts nonprofit organization ArtSpring.

Roshanda Melton was recently released from prison in 2014. She writes: "I am born in the wind and raised in the storm, a mother I was even before the baby was born. My story is etched in-between blurred lines, a diamond in the rough with a heart that shines."

Mia spent time in Cook County Jail, Chicago, and is a writer.

Patricia O'Brien is an associate professor at the University of Illinois at Chicago, Jane Addams College of Social Work, teaching practice methods, group work, and practice with women. Her practice background is in working with battered women and their children. Her current scholarship and publications describe the complex and overlapping factors that relate to women's criminal behaviors and the pathways of reentry after incarceration. She is the author of *Making It in the "Free World": Women in Transition from Prison.*

Shelley Goldman, a/k/a S. Phillips is the mother of one beautiful child. She enjoys theatre, art, writing and any creative outlet. Her hobbies are exercising and bragging about her son Robert. She is supported by her family and friends Laurie, Sami, and Amanda.

Helen Prejean, C.S.J. is an award-winning Roman Catholic nun and a leading American advocate for the abolition of the death penalty. She is author of the acclaimed book, *Dead Man Walking,* which also became a film directed by Tim Robbins. She is also author of *The Death of Innocents: An Eyewitness Account of Wrongful Executions*.

Sadie Reynolds founded and directs the Inside Out Writing Project, a jail-based writing program for women in Santa Cruz County, California. She is an instructor of sociology and with the Academy for College Excellence at Cabrillo College. A former prisoner, Reynolds's scholarly work is informed by firsthand experiences of criminalization and confinement, as well as her commitment to active struggle for social justice—particularly justice for women prisoners.

Samsara is a writer in Colorado for whom writing has been a tool for exploring life's joys and pains. She is deeply committed to using her voice to reclaim control over her life.

Sarah is a small business owner in a Midwestern city, "creating things, and trying to create social change." She is also an exhibited photographer, a gardener, a furniture maker, and a self-published writer. She has worked in the past as an alcohol/drug counselor working with battered women. "I try every day to slow down, to be open, to acknowledge the gifts I've been given, to work for a better world how I can."

Judith Scheffler is an professor of English at West Chester University. She has published several articles on women's prison literature. Her anthology of women's prison writings, *Wall Tappings*, has recently been released in its second edition. The first edition of *Wall Tappings* won the Susan Koppelman Award for Popular Culture.

Gretchen Schumacher was formerly held at the Coffee Creek Correctional Facility in Wilsonville, Oregon, and is founder and president of Water Under the Bridge, a nonprofit for formerly incarcerated women.

Ann Folwell Stanford is Vincent DePaul Professor of Multidisciplinary and Literary Studies at the School for New Learning, DePaul University. A poet, she founded and directed the DePaul Project on Women, Writing, and Incarceration after having written poetry with women at Cook County Jail for over seven years. Her book, *Bodies in a Broken World: Women Novelists of Color*

& the Politics of Medicine, was published in 2003. Her articles have appeared in *African American Review, American Literature, Literature and Medicine, Feminist Studies*, and other journals and books.

Sandy Sysyn is a feminist and a humanitarian. She loves animals and wildlife. She believes in eternal learning. If not for the restraint of prison, she would love to pursue more academics and advocacy. However she still dreams of the things she could do one day so as never to lose sight of the possibilities. She strives for self-betterment in the hope of transforming the judgment of her captors.

Velmarine Oliphant Szabo is an African American woman and the mother of three children. She is a military veteran and a student at the Sam Houston University where she maintains a 4.0 grade point average. She spent seven of eight years writing during her incarceration.

Jean Trounstine is an activist, author, and professor at Middlesex Community College in Lowell, Massachusetts. She worked at Framingham Women's Prison for ten years where she directed eight plays and wrote extensively about women offenders. Her book, *Shakespeare Behind Bars: The Power of Drama in a Women's Prison* (2001), was featured on NPR and has recently come out in paperback in 2004. She coedited *Changing Lives through Literature* (1999) and a book of poetry, *Almost Home Free* (2003).

Appendix

Resources for Facilitating Prison Writing Workshops

Many writing opportunities for prisoners are sponsored by teachers and program volunteers who learn about the complexities of working behind bars as they gain experience. We offer the following observations and suggestions based upon our years of training writing workshop facilitators and teaching inside.

Establishing Your Role as Writing Workshop Teacher / Facilitator behind Bars

- **Remember that your primary role is that of a writer:** It is important to recognize that you are working with a population that has undergone some level of crisis, and that we do not provide training for you to offer advice to writers beyond your expertise as a writer. Establishing a writing relationship and a subsequent community of writers is a rich opportunity for conversation, creativity, and critical and supportive feedback.
- **Acknowledge diverse writing histories:** Consider the role writing might play in the writer's life now. For many of us writing is an academic activity,

or a means to tell a story, but for others it might also represent companion-
ship, voice, possibility, validation (of experience and/or writing ability),
growth, moments of clarity, freedom from "school" or social conventions,
emotional release, a chance to imagine (or plan) the future, a risky disclosure. It might represent a sustained effort, a reality check, hope, an opportunity to share an alternative story, or a desire for change. It might also carry
a weighty and painful past if former writing attempts weren't embraced/
supported (e.g., poor school experiences).

- **Create a community of writers**: We understand writing to be a collective
  and recursive endeavor; that is, writing often happens in communities
  (informal and formal). Writing programming often creates regular opportunities for writers to be together. A community of writers can be a lifeline
  of encouragement for those trying to explore writing beyond school for the
  first time.

- **Focus on writing-as-craft:** We want to support the development of deep-
  ened understandings of the forms writers choose for expressing their
  thoughts. Writers might choose prose, memoir, poetry, or a blend of any
  number of written forms to express their ideas, and all can be embraced. In
  both group and individual contexts, work that shows promise for development can be encouraged. Surface level concerns (e.g., grammar, spelling)
  should be a secondary concern unless the writer has expressed specific
  interest in improving this area or you are helping the writer polish the
  writing for publication. Sometimes simple questions about clarification can
  encourage writers to deepen how they address a topic or enhance the style
  they've chosen to experiment with. There are many terrific print and online
  resources that begin with the craft of writing that lend themselves well to
  writing in confined spaces.

- **Foster space for conversation about writing:** We can do this by taking
  writing seriously and modeling verbal commentary that will both help writers grapple with their work as a meaningful piece of text and demonstrate
  that strong writing emerges from revision and multiple readings. When
  offering suggestions, it is useful to frame them as possibilities rather than
  mandates through respectful observations or questions. Often the group of
  writers will pick up this technique and begin to practice it with each other.

- **Facilitation and expertise:** For many, commenting on a writer's creative
  work can prove intimidating, especially if the facilitator has little or no ex-

perience studying the craft. Keep in mind that facilitators do not need to be experts. Consider the creative writing elements that you are familiar with: word choice, description, rhyme, theme. Focus on one or two elements. If facilitators want to learn more about specific craft elements, they can find myriad resources online or through fellow teachers.

- **Returning writers' work:** Since many of the submitted writings are hand-written or unable to be reproduced (e.g., are not electronically saved), writers often highly value receiving typed copies of their work. We recommend offering writers their original work along with two typed copies (one with comments, one clean). Alternatively, sticky notes can be used to offer comments and feedback to writers. A timely response (one week) is the best way to validate their effort and encourage them to continue writing.
- **Encourage multiple drafts:** Remind writers that great writing surfaces after it has undergone various revisions. Encourage writers to revise and resubmit one or two pieces of writing after reviewing feedback from peers and facilitators.
- **Provide writing samples and resources:** Based on the writing and/or responses you receive from writers, you may want to provide samples of writing that are similar stylistically or thematically that might assist writers in developing and revising their work. Samples may include: excerpts from novels, short fiction, poems, op-ed pieces, essays. These samples might include work from a wide range of writers from diverse backgrounds. That said, please carefully consider the amount and appropriateness of the material to avoid overwhelming writers.

Techniques for Responding to Written Work

- Be open to all types of writing.
- Ask the writers to suggest where they would like feedback and encourage open conversation about response with the group.
- Discuss the role of first person in shared writing and offer writers the option of fictional narratives. That is, in responding to writers' work, try not to

assume that the use of "I" necessarily equates disclosure or even ownership of the actions or stories being described. We all deserve the right to explore the diversity of life through fiction. The writers we work with might have a strong desire to claim ownership over the narratives they share; they might also enjoy writing as an opportunity to write through life experiences that are not their own. Embrace both through creative responses.

- Acknowledge difficult disclosures by making space for other writers to react to the writing/content. Offer time for candid discussion, if the writer seems to want that. If not, move on to another writer/activity. Recognition of a sensitive disclosure can also happen through individual acknowledgment or written feedback.
- Demonstrate empathy. Allow your comments to show that you are listening. Acknowledge the courage and emotional risk in the disclosure of difficult subject matter. ("It must have taken a lot of courage to write this poem. Thank you for sharing it.")
- Ask the writer intentional questions. ("Can you say more about this?" or "It seems like there is more to this story. Do you have more to say?" or "I love the part about ___; can you add more details about ____?" or "This is working really well. It might make a great series. Can you extend it a bit? Maybe with similar narratives?")
- Connect to other writers (compare writing to another writer's work or style) or connect to something in pop culture (point to a relevant current event).
- Make observations about writing style and form. For example, you might point to strong lines and the techniques used (i.e., repetition or word choice) or you might focus on form on the page (i.e., line breaks, spacing, use of white space).
- Validate the writer/narrator's experience (whether it's theirs or not). ("This is an amazing story." Or, "This experience must have been difficult to get through.")
- Encourage more writing. ("This narrative is great so far. I'd like to know more about___; is there more to tell?").
- Narrate your reading/response experience. ("This line made me stop and think about . . .").
- Make connections ("I had a similar experience when . . ."), but be careful not to take over with your story.

- Comment on strength of voice. Be specific. ("This line represents a really powerful voice. It reminds me of . . .")
- Comment on the power of publication. Let writers know that there are many kinds of community writing publications and literary magazines that they might submit their work to.
- Communicate regularly with other workshop facilitators in your program to ensure consistent amount and type of feedback is offered to writers.
- If/when appropriate, offer resources. For example, you might suggest contacting a social service provider or talking with a staff person about resources. This is a delicate line to cross. Ask program staff, if you are uncertain about how/if to offer resources. Hard as it might be sometimes, we must resist the urge to solve problems for writers; we often aren't trained for counseling, therapy or social work and have only a small window into each writer's life circumstances. Remember that we can leave and have access to any resources we might need to help us with issues raised in or by the workshop experience. The women inside cannot.

Selected Bibliography

Articles

Allred, Sarah L. 2009. The inside-out prison exchange program: The impact of structure, content, and readings. *Journal of Correctional Education* 60 no. 3: 240–58.

Berry, Patrick W. 2014. Doing time with literacy narratives. *Pedagogy: Critical Approaches to Teaching Literature, Language, Composition, and Culture* 14 no. 1: 137–60.

Billington, Josie. 2011. Reading for life: Prison reading groups in practice and theory. *Critical Survey* 23 no. 3: 67–85.

Biscoglio, Frances. 2005. In the beginning was the word: Teaching pre-college English at Bedford Hills Correctional Facility. *Writing on the Edge* 16 no. 1: 23–43.

Boudin, Kathy. 1993. Participatory literacy education behind bars: AIDS opens the door. *Harvard Educational Review* 63 no. 2: 207–32.

———. 1995. Critical thinking in a basic literacy program: A problem-solving model in corrections education. *Journal of Correctional Education* 46 no. 4 (December): 141–45.

Butler, Paul. 2007. The GED as transgender literacy: Performing in the learning/acquisition borderland. *Reflections: A Journal of Public Rhetoric, Civic Writing, and Service Learning* 6 no. 1 (Spring): 27–39.

Carr, Barbara Allen. 2000. Behind the fences: Case study of a literacy teacher in a prison classroom. *ERIC*. Web. 31 May 2012.

Clary, Jordan. 2001. The posture of the key: Teaching Emily Dickinson to prisoners. *Teachers & Writers* 33 no. 1: 5–9.

Clemente, Angeles, Michael James Higgins, and William Michael Sughrua. 2011. I don't find any privacy around here: Ethnographic encounters with local practices of literacy in the state prison of Oaxaca. *Language and Education* 25 no. 6: 491–513. *ERIC*. Web. 30 May 2012.

Conrath, Richard C. 1986. New partnerships: The community college in prison. *Issues and Trends in Corrections Education. ERIC*. Web. 4 June 2012.

Corcoran, Farrel. 1985. Pedagogy in prison: Teaching in maximum security institutions. *Communication Education* 34 no. 1: 49–58.

Cordero, Iris, and Alicia Pousada. 1995. Until I learn English, I will always live in a prison: Teaching E.S.L. to Hispanic women inmates. *ERIC*. Web. 30 May 2012.

Cotto, Maxwell. 2009. Creative writing in the culture of the American prison. *Salamagundi* 162–163: 160–81.

Cowser, Robert. 2003. Writing in jail: A chance for reflection. *Adult Learning* 14 no. 2: 25.

Elliott, Anne, Patricia Williams, and Toronto (Ontario) Canadian Congress for Learning Opportunities for women. 1995. Isolating the barriers and strategies for prevention: A kit about violence and women's education for adult educators and adult learners. *ERIC*. Web. 30 May 2012.

Fewell, Peter. 2011. Peter, you are a writer. *Adults Learning* 23 no. 1: 12–13.

Foran, Frances. 1998. "Con/versions: Women re-signing from prison." Master's thesis. McGill University (Canada). Canada: *ProQuest Dissertations & Theses (PQDT)*.

Gavin, Madeleine, Judith Katz, and Gary Sunshine, Dirs. 2003. *What I want my words to do to you*. PBS Home Video.

Geraci, Pauline M. 2000. Reaching out the write way. *Journal of Adolescent & Adult Literacy* 43 no. 7: 632–34.

Graham, Michael. 2008. Notes on teaching in a prison. *North Dakota Quarterly* 75 no. 2: 88–97.

Gready, Paul. 1993. Autobiography and the "power of writing": Political prison writing in the apartheid era. *Journal of Southern African Studies* 19 no. 3: 489–523.

Haigler, Karl, Caroline Harlow, Patricia O'Connor, and Anne Campbell. 1994. Literacy behind prison walls: Profiles of a prison population. Washington, DC: U.S. Department of Education office of Educational Research and Improvement. http://nces.ed.gov/pubs94/94102.pdf.

Hall, Renee Smiling, and Jim Killacky. 2008. Correctional education from the perspective of the prisoner student. *Journal of Correctional Education* 59 no. 4: 301–20.

Harlow, Caroline Wolf. 2003. Education and correctional populations. Bureau of Justice Statistics Special Report. January. http://www.ojp.usdoj.gov/bjs/pub/pdf/ecp.pdf. 25 January 2006.

Hastings, Phyllis G. and Jim Morrison. 2004. Do you hear what I hear? Voices from prison composition classes. *Reflections: A Journal of Public Rhetoric, Civic Writing, and Service Learning* 4 no. 1: 101–13.

Herrington, Margaret, and Tom Joseph. 2001. Literacies within prison settings: A fourth space? *Rapal Bulletin* 43: 12–17.

Higgins, Jane. 2004. Sharing sociological stories: Reflections on teaching sociology in prison. *International Journal of Lifelong Education* 23 no. 3: 243–57.

Hill, Margaret H., and Leigh Van Horn. 1995. Book club goes to jail: Can book clubs replace gangs? *Journal of Adolescent & Adult Literacy* 39 no. 3: 180–88.

Hinshaw, Wendy Wolters. 2010. "Incarcerating rhetorics, publics, pedagogies." Dissertation. The Ohio State University. *ProQuest Dissertations & Theses (PQDT)*.

Jackson, Chuck. 2009. What looms: The university, the jailhouse, and pedagogy. *Pedagogy: Critical Approaches to Teaching Literature, Language, Composition, and Culture* 9 no. 2: 315–24.

Jackson, Spoon. 2007. Speaking in poems. *Teaching Artist Journal* 5 no. 1: 22–26.

Jacobi, Tobi L. 2003. "Contraband literacies: Incarcerated women and writing-as-activism." PhD dissertation. Syracuse University. New York: ProQuest Dissertations & theses (PQDT).

———. 2008. Slipping pages through razor wire: Literacy action projects in jail. *Community Literacy Journal* 2 no. 2: 67–86.

———. 2008. Writing for change: Engaging juveniles through alternative literacy education. *The Journal of Correctional Education* 59 no. 2: 71–93.

———. 2009. Writing workshops as alternative literacy education for incarcerated women. *Corrections Today* (February): 52–55.

———. 2011. Speaking out for social justice: The problems and possibilities of U.S. women's jail writing workshops. *Critical Survey* 23, no. 3: 40–54.

———. 2012. Twenty year sentences: Writing workshops and women in prison. In *Feminist popular education in transnational debates: Pedagogies of possibilities.* Edited by Linzi Manicom and Shirley Walters. New York: Palgrave-Macmillan: 111–28.

Jonietz, Patricia. 1995. A creative writing class in the detention setting. *Journal of Emotional and Behavioral Problems* 3 no. 4 (Winter): 4–7.

Juska, Jane. 1999. The writing process goes to San Quentin. *Phi Delta Kappan* 80 no. 10: 759–62.

Kerr, Tom. 2004. Between ivy and razor wire: A case of correctional correspondence. *Reflections: A Journal of Public Rhetoric, Civic Writing, and Service Learning* 4 no. 1 (Winter): 62–75.

Lakshmi, Aparna. 2012. Teaching the prison industrial complex. *Rethinking Schools* 26 no. 2: 38–43.

Laughlin, Thomas. 1996. Teaching in the yard: Student inmates and the policy of silence. *Teaching English in the Two-Year College.* 23 no. 4: 284–90.

Lockard, Joe, and Sherry Rankins-Robertson. 2011. The right to education, prison-university partnerships, and online writing pedagogy in the US. *Critical Survey* 23 no. 3: 23–39.

Maher, Jane. 2004. "You probably don't even know I exist": Notes from a college prison program. *Journal of Basic Writing* 23 no. 1: 82–100.

Martin, Keavy, and Sam McKegney. 2011. Inuvialuit critical autobiography and the carceral writing of Anthony Apakark Thrasher. *Canadian Literature* 208: 65–83.

Mastrangelo, Lisa. 2004. First year composition and women in prison: Service-based writing and community action. *Reflections: A Journal of Public Rhetoric, Civic Writing, and Service Learning* 4 no. 1 (Winter): 43–50.

Oppenheim, Rachel Leffler. 2010. "Calculating females: Incarcerated women, correctional education, and the struggle for self-preservation." Dissertation. Teachers College, Columbia University. *ProQuest Dissertations & theses (PQDT).* Web.

Parkinson, Deirdre. 2007. Let me tell you a story. *Adults Learning* 19 no. 2: 18–20.

Parrotta, Kylie L. and Gretchen H. Thompson. 2011. Sociology of the prison classroom: Marginalized identities and sociological imaginations behind bars. *Teaching Sociology* 39 no. 2: 165–78.

Paup, Elizabeth Gail. 1995. Teachers' roles in the classroom: Adopting and adapting to the paradox of education within a prison institution. *ERIC*. Web. 4 June 2012.

Pompa, Lori. 2004. Disturbing where we are comfortable: Notes from behind the walls. *Reflections: A Journal of Public Rhetoric, Civic Writing, and Service Learning* 4 no. 1 (Winter): 24–34.

Rhodes, Lisa. 2002. Poetry and a prison writing program: A mentor's narrative report. *Journal of Poetry Therapy* 15 no. 3: 163–68.

Rimstead, Roxanne, and Deena Rymhs. 2011. Prison writing/writing prison in Canada. *Canadian Literature*: 6+.

Rodríguez, Dylan. 2002. Against the discipline of "prison writing": Toward a theoretical conception of contemporary radical prison praxis. *Genre: Forms of Discourse and Culture* 35 no. 3–4: 407–28.

Rogers, Laura. 2004. Where lifelines converge: Voices from the Forest Correctional Creative Writing Group. *Reflections: A Journal of Public Rhetoric, Civic Writing, and Service Learning* 4 no. 1: 12–23.

———. 2009. Diving into prison teaching: Mina Shaughnessy, teacher development, and the realities of prison teaching. *Reflections: A Journal of Public Rhetoric, Civic Writing, and Service Learning* 8 no. 3: 99–121.

Rothman, Juliet C. and Reginald Walker. 1997. Prison poetry: A medium for growth and change. *Journal of Poetry Therapy* 10 no. 3: 149–58.

Rymhs, Deena. 2009. "Docile bodies shuffling in unison": The prisoner as worker in Canadian prison writing. *Life Writing* 6 no. 3: 313–27.

Salzman, Mark. 2003. The writing class. *American Scholar* 72 no. 4: 13–33.

Shafer, Gregory. 2001. Composition and a prison community of writers. *English Journal* 90 no. 5: 75–81.

Sheffield, Reggie. 2003. Volunteer mends relationship between girls, inmate mothers. *Sunday Patriot News* (Harrisburg, PA), 27 June. http://lifeesteem.org/inthenews2.html.

Smitherman, Tracy, and Jeanie Thompson. 2002. "Writing our stories": An anti-violence creative writing program. *Journal of Correctional Education* 53 no. 2 (June): 77–83.

Sparks, Leigh Pryor. 2008. "The creative writing process as a means for a woman inmate to cope with her incarceration, rehabilitate herself within the prison setting, and prepare for her reentry into society." Dissertation. University of Arkansas. *ProQuest Dissertations & theses (PQDT).* Web.

Spaulding, Susanna. 2011. Borderland stories about teaching college in prison. *New Directions for Community Colleges* 155: 73–83.

Stanford, Ann Folwell. 2004. More than just words: Women's poetry and resistance at Cook County Jail. *Feminist Studies* 30 no. 2: 277–301.

———. 2005. Where love flies free: Women, home and writing in Cook County Jail. *Journal of Prevention & Intervention in the Community* 30 no. 1–2: 49–56.

Steurer, Stephen J. 2001. Historical development of a model for correctional education and literacy. *Journal of Correctional Education* 52 no. 2: 48–51.

Stino, Zandra, and Barbara Palmer. 1995. Writing as therapy in a county jail. *Journal of Poetry Therapy* 9 no. 1: 13–23.

———. 1999. Motivating women offenders through process-based writing in a literacy learning circle. *Journal of Adolescent and Adult Literacy* 43 no. 3 (November): 282–91.

Swanson, Cheryl, Kate King, and Nicole Wolbert. 1997. Mentoring juveniles in adult jail: An example of service learning. *Journal of Criminal Justice Education* 8 no. 2 (Fall): 263–71.

Trounstine, Jean. 2008. Beyond prison education. *PMLA: Publications of the Modern Language Association of America* 123 no. 3: 674–77.

Vinz, Ruth, et al. 2007. Writing out of the unexpected: Narrative inquiry and the weight of small moments. *English Education* 39 no. 4: 326–51.

Wade, Stephen. 2008. Reflections on writing good sentences in prison. *PN Review* 34 no. 3 [179]: 11–12.

Williams, Rachel, and Janette Y. Taylor. 2004. Narrative art and incarcerated abused women. *Art Education* 57 no. 2: 46–52.

Willingham, Breea C. 2011. Black women's prison narratives and the intersection of race, gender, and sexuality in U.S. prisons. *Critical Survey* 23 no. 3: 55–66.

Wilson, Anita. 1996. Speak up—I can't write what you're reading: The place of literacy in the prison community. *Journal of Correctional Education* 47 no. 2 (June): 94–100.

———. 1999. There is no escape from third-space theory: Borderland discourse and the in-between literacies of prisons. In *Situated literacies: Reading and writing in context*. Edited by David Barton, Mary Hamilton, and Roz Ivanic. London: Routledge, 54–69.

———. 2004. Four days and a breakfast: Time, space and literacy/ies in the prison community. In *Spatializing literacy research and practice*. Edited by Kevin Leander and Margaret Sheehy. New York: Peter Lang.

Wiltse, Ed. 2011. Doing time in college: Student-prisoner reading groups and the object(s) of literary study. *Critical Survey* 23 no. 3: 6–22.

Wright, Randall. 2004. Care as the heart of prison teaching. *Journal of Correctional Education* 55 no. 3: 191–209.

———. 2005. Going to teach in prisons: Culture shock. *Journal of Correctional Education* 56 no. 1: 19–38.

Books and Chapters

Alessi, Lauren, and Tobi L. Jacobi. 2014. The limits of (critical) expressive writing in prisons and jails. In *Expressive writing: Classroom and community*. Edited by Kathleen Adams. Lanham, MD: Rowman and Littlefield.

Alexander, Buzz. 2010. *Is William Martinez not our brother? Twenty years of the prison creative arts project*. Ann Arbor: U Michigan P.

Alexander, Michelle. 2010. *The New Jim Crow: Mass incarceration in the age of color blindness*. New York: New Press.

Atwood, Jane Evelyn. 2000. *Too much time: Women in prison*. London: Phaidon.

Buck, Marilyn. 2012. *Inside/out: Poems.* San Francisco: City Lights.

Chevigny, Bell Gayle. 2011. *Doing time: 25 years of prison writing—A PEN American Center Prize Anthology.* New York: Arcade.

Davis, Angela. 2003. *Are prisons obsolete?* New York: Seven Stories Press.

El Saadawi, Nawal. 1994. *Memoirs from the women's prison.* Berkeley: University of California Press.

Enos, Sandra. 2001. *Mothering from the inside: Parenting in a women's prison.* Albany: State University of New York Press.

Faith, Karlene. 1993. *Unruly women: The politics of confinement and resistance.* Vancouver, BC: Press Gang.

Fraden, Rena. 2001. *Imagining Medea: Rhodessa Jones and theater for incarcerated women.* Chapel Hill: University North Carolina Press.

Franklin, Bruce H. 1998. *Prison writings in 20th century America.* New York: Penguin.

Gottshalk, Marie. 2006. *The prison and the gallows: The politics of mass imprisonment.* New York and London: Cambridge.

Herivel, Tara and Paul Wright. 2003. *Prison nation: The warehousing of America's poor.* New York: Routledge.

Jacobi, Tobi, and Elliott Johnston. 2008. Writers speaking out: The challenges community publishing from spaces of confinement. In *Circulating communities: The tactics and strategies of community publishing.* Edited by Paula Mathieu, Steve Parks, and Tiffany Rousculp. Lanham, MD: Lexington.

Johnson, Paula C. 2003. *Inner lives: Voices of African American women in prison.* New York: New York University Press.

Lamb, Wally. 2008. *I'll fly away: Further testimonies from the Women of York Prison.* New York: Harper/Perinneal.

Lamb, Wally, and the Women of the York Correctional Facility. 2003. *Couldn't keep it to myself: Testimonies from our imprisoned sisters.* New York: HarperCollins Publishers.

Lawston, Jodie Michelle, and Ashley E. Lucas, Eds. 2011. *Razor wire women: Prisoners, activists, scholars, and artists.* Albany: State University of New York Press.

Levi, Robin, and Ayelet Waldman. 2011. *Inside this place, not of it: Narratives from women's prisons*. San Francisco: McSweeney's/Voice of Witness.

Mauer, Marc, and Meda Chesney-Lind. 2002. *Invisible punishment: the collateral consequences of mass incarceration*, New York: New Press.

Moses, Claire G. et al., Eds. 2004. *The prison issue. Feminist Studies* 30 no. 2.

O'Brien, Patricia. 2001. *Making it in the "free world": Women in transition from prison*. New York: State University of New York Press.

O'Connor, Patricia E. 2000. *Speaking of crime: Narratives of prisoners*. Lincoln: University of Nebraska Press.

O'Shea, Kathleen. 2000. *Women on the row: Revelations from both sides of the bars*. Ithaca, NY: Firebrand.

Owen, Barbara. 1998. *In the mix: Struggle and survival in a women's prison*. Albany: State University of New York Press.

Parenti, Christian. 1999. *Lockdown America: Police and prisons in the age of crisis*. London: Verso.

Reiter, Sherry. 2009. *Writing away the demons: Stories of creative coping through transformative writing*. St. Cloud, MN: North Star Press.

Rich, Adrienne. *The Dream of a Common Language: Poems 1974–1977*. New York: W.W. Norton, 1977.

Ritchie, Beth. 1996. *Compelled to crime: The gender entrapment of black battered women*. New York: Routledge.

Salzman, Mark. 2003. *True notebooks*. New York: Knopf.

Schaafsma, David. 1993. *Eating on the street: Teaching literacy in a multicultural Society*. Pittsburgh: U of Pittsburgh.

Scheffler, Judith A. 2002. *Wall tappings: An international anthology of women's prison writings 200 to the present*. New York: Feminist Press at the City University of New York.

Smith, Richard, and Friends. 2003. *"Only be strong and courageous": A conversational cookbook on how to conduct a creative writing workshop in a correctional facility*. 10 April 2003. http://www.umich.edu/%7Eocsl/Proj_Community/coord/only.html.

Solinger, Rickie, et al., Eds. 2010. *Interrupted life: Experiences of incarcerated women in the United States*. Berkeley: University of California Press.

Tannenbaum, Judith. 2000. *Disguised as a poem: My years teaching poetry at San Quentin*. Boston, MA, Northeastern University Press.

Trounstine, Jean. 2001. *Shakespeare behind bars: The power of drama in a women's prison*. New York: St. Martin's Press.

Watterson, Kathryn. 1996. *Women in prison: Inside the concrete womb*. Boston, MA: Northeastern University Press.

Williams, Rachel Marie-Crane. 2003. *Teaching the arts behind bars*. Boston, MA: Northeastern University Press.

Williford, Miriam, Ed. 1994. *Higher education in prison: A contradiction in terms?* Phoenix, AZ: Oryx Press.

Index

CPSIA information can be obtained
at www.ICGtesting.com
Printed in the USA
BVHW032112050121
597094BV00007B/39